WELFARE IN AMERICA

WELFARE IN AMERICA

How Social Science
Fails the Poor

WILLIAM M. EPSTEIN

The University of Wisconsin Press

The University of Wisconsin Press
2537 Daniels Street
Madison, Wisconsin 53718

3 Henrietta Street
London WC2E 8LU, England

A portion of chapter 5 appeared in William M. Epstein, *The Dilemma of American Social Welfare* (New Brunswick, NJ: Transaction Publishers, 1993), 122–125. Reprinted by permission of Transaction Publishers. Copyright © 1993 by Transaction Publishers; all rights reserved. A portion of chapter 6 appeared in William M. Epstein, *The Illusion of Psychotherapy* (New Brunswick, NJ: Transaction Publishers, 1995), 56–58. Reprinted by permission of Transaction Publishers. Copyright © 1995 by Transaction Publishers; all rights reserved.

Library of Congress Cataloging-in-Publication Data
Epstein, William M., 1944–
    Welfare in America: how social science fails the poor /
William M. Epstein.
    278 pp.   cm.
    Includes bibliographical references and index.
    ISBN 0-299-15590-0 (cloth: alk. paper)
    ISBN 0-299-15594-3 (pbk.: alk. paper)
    1. Public welfare—United States—Philosophy.   2. Public welfare—
Government policy—United States.   3. Social sciences—Philosophy.
4. Poverty—United States.   5. Social problems—United States.
6. United States—Social policy.   7. United States—Economic policy.
I. Title.
HV91.E69   1997
361.973—dc21   97-14661

My Father
Harry Epstein
1912–1996

Contents

Acknowledgments

I am very grateful for comments from Ronald A. Farrell, Carol Case, R. Keith Schwer, Robert Morris, Marvin Bloom, Robert Dippner, David Stoesz, Gage Chapel, Anthony Grasso, Gerald Rubin, Malcolm Wilson, Douglas Imig, Colin T. Loader, Chau Kiu Cheung, Karmen Smith, and Janie Ostlund. The errors that remain are all mine. I also wish to thank the staffs at the University of Nevada–Las Vegas library, especially its former dean, Matthew J. Simon, and at the Library of Congress, one of the great institutions of American scholarship. Although frequently critical of the work coming out of the Institute for Research on Poverty and those associated with it, this book would not have been possible without that work. I owe a special intellectual debt to Robert Haveman, Robert Moffitt, Barbara Wolfe, Robert Plotnick, Irwin Garfinkel, Sheldon Danziger, and their colleagues. I also wish to thank the staff at the University of Wisconsin Press—their senior editor Rosalie M. Robertson, editor Raphael Kadushin, and Rozlyn Coleman, their copy editor. Finally, the manuscript benefited from the careful work of my graduate assistants, Amy Burger and Jennifer C. Duddy.

WELFARE IN AMERICA

Introduction: Absence of
Rational Authority

This is a book about social welfare policy and poverty in the United States, but more important it is about the conduct of the nation's intellectual life. That life is bound up with American civic culture. Social welfare is one of its central themes.

The policy issues of American welfare can be narrowly construed as the few federal entitlement programs designed to meet the needs of poor able-bodied Americans: Aid to Families with Dependent Children (AFDC), Food Stamps, and to a much smaller degree Medicaid. Yet, more broadly conceived, social welfare refers to all public and private arrangements to secure the common good. The importance of the debate over welfare policy lies in its implications for this broader meaning of social welfare.

Because of the tightly interwoven character of American society and the imposing logic of social welfare, the way that the nation designs relief for the 10–15 percent of its poorest citizens powerfully affects the many millions of its citizens—perhaps more than half of all Americans—whose lives are economically and socially precarious and who must depend upon the public sector for many supports. Each policy decision has telling ideological implications for the causes of social problems, the manner to address them, rights to benefits, and the level at which they are to be provided. In this way, the analysis of welfare policy for poor people has meaning for the rest of the nation; the narrow sense of social welfare becomes a synecdoche for the nation's deepest concerns and its most intimate social relations.

An immense amount of material is pertinent to a discussion of social welfare policy in the United States. In many areas this book has little to add to what has already been admirably presented by a large number of capable scholars. Libraries of impressive scholarship have described social problems and their relation to a variety of competitive political positions—notably the liberal vision and the conservative vision. The literature of social welfare, even the best of it, is so vast that some strategy of selection must be employed in order to produce a work that is more than an annotated bibliography.

This work traces the social welfare proposals of the past few decades, including the current welfare legislation enacted in 1996, back to the source of their authority, their basic evidence. This authority is most frequently presented in systematic, social scientific studies that claim either to have discovered the causes of poverty or to have demonstrated the effectiveness of some programmatic strategy to address poverty and dependency. In this way, the proposals are evaluated on the basis of their claims to rationality. By extension this strategy also allows the public debate to be critiqued on the grounds of its scientific credibility and not simply on the grounds of its character.

The book is necessarily limited by the immensity of information that describes social welfare programs and, at the same time, the desire to come to generally applicable conclusions about the notion of welfare in America. It attends only to the core programs of the welfare state targeted on the poor, and largely on those who do not have long attachment to the labor force. The book largely ignores the role that Social Security (Old Age, Survivor, Disability, and Health Insurance, OASDHI) has played in reducing poverty. The broader effects of the welfare state on the economy and business, working through the Federal Reserve and a variety of other regulatory agencies, also are not considered. The book further avoids comparisons between the United States and other modern industrial nations; a variety of scholarly works treat the comparative picture well, although they are hampered by many problems of data and interpretation (see as two examples McFate, Lawson, and Wilson 1995; Rein and Rainwater 1986). Yet, in spite of its limitations, the conclusions of this work may well transcend its narrow focus on public welfare to speak broadly about the social climate of the United States.

In spite of the vast scholarship describing poverty, dependency, crime, health and mental health, and so forth, the true value of the social sciences resides in their fundamental ability to provide objective and reliable information for public discussion of social problems. In essence, this implies that solutions for such problems need to be credibly tested, which in turn implies that scholarship exhibit particular methodological characteristics as well as a commitment to objectivity.

Yet the most objective descriptions of social conditions are frequently proxies for what appears to be society's real thirst: data that depict the moral dimensions of a social problem. If good could be distinguished from evil, thus setting a true test of deservingness, then the problem of relief could be greatly simplified. Even the most loathsome criminal may be able to offer some exculpating cause for his or her behavior—a genetic compulsion toward violence, a ferocious background of abuse—which mitigates personal responsibility. In these cases, the problem shifts subtly from one of identifying initial cause to one of providing effective interventions whatever the cause. Unfortunately, the ability to identify cause has eluded social scientists even when it has been technically possible. The effects of this failure have both undercut their authority as policy advisors and deprived the policy debate of important information about social problems.

Ignorance is frequently quite informative. Society may hold on to false evidence that at least some progress is possible against social problems. In spite of the great degree to which policy proposals differ in their budgetary implications, and consequently the role of the public sector, they may still hide the true amounts that are needed to correct grievous social problems in the United States. In this sense, the scholarship of social welfare in spite of its impressive demography may remain trapped in ideology.

All this implies that solutions for America's social problems may lie outside the current tolerances to fund social welfare and social services. While any perspective on social welfare that calls for greater amounts of new resources is certainly not a practical entry into contemporary politics, it may still define an important point of reference for the debate over poverty and insufficiency, looking past the current stultifying political climate to a time when both greater imagination and greater resources are feasible.

There may not be easy remedies for the large social problems in the United States, nor even any reasonable statements to make about the effectiveness of prior attempts to deal with them. In this way, the notion of even a limited rationality—the province of the social sciences—to resolve issues of social equity seems a bit presumptive. The epistemic fix of welfare—bleaker even than Braybrooke and Lindblom (1963) but not nihilistic—sets the problem back onto a social and political footing while reopening the debate over rationality in public discourse. Rationality in public discourse was, after all, the abiding hope of the Enlightenment for this American experiment in democracy.

The scholarship of social liberals has greatly undermined the conservative position. Ellwood (1988) on Murray (1984), a host of criticisms of *The Bell Curve* (1994), and the enormity of the scholarship that identified the antisocial tendencies of the market, unmasking its pretensions to charitability, justify the strong political inclination to regulate the free enterprise system.

The conservative position has focused on the failure of liberal programs, largely expressed in the initiatives of the 1930s and 1960s, that constitute America's welfare state. In turn, liberals, as just mentioned, have produced a variety of defenses of these programs and taken new steps to augment their position. To a great extent, the authority for these positions has rested upon social science proofs of the programs' actual and potential effectiveness. However, the credibility of the social science evidence that underpins these analyses, and hence the social desirability of the programs, have escaped criticism. Stripped of its humanitarian trappings, the liberal position may not be any more capable of handling profound social problems than the conservative approach of neglect, since both may have made peace with the political constraints that deny the necessary resources to address social ills. The social sciences and their promises to provide an objective, credible source of policy information may be hopelessly compromised by political pressures to affirm existing power relationships.

This book is not intended as a definitive commentary on liberal and conservative thought nor as a history of social welfare and welfare reform in the United States. Rather, it meditates on the value of social welfare proposals that are inspired by these ideologies, raising questions about the development of social policy in the United States and the contribution of the social sciences to the debate over public policy.

SUMMARY AND PLAN OF BOOK

The uncertainty of evidence undercuts all of the proposals for reforming America's social welfare system. The fundamental debate over initial cause—subcultural versus structural versus genetic versus nonrational—is inherently irresolvable. Applied and policy-directed research also has failed to provide scientifically credible evaluations of social interventions. The nation believes because it needs to believe and not because it possesses any rational information that identifies the causes and effects of human behavior or that assesses the efficacy of the interventions themselves. This delusion erodes the pillars of the social welfare debate. It also undermines much of the social authority of the policy community and the social sciences, especially their claims that they occupy important roles in the production of objective information for democratic decision-making.

The welfare debate has focused on the ability of programs—both public and private—to achieve specific values that are central to the American ethos: work and economic self-sufficiency, strong families, and social adjustment. These values also can be interpreted as instrumental in achieving broader visions, usually social tranquility, public civility, and a wide consensus on American democracy itself. This is essentially a debate over socialization, the reduction of deviant behaviors such as lassitude, illegitimacy, crime, mental disease, "oppositional subcultures" (to use Massey and Denton's [1993] phrase), and so forth.

The politics of social welfare policy are created when normal socialization fails and the public moves along to consider a variety of alternative strategies for restoring tranquility. These strategies have focused on improving market behaviors, such as work, through changes in the market itself or in the capacities of the worker; protecting or creating functioning families; and directly challenging deviant personal behaviors, through intensive casework, case management, and psychotherapy, to name a few.

As many note, poverty has long been viewed as a problem of labor force participation. Yet, the incentive effects of welfare, particularly on work and family structure (marriage, divorce, childbearing), are poorly understood and hardly endorse any particular intervention. Indeed, the weakness of almost all social welfare interventions—the miserably low levels at which they are funded to achieve their goals—would intuitively argue for simply higher levels of care. Still, ignorance of effects has not inhibited a ferocious and seemingly interminable debate between liberals and conservatives over the wisdom of their separate visions. In this light, their differences are better understood as frank political plays to a partisan audience than as any sort of high-minded pursuit of the common good.

The descriptions and analyses throughout this book are initially presented in simple form and addressed with increasing complexity in succeeding chapters. The chapters are organized along the lines of the thematic evidence: labor supply, family structure, training programs for welfare recipients, and the personal social services. Chapter 1 lays out the difficulties of addressing poverty, economic and social inequality, and their associated problems in the United States. It states the terms of the analysis. While the argument focuses upon the narrow range of programs commonly considered to constitute welfare, the purpose is to comment on the broader sense of social welfare policy. Chapter 2 presents the current range of policy proposals for reforming welfare, including the Clinton Administration's 1996 ratification of conservative legislation—the Personal Responsibility and Work Opportunity Reconciliation Act of 1996. The chapter traces the rational authority of the different proposals back to their empirical claims and sets the analytic tasks for subsequent chapters.

Chapter 3 analyzes the impact of welfare on work, specifically addressing current programs and, more generally, the theoretical interactions between the two. Chapter 4 considers the possible effects of direct welfare on family structure, addressing one of the central supports for the moral-hazards argument. The moral-hazards argument implies that direct welfare in pursuing a reduction of poverty creates perverse incentives that undermine the traditional virtues, such as personal responsibility and modesty, family loyalty, devotion to children, ambition, and the central social institutions—among them, family, community, and work. The chapter also considers whether any of the proposed welfare reforms have any ability to address the continuing existence of dysfunctional families.

Work training is frequently posed as an alternative to direct relief. Chapter 5 extends the concern with work to specific programs designed to improve the capacity of low-skilled workers and long-term welfare recipients to enter the job market. Chapter 6 analyzes the impact of personal social services—psychotherapy, social work, and a variety of other targeted programs—on welfare recipients and other poor groups. It considers the ability of therapeutic social services to achieve socialization in the absence of traditional social institutions, namely functioning families, supportive communities, effective education and vocational preparation, and the availability of work.

The conclusions, Chapter 7, of this bleak and ambiguous study in gray collect the separate chapters to support a summary that largely negates any pretense to rationality in this forum of American social policymaking. The ignorance of the social science literature relates to two underlying problems: the practical impossibility of determining either social causation or the effects of state intervention and the failure of the intellectual community to provide an adequate constituency for the goal of greater equality. These two failures have conspired with an increasingly conservative popular will to determine the contemporary politics of poverty, expressed in the 1996 reform law. Yet, the social science community's failures impede the development of effective social welfare policy, rebuking its pretenses to leadership and rationality.

The conclusions also consider the role of the social sciences in policy development and their relation to the problems of a deteriorating American civic culture. At least in the arena of welfare policy, the social sciences do not appear to have achieved a satisfying compromise with rationality. Neither its statements concerning human behavior nor its evaluations of social programs constitute a practice of limited rationality that provides scientifically credible information for public decisionmaking. The social sciences seem to be creating politically obedient myths of governance that endorse the impossible hope of social efficiency: the notion that social problems can be resolved inexpensively and with little disruption of customary social institutions.

The logic of these conclusions does not fall victim to its own critique; the conclusions are no more rational than the positions they seek to replace. Nevertheless, they embrace political values that the established orthodoxies cannot refute. Contemporary social authority in the United States has not defined the welfare of citizens correctly, a failure that justifies any number of alternatives, notably generosity.

The book is a systematic attack both on the conservative's vain hope that neglect is therapeutic and on the liberal's conceit that a little bit of assistance is sufficient. Much greater expenditures are probably needed if any progress is to be made in realizing a just, safe, and satisfying society. Yet, generosity is lamentably millenarian even if quite timely.

1 The Rhetoric of Welfare

Never edenic, social conditions in the United States are deteriorating, and solutions for social problems are demanding attention. However, the difficulties of verifying either the causes of these problems or the effects of implemented solutions have produced an epistemic fix in the social sciences that inhibits their ability to inform social welfare policy: no general strategy enjoys clear rational support. Preferences for one course of action over another remain largely ideological. Moreover, a pragmatic compromise between competing social visions is impeded by a strategic conundrum: the lack of certainty over program effectiveness counsels caution while extensive social need pushes for boldness.

The history of social welfare in the United States is one of neglect and timidity. There are no credible success stories for the poor, no forceful attempts to interrupt the patterns of social failure and economic dependency. The one untried policy option—generosity—has never been instituted. The United States is certainly wealthy enough to afford a policy of generosity, but the form it should take is ambiguous since neither the social sciences nor any political camp have cleared a path to viable programs. Still, the political improbability of generous solutions does not diminish their desirability.

With rare exceptions, it seems improbable that any of the interventions on the table—even the most thoroughgoing—will be able to address American society's fundamental problems. The proposals are focused more on reducing dependency than on reducing poverty. Moreover, in the few instances when they seem to focus on poverty, the proposals tend only to address its most superficial manifestations—the absence of minimally adequate standards of living. Yet filling even this measure of the poverty gap while maintaining commensurate rewards for the near poor and the working class would require massively greater public expenditures than contemporary politics or for that matter political tolerances at any time during the past are willing to ante up. Nevertheless, even at these levels of public expenditure there is little assurance, or even reason to believe, that the underlying causes of social problems, or more carefully stated, the more threatening social problems associated with poverty and inequality, will be addressed. As a consequence, the bad things that happen all too often in America will continue; our little murderers, orphans, and street people will simply be a bit better fed and clothed.

Even if economic inequalities are reduced to the point at which few live below the poverty line, many people will still be brought up without viable families; violent unprotected neighborhoods will continue to trap their residents in "oppositional" and dysfunctional subcultures; many will remain unemployed; the underground economy will grow; millions will continue to be addicted to drugs and alcohol; and, in the end, many more will lead desperate, unrewarding, and sterile lives, a danger to their neighbors and a burden to themselves. Filling these deficits in basic social institutions would require annual expenditures far, far in excess of even what the most liberal proposals of the past decades have advocated. Indeed, the nation would have to embark upon a generous program of publicly targeted jobs to rectify the appalling failures of its culture.

This is a very different story than the one that the social sciences are telling. The professions of objective truth seem mired in disciplinary formalism and ideological battles over the wisdom of their politically tempered solutions. Few if any of the proposed solutions have any ability, however, to achieve their avowed goals or to affect the underlying social concerns that propel the search for effective interventions.

THE RHETORIC OF SOCIAL WELFARE

The rhetoric of social welfare customarily begins with recognition by influential social groups of a problem, often based upon evidence that the norms of society have been violated. The argument then proceeds to identify causes of the violation; on the strength of these causes, it recommends interventions that usually have proved in preliminary tests, analyses, or historical reconstructions to be effective. The sticking point in almost all social welfare constructions, however, is the difficulty of credibly establishing the causes of social conditions. This ambiguity of cause—the essential issues of fact—together with differences over basic social values promote the factionalism of political debate.

Information remains the crucial component of the rhetoric of public policy. It determines the relative values of goals, the causal roles of different factors, and the power of interventions to master those factors. Policy information, usually cultural, frequently aspires to be rational, and the policymaking process customarily combines the two qualities. Although the importance of goals is often assessed implicitly through personal and collective experience, their centrality and their relationship to each other are also tested through social scientific opinion surveys, historical analyses, and a variety of tests of their causal influence. The demonstration of cause itself requires formal proof but, again, personal experience and social tradition often validate particular factors that in the end prove decisive for policymaking. The case for the effectiveness of interventions is built, then, by belief and tradition as well as by more formal evidence.

THE CONTEMPORARY DEBATE

The contemporary welfare debate in the United States is framed by growing social problems and an intensifying competition over scarce public resources. At its most apparent level, the problems are captured by demographic measures that assess the vitality of basic social institutions of American society and the society's capacity to support those institutions. More profound, these measures also evaluate American progress in achieving its fundamental social goals—fairness, social tranquility, justice, adequacy, and equality.

Scarcity drives the policy debate. If resources were plentiful, at least relative to desires, there would be little social conflict. However, human appetites seem insatiable, and at every level of society an intense competition exists to maintain control of private resources and decisive influence over public expenditures.

Competing visions of public policy—the market versus government—have played out in the intellectual life of the United States. An enormous portion of modern scholarship is devoted to the antagonistic claims of these political poles, each leading to different empirical statements about the causes and solutions for social problems. Because these solutions can entail vastly different tax encumbrances and public benefits, they define the large stakes in policy outcomes.

The federal budget deficit has precipitated the battle lines of recent social politics. Previous decades have chosen other superordinate imperatives—war, inflation, growth, the environment, poverty, and equality. Whatever their merits as unifying social themes, it is clear that each captured the political imagination of its time, defining both contemporary social dialectics and the opportunities for factional organization. These overarching political issues structure what seems to be the permanent competition over American social welfare priorities.

Social welfare can be construed narrowly in terms of the interests of society's most dependent citizens—the poor and the physically and mentally incapacitated. Or it can more profitably be broadened to include the far greater number of citizens who lead precarious economic and social existences and are at risk of poverty and dependency. In its widest sense, social welfare is the general notion of the public good, encompassing the relationships among citizens and between them and their government.

In the narrow sense, the welfare debate targets perhaps 10–15 percent of Americans; in its broad sense, social welfare policy probably touches the lives of more than half of the American population. Thus, it inescapably affects the tenor of contemporary society. Yet even in its narrow sense, any proposal to address the needs of the most dependent population, especially when their problems appear to be related to social deficiencies as opposed to medical or mental incapacities, necessarily implies a consideration of the broader rights and obligations of many more people. This becomes apparent in the debate over federal fiscal policy, the issue of who should pay the bills and who should benefit. If social welfare policy moves to include more and more people, its size and costs naturally increase with the result that taxes become a pressing political issue. Its impact on some sense of the natural order of society also increases.

EMPIRICAL VERIFICATION AND SOCIAL DIALECTICS

The rhetorical heart of the social welfare debate invariably contains contending claims that the causes of a social problem, emergent or actual, have been identified and that the proferred solution can deal with that cause. In the rhetoric, both the cause of a social problem and its solution are typically factual claims that are amenable to empirical testing, at least in principle. The possibility of verification has justified the modern and increasingly quantitative practice of the social sciences. At the same time, the definition of a social problem is also a normative and ideological choice.

Social dialectics for some time now have arbitrated between the liberal vision of American society, favoring government intervention, and the conservative vision, with its faith in market solutions. By adhering to incompatible assumptions about society, the different outlooks naturally lead to different fiscal strategies: their policies benefit different groups and distribute the burden of paying for those benefits differently.

The alternative visions naturally attract competitive constituencies. The conservative ideology, emphasizing characterological deficiency as the source of social failure, draws support from among the traditional low-tax, low-expenditure business community and the new right that is animated by a vision of small, unobtrusive government. In contrast, the liberal constituency has largely consisted of those who seek to control market forces through government action.

The liberal vision locates individual failure in the imperfections of social institutions—the economy, the family, the community—over which the individual has little control. In the logic of liberalism, the unregulated market produces a variety of social problems—monopoly, unemployment, environmental degradation, and abuses of power and wealth—that necessitate government intervention. In contrast, the conservative vision worries over the possible tyrannies of government, its power not simply to impede market productivity and to threaten private wealth but also to arbitrarily limit personal and political freedoms. The potential effects of state action are therefore central to the arguments of both sides.

The criteria to evaluate state action, and by extension the welfare state generally, have become formal and, with the proviso of Pareto optimality, broadly accepted (Barr 1993). State intervention—regulation, finance, the direct production of goods and services, and income transfers—is preferable to the private market to the extent to which it is economically efficient or to which it achieves a variety of nonmarket goals (such as security, justice, equality), or both. Indeed, security, in the sense of social insurance, is a main justification for the welfare state. Economic efficiency is broadly conceived to be "a Pareto improvement . . . [that] takes place if any change in production or distribution makes one person better-off without making anyone else worse-off" (Barr 1993:105).

However, the notion of welfare includes more than economical aid, embracing also the less tangible benefits of social justice. Ideological factions have formed over what constitutes social justice—liberty for libertarians, utilities for liberals, and equality, freedom, and fraternity for socialists—and the degree, if any, to which these ideals justify the sacrifice of economic efficiency. Still, "an increase in efficiency which does not impair social justice is an unambiguous gain under *any* theory of society" (Barr 1993:428). With this in mind, state intervention is justified where the standard assumptions of the "invisible hand theorem" fail and room exists to improve efficiency through state action without injury to social justice (Barr 1993).

This theory of state action, tied to the seemingly tangible idea of economic efficiency, is intended to create a rational test for welfare interventions and thereby for the value of state intervention relative to the workings of the private market. Yet even while disciplined by a formal definition of benefit, the notion of welfare remains curiously imprecise, allowing for new political goals to arise as social imperatives and preferences evolve. This slippery notion of welfare begs the issue of rationality by leaving the door wide open to possible inefficiencies, such as social insurance and social justice that function as received values in the welfare state but cannot be shown to promote efficiency. In this way, general formulations of the welfare state become necessarily limited when goals cannot be rationally derived and must be accepted largely as cultural norms (and therefore nonrational) (Merton 1957).

The choice between markets and government is often characterized in terms of their defining strengths and failures: markets maximize economic efficiencies and fail at distributional equities; government can achieve nonmarket goals but at the price of efficiency (Wolf 1988). Markets tend toward economic injustices, such as monopoly, price fixing, and the perturbations of the business cycle (unemployment and inflation, among others); governments tend toward the failures of political power. Wolf (1988), for one, hopes that each is the antidote for the other, but this too is simply the same problem of knowing the optimal mix.

If the choice between markets and government is to be rational, then one is obliged to assess the impact of market control relative to state intervention. However, without an empirical test of their relative effect, interventions may be *understandable* only in principle. Without verification, they remain nonrational speculations about true cause even while they may have decisive political importance. In this way, constructs such as race, class, gender, regionalism, and so on—even while failing to rationally explain a variety of outcomes—may yet achieve graphic standing because of their symbolic prominence in factional disputes.

With this in mind, can social welfare policy be understood rationally? Probably not, with the result that social policymaking will remain proportionately political. Moreover, without an ability to measure the effects of market-based approaches versus state action, the policy sciences themselves, predicated precisely upon objective analysis, cannot reach intellectual maturity. Without the ability to judge policy effectiveness decisively, policy research comes to fulfill a literary role, advocating one cultural value over another, its research studies creating mythic belief.

A QUICK PROFILE OF U.S. SOCIAL CONDITIONS

While the U.S. economy has grown over the past few decades, poverty has increased along with a variety of other problems. Poverty rates that declined from roughly 22 percent in 1960 to about 11 percent in 1973, stayed persistently high throughout the 1980s, reaching a peak of 15 percent in 1984 and dropping only slightly to 14 percent by 1989 (U.S. Bureau of the Census 1995). Large economic disparities persist among blacks, Hispanics, and whites with poverty rates in 1993 of 33 percent, 31 percent, and 12 percent respectively (Bureau of the Census 1995). Nevertheless, it is possible that the official statistics exaggerate the extent of poverty, at least as measured by the official poverty threshold— $14,763 for a family of four in 1993.[1] Still, the poverty line in the United States is very low, fixated on an absolute consideration of need that has changed little since the 1960s. A more accurate estimate, which looks at relative poverty and reflects increased standards of living in the United States since the 1960s, raises the extent of poverty proportionately (Citro and Michael 1995).

Real per capita income has risen steadily over the past few decades from about $10,500 in 1969 to over $15,000 in 1991, but income per employed person has not been as robust, rising from about $27,000 to only $33,000 in the same period (all in 1989 dollars). Levy (in Farley 1995a; Levy 1987) explains this apparent disparity between per capita income and income per employed person in terms of demographic trends—the greater work participation of women, the entry into the work force of the large baby boom generation, and declining family size. Yet, it is not clear that the additional work effort of women is entirely voluntary or that it has translated into a higher standard of living, especially for poorer families. The frequently forced trade-off between family involvement and work, especially for mothers, may be at the root of increasing family problems (Hernandez 1993).

While productivity growth has slowed nationally (Levy in Farley 1995a), wage earners at the bottom of the skill ladder have suffered the most (Cancian, Danziger, and Gottschalk in Papadimitriou and Wolff 1993). The worsening position of less trained workers means that the great economic growth of the 1980s was not widely shared (Blank in Papadimitriou and Wolff 1993; Wetzel in Farley 1995a). Recent economic growth has not created the tide to lift all boats (Tobin in Danziger, Sandefur, and Weinberg 1994; Danziger and Gottschalk 1986); "trickle-down is dead, that is, there has been a surprising decline in the responsiveness of earnings to the macroeconomy" (Weinberg in Papadimitriou and Wolff 1993).

Along with an absolute decline in living standards among some socioeconomic groups, relative inequality, arising out of a competition over

---

1. Citro and Michael (1995), and see Haveman in Papadimitriou and Wolff (1993) for descriptions of these problems. Moreover, Edin's (1991) suggestion that many official sources including the major income surveys persistently undercount income for those receiving AFDC is handled in some detail in the next chapter.

scarce resources, appears to be a crucial consideration in explaining rising social tensions. A variety of sources have documented the growing income and wealth inequalities in the United States. One excellent summary states,

> Wealth inequality is today and has always been extreme and
> substantially greater than income inequality. Indeed, the top
> 1 percent of wealth holders has typically held in excess of
> one-quarter of total household wealth, in comparison to the
> 8 or 9 percent share of income received by the top percentile of the
> income distribution. . . . Thirty-seven percent of the total real income
> gain between 1983 and 1989 accrued to the top 1 percent of income
> recipients (in contrast to 62 percent of the marketable wealth gain),
> 39 percent went to the next 19 percent of the income distribution,
> and 24 percent accrued to the bottom 80 percent (versus only
> 1 percent of the marketable wealth gain). While not as powerfully
> as in the case of wealth, these results for income show again that
> the growth in the economy during the 1980s was concentrated in
> a surprisingly small part of the population. . . . The starkness of these
> numbers suggests a widening fissure separating the strata within our
> society. (Wolff 1995:27)

Since the mid-1970s the earnings share of the poorest quintile of the income distribution has actually declined 9 percent while the next two quintiles have also lost substantial ground. In short, over 60 percent of Americans have seen their relative standards of living decline since 1969.

Declining standards of living are frequently associated with an increase of social instability. Indeed, it is not at all clear whether the declining standards of living for most Americans are the cause or the effect of persistent social problems. For example, the fact that wages for the less well educated have fallen over the past few decades might be linked to a greater demand for education or a greater resistance among the poor to educational opportunities.

While income is a crucial consideration in poverty, it is not a full measure of social well-being (Rainwater 1974). The problem in using a poverty line based almost entirely on food, clothing and shelter costs misses the critical concern of participation in the basic institutions of society that is necessary for successful socialization, citizenship, and social cohesion. Indeed, inadequate participation in these institutions—that is, cultural deprivation—may be the principal reason for pressing social problems, perhaps producing the material differences that translate into economic hardship (Chan 1990). The official measures of poverty, and most of the proposed substitutes for them, largely consider financial status, assuming that economic deprivation drives social deprivation;[2] such measures are very attractive and lend a coherence to social policy debates. Yet economic failure in itself may be as much a result of poor socialization as its cause. Certainly this issue has not been settled in spite of the long popularity of economic causation as an explanatory tool.

Relative cultural poverty and not any fixed level of economic deprivation is the more robust concept for explaining the epidemiology and etiology of social problems. Cultural poverty assumes that inadequate participation in the institutions of society—family, school, community, work, civic culture, and so forth—explains the problems customarily associated with money poverty. The failure of families to appropriately socialize and motivate children interferes with their education, their interaction with peers, their mental and emotional health, and ultimately hobbles their earning capacity and their contribution as citizens. Indeed, the inability to distinguish rationally between economic and social causation has provided a compelling reason to press for human capital investment, although the conditions for successful investments of this kind are still uncertain. Nevertheless, the continuing growth of social problems, particularly among those at the bottom of the income ladder, commands attention to cultural insufficiency in addition to simple money poverty.

It is a cause for alarm that social institutions in the United States seem to be deteriorating. Housing, for example, is important both for its economic influence as well as for its social impact on family and community life. Myers and Wolch (in Farley 1995a) report that between 1980 and 1990, and for the first time since the 1930s, overcrowding increased. Moreover, even after controlling for income and other variables, the overcrowding was "strongly related to race-ethnicity" perhaps "reflecting different cultural tolerances" (Farley 1995a:324). Also during the 1980s, overall ownership rates declined while the proportions of both the "precariously housed" and the "most generously housed" grew:

> In general, the young, minorities, female-headed households, immigrants, and those not in the labor force or unemployed were overrepresented among the precariously housed and faced the greatest risks of becoming precariously housed. For most groups, these risks increased over the decade of the 1980s. (Farley 1995a:325)

The numbers of short-term and long-term homeless have also grown apace with federal cutbacks in housing programs and community mental

2. See Haveman's net earnings capacity in Papadimitriou and Wolff (1993), and Citro and Michael's (1995) assortment of alternatives.

health centers. While as many as two million people may have been homeless at some point during 1990, it has been estimated that at any point in time as many as 300,000 to 400,000 may be homeless (Danziger, Sandefur, and Weinberg 1994:279). Moreover, racial minorities and multiproblem families (those that have been dependent on welfare over generations and headed by young, poorly educated mothers) are overrepresented among the homeless.

Housing patterns have become notably more segregated over the past fifty years. In almost every major urban center in the nation, blacks were more isolated in 1980 than they were in 1940. Massey and Denton (1993) suggest that spatial segregation leading to social isolation is at the root of many other social problems, not the least of which is a growing American underclass, whatever its definition, and intensifying ghetto poverty (also Mincy in Danziger, Sandefur, and Weinberg 1994).

The declining situation of youth is particularly symptomatic of declining family life. In a classic study focusing on the five national censuses between 1940 and 1980 and supplemented with additional survey data, Hernandez (1993) reports large increases since the 1970s in the proportion of American children living in absolute and relative poverty. The absolute poverty rate for children reached a low of 16 percent between 1969 and 1979 and then rose to over 22 percent in the 1990s (Hernandez 1993; Committee on Ways and Means 1994). However, the relative poverty rate is a better measure of cultural deprivation and probably a more useful estimate of social problems. As Galbraith argues,

> [p]eople are poverty-stricken when their income, even if adequate
> for survival, falls markedly behind that of the community. Then they
> cannot have what the larger community regards as the minimum
> necessary for decency; and they cannot wholly escape, therefore,
> the judgment of the large community that they are indecent. They
> are degraded for, in a literal sense, they live outside the grades
> or categories which the community also regards as respectable.
> (Hernandez 1993:241)

In a more material sense, people who are relatively poor probably cannot purchase or in other ways lack critical experiences in the basic social institutions required for successful lives.

Employing a relative poverty threshold of 50 percent of the median family income, adjusted for family size, Hernandez (1993) estimates that 27 percent of American children and 30 percent of preschoolers lived in poverty in 1988, well above the post–Great Depression low of 23 percent in 1979. Fully 52 percent of children in relative poverty live in families that are wholly self-supporting; only 18 percent of the relatively poor are wholly dependent on welfare. The relative poverty rate has been increasing during the 1990s with the result that the United States has made hardly any progress in equality since the 1930s. At the same time, tax changes during the past few decades have favored the wealthy (Slemrod 1994). While it is apparent that the poor today have more possessions than they had in the 1930s, it is not at all apparent that they are better off socially or that society has become more cohesive. To the contrary, social fissures are deepening, and material progress past a certain minimum apparently provides no assurance of social progress.

Hernandez (1993) offers the observation that the rise of "dual-earner or one-parent" families has occasioned great instability for children. "By 1980, in fact, about 60 percent of all children lived in dual-earner or one-parent families" (10). The resultant need for alternative child care did not in itself produce harmful consequences. Yet, Hernandez adds,

> the quality of care received appears to have important consequences, and children from low-income families are especially at risk. In general, the time that mothers devoted to child care as a primary activity increased between the 1920s and the early 1960s, but since then it has declined. (Hernandez 1993:11)

Moreover, education has not acted as an adequate social leveler in that levels of attainment are perpetuated within families. Society seems to be tracking in divergent directions with children of better educated parents increasingly differentiating themselves economically and socially from children of poorly educated parents:

> In both the short term and the long run, parents' relatively high educational attainments represent an important resource from which children benefit—a steppingstone to success. Conversely, children whose parents have completed relatively few years of school were found to be comparatively disadvantaged in their chances of achieving success. (Hernandez 1993:192)

Hernandez's (1993) bleak portrait of American youth has been echoed in a variety of prominent reports and studies (see, among others, Carnegie Council on Adolescent Development 1995; National Commission on Children 1991).

Increasing crime and substance addiction are also notable signals that basic social institutions—the family, the community, and schools—are failing in their basic socialization functions. The prominent conservative, William J. Bennett, has trenchantly summarized these trends (Bennett

1994). Between 1960 and 1992, the overall crime rate tripled while the violent crime rate more than quadrupled from 16 to 76 episodes per 100,000 population. Murders committed by juveniles, especially blacks, have skyrocketed along with the probabilities of becoming a juvenile victim, generally among the poor. The lifetime probability of victimization is startling: there is an 83 percent probability that a twelve-year-old in 1987 will suffer one or more violent crimes in his or her lifetime; a 40 percent probability of suffering a robbery or assault resulting in injury; and an 87 percent chance of experiencing three or more thefts (Siegel and Senna 1991). Juvenile arrests as well as incarceration rates have increased proportionately, again particularly among blacks. Piel (1993) has commented wryly that the United States "crowds more than a million convicts into its prisons, among them 40 times as many black prisoners, proportionately, as South Africa at the peak of apartheid" (117).

Indeed, Tonry (1995) has pointed out that blacks are six times more likely to be in prison than whites, a disparity that does "not result from increases in the proportions of serious crimes committed by blacks" (28). It is startling that in 1990 23 percent of black males in the United States between the ages of twenty and twenty-nine were under the control of the criminal justice system—in jail, on parole or probation, or on bail or recognizance while awaiting trial. In Washington, D.C., 42 percent of black males between eighteen and thirty-five were under control of the justice system in 1991, and in the same year the corresponding figure for Baltimore was 56 percent (Tonry 1995:29–30).

Bennett (1994) details the growing prevalence of illicit drug use. While overall drug use appears to have declined since its peak in 1979, the number of hard-core addicts has stayed relatively stable. Nonetheless, the decline in reported drug use may be unreliable since self-reports from the national surveys of drug use are notoriously reactive to a variety of respondent biases (Sidney 1990). Still, the 1988 National Household Survey on Drug Abuse reports an immense amount of illicit drug use, notably among youths and young adults. Among those under the age of twenty-six, 500,000 reported taking illicit drugs intravenously; 800,000 may have taken hallucinogens such as LSD; 300,000 used crack cocaine; 1.5 million used cocaine; six million smoked marijuana.

Other indicators of the social good and the health of the civic culture are also troubling. Youth suicide is increasing, as is the rate of out-of-wedlock births. Divorce and family dissolution are at all-time American highs. Child abuse and neglect are common, persistent problems. Civic participation also appears to be thinner: voter turnout, especially among poorer voters has declined, as has active membership in political parties and unions, charitable giving, and church membership.

Educational attainment has not progressed much in the past twenty-five years. Overall graduation rates from high school have not improved since the 1960s, with regular graduation rates having declined slightly and the GED (General Equivalency Degree) rate increasing (Jencks and Peterson 1991:63). While the dropout rate for blacks improved between 1970 and 1988, the overall rate including a high Hispanic dropout rate has held steady.

In short, social problems in the United States seem to be rising along with economic disparities. Yet modern industrialization does not explain the severity of these problems; other contemporary industrialized democracies do not appear to be suffering these problems to the same extent.[3] Moreover, the chance to mount an adequate public response may be lost in the competition over scarce resources, increasingly driven by the politics of the national deficit and an increasingly aging population. Social and economic inequalities—and the growing amount of frank need—seem to be running beyond the meager provisions of the welfare state and the sympathies of its citizens.

THE STATE RESPONSE TO POVERTY

Portions of the welfare state, particularly its regulatory apparatus and to a lesser extent its tax structure, are designed, at least in part, to prevent poverty.[4] In contrast, its social welfare components, including transfer programs as well as a variety of social services, are geared to handle the consequences. These programs, notably Aid to Families with Dependent Children and Food Stamps, are at the center of the political controversy surrounding poverty and dependency.

Since the 1960s, a large number of programs have been developed to handle poverty and its associated social problems. In 1995, $177 billion was spent on federal means-tested entitlement programs, which comprise the core of the welfare state's efforts for poor people. Approximately half, $82 billion, was spent on Medicaid, the largest of these programs,

---

3. A variety of studies and reports have suggested that America's social problems are disproportionately large compared with other industrialized nations: McFate, Lawson, and Wilson (1995); Osberg (1991); Rainwater and Smeeding (1995); Rainwater, Rein, and Schwartz (1986); Smeeding, O'Higgins, and Rainwater 1990; Townsend 1992.

4. The effects of these programs are outside this book's consideration, which focuses on programs directed at poverty and low income.

of which fully 72 percent was used for the elderly and disabled (Parrott 1995).[5] Indeed, in 1995 only about $17 billion, or about 1.6 percent of all federal outlays, was spent on the nonworking poor for AFDC, child care, and child support enforcement (Parrott 1995); the states matched the federal share with approximately $12 billion (Committee on Ways and Means 1994:389). An additional $25 billion was spent on Food Stamps of which a large portion, perhaps 60 percent ($15 billion), was spent on AFDC recipients (Parrott 1995). Moreover, AFDC recipients accounted for a very small portion of the $9 billion spent on other entitlement programs (Parrott 1995). In 1995, another $63 billion was appropriated for a multitude of discretionary programs targeted at the low-income population, including the poor and near-poor disabled, children, elderly, and adults as well as people living in poor neighborhoods (Parrott 1995). In the end, a very small amount of money—perhaps $50 billion (in total AFDC and family support expenditures, Food Stamps, housing, and other discretionary and nondiscretionary programs) plus Medicaid—is spent on the AFDC caseload. Thus, the classic welfare recipients of the popular imagination consume far less than 10 percent of the federal budget and only a tiny fraction of the wealth of the nation. Yet the welfare debate is curiously intense.

As the forum to discuss the conditions of deservingness—that is, the priorities for establishing rights to public compensation and relief—the symbolic importance of AFDC is far out of proportion to the size of its budget. The program has become the bellwether for all antipoverty programs, many of which are specifically tied to its standards of eligibility. Within broad guidelines, eligibility for AFDC is set individually by the different states. The small AFDC-UP (Unemployed Parents) program pays benefits to two-parent families, while the much larger AFDC program is restricted to single parents who meet its income criteria, which the states customarily set below the poverty level. In 1993, the average family on AFDC (approximately three people) received about $373 a month, a considerable cut from the average 1970 payment of $676 a month (in 1993 dollars) (Committee on Ways and Means 1994:325). Moreover, taking AFDC payments together with maximum Food Stamp allotments for a family of three (approximately $200 a month in 1993 after calculating the reduction for AFDC), it appears that combined bene-

---

5. Moreover, much of Medicaid is spent on patients in nursing homes who have taken advantage of liberal transfer provisions to divest themselves of their assets in order to qualify for coverage. These people, who are only formally needy, distort the role of Medicaid, exaggerating its coverage of the poor.

fits—the basic welfare package—have decreased substantially since 1970 (and even more since the peak years of welfare in the mid-1970s). The typical welfare family therefore receives about $6,400 a year (about $530 a month) in cash and Food Stamps in addition to Medicaid.

Another small percentage of recipients, less than 10 percent lives in public housing while perhaps another 14 percent receives housing subsidies (Committee on Ways and Means 1994:402, 409). Still others receive some social services, including day care. However, in 1992 welfare payments removed only about 12 percent of poor people from poverty; in contrast, the social insurance program, notably Social Security, removed fully 30 percent of the poor from poverty (Committee on Ways and Means 1994:1171). Put in other terms, social insurance reduced the poverty gap by 44 percent while means-tested welfare payments reduced it by only 24 percent (Committee on Ways and Means 1994:1172).

It is also notable that the National Academy of Sciences suggested a modest increase in the poverty threshold, of between 14 percent and 24 percent (Citro and Michael 1995:54–55). Others have argued for much greater increases. Against a higher poverty threshold, the effectiveness of public transfer programs in removing people from poverty declines dramatically.

The AFDC rolls have grown enormously, almost doubling from about 7.5 million recipients in 1970 to about 14.1 million in 1993 (Committee on Ways and Means 1994:325).[6] Typically, two-thirds of recipients are children. The participation of eligible families seems to have doubled since 1967 when the rate was about 40 percent, leveling out at about 80 percent in the 1980s (Giannarelli and Clark 1992; Ruggles and Michel 1987). The increased enrollment is variously attributed to broadened eligibility criteria; increased need; changing social mores, particularly related to out-of-wedlock childbearing; and relaxed social attitudes toward dependency. In response, a considerable amount of research has been conducted to describe, and perhaps explain, the dynamics of welfare use: reasons for reliance on welfare, conditions under which people exit, and the length of use.

Bane and Ellwood (1994) estimated that about 42 percent of first-time AFDC spells took place because divorce, separation, or death made a woman into the single head of her family's household. Another 39 percent began welfare because they bore a child out of wedlock. Only about 7 percent of first-time spells resulted from a fall in earnings. The average

---

6. The modest decrease in the AFDC rolls since 1993—perhaps 9 percent—may be due more to mechanical changes in eligibility and other administrative decisions than to any change in the economy, social attitudes, or characteristics of the poor themselves.

duration of first-time spells is 4.4 years with about 55 percent of first-time recipients expected to use welfare for four years or less during their lifetime. Those with less education who have never been married are expected to rely upon welfare to a greater extent than the better educated who have been married. Of all those who exit AFDC, 30 percent leave because they marry, and another 25 percent leave because they find jobs. About 11 percent age out of the system, presumably without finding a spouse or a job, when their youngest child reaches age eighteen. Thus, Bane and Ellwood (1994) painted an AFDC picture in which most recipients, perhaps two-thirds, rely upon welfare for a relatively short period of time; another smaller group, presumably less skilled and perhaps more socially debilitated, rely upon welfare for a considerable period. Bane and Ellwood's (1994) view of welfare utilization is widely accepted, although estimates of time on welfare and exits from it have varied.[7]

All parties to the controversy over welfare seem to accept that the current welfare program has failed to adequately abate poverty and that too many Americans remain poor and dependent for too long upon public relief. The Family Support Act (FSA) of 1988 that preceded the 1996 welfare reform—the Personal Responsibility and Work Opportunity Reconciliation Act of 1996—has failed to resolve either dependency or poverty. The welfare rolls remained stubbornly high in spite of FSA's provisions for job training, and the benefits themselves, provided at levels well below the official poverty line, were rarely enough to cover basic needs, much less eliminate poverty.

SOCIAL SCIENCE AND THE ISSUE OF CAUSE

The social sciences have drawn their public authority from the production of rational information for the policymaking process. They claim to provide scientifically credible information to evaluate goals, to identify the causes of social problems, and to assess the effectiveness of policy interventions in achieving those goals. The authority of the social sciences is derived at least formally from adherence to the rules of scientific ration-

---

7. Yet Stevens (1994) has shown that mobility out of poverty spells has generally declined between 1970 and 1987. In contrast with Bane and Ellwood (1994), Harris (1993) insists that fully two-thirds of exits from AFDC take place through work and accordingly argues for greater human capital investments. A variety of others, notably Blank and Ruggles (1993) and Ruggles and Michel (1987), have reported a range of differences. It is important, however, to note that these differences fluctuate with the different ways that work, in particular, is defined and measured—the shorter the time span of work, the higher the percentage of recipients who are reported to work. The reasons for welfare utilization, that is, the interpretation of use, have been hotly contested.

ality, and, indeed, the social sciences reject the subjective, implicit, immeasurable, and incoherent policymaking processes of culture. Instead, they offer a rational alternative: impartial and logically connected evidence to inform the "intelligence of democracy."

Demonstration of the instrumental value of social policy requires the assessment of outcomes. Each proposition about the relative value of government versus market solutions must therefore be amenable to empirical verification. In contrast, self-certifiable truths are beyond any objective process of verification. Empirical verification requires that rational methods exist and that they can be appropriately applied. In turn, methodological adequacy is measured against the scientific canon of controlled experimentation. Yet, the social scientist, in pointed distinction to the natural scientist, faces serious practical and situational obstacles to creating controlled experimental environments; the full epistemological maturity of his or her art is questionable. The absence of rational techniques for evaluating interventions or the failure to execute research without bias undercuts the possibility of scientifically credible policy information.

Glazer (1988) acknowledges that the causes of social problems have proven elusive. He argues that "the most significant limitation on the effectiveness of social policy is simply lack of knowledge" (6) and that information itself is limited by the insuperable complexity of underlying problems as well as by cost. The stubborn absence of rational information has evoked a lament to end ideology, a lament, often expressed about the War on Poverty, that the social sciences would "relegate the ideological conflicts between conservatives and liberals and radicals to the past because we now knew more and because we had the tools, or were developing them, to do better" (Glazer 1988:1). At the heart of the disenchantment with the rational promise of the social sciences is the observation that truth—the identification of social causation—has many profound contingencies. Most notably, perhaps, the solutions themselves seem to create unanticipated new problems, which, from the conservative perspective, subvert traditional social structures, notably the family and the neighborhood.

There are two basic types of cause: causes that initiate a problem and causes that sustain it. They may be the same, but frequently a social problem is sustained by factors other than those that produced it. Many liberals believe that poverty is both an initial cause and a sustaining one in such contemporary social problems as drug addiction, delinquency, school truancy, and illegitimacy. These problems may be sustained, however, by additional factors, such as peer pressure, family dissolution, and so forth. Other factors rooted in the family's wider environment—technological displacement, discrimination, and social neglect—may also account for social problems. In this way, transfer programs that address only money poverty will have little impact on social problems. Likewise, if poverty is produced by the deviant behaviors of underclass subcultures, then addressing poverty as a result of institutional factors, such as unemployment and lack of skills, will also fail to reduce social problems.

While resolving existing social problems requires only the identification of sustaining causes, preventing social problems entails the discovery of initial causes. Yet the choice to handle only emergent problems may be less expensive and less socially invasive than a strategy of prevention. Initial causes may be embedded in the culture, and the cost of prevention may exceed its benefits since the number of people at risk of a problem may be far greater than the number who eventually suffer from it; thus, paying for the effects of a problem may cost less than paying to prevent its emergence.

METHOD AND RATIONALITY

Classical experimentation—the randomized controlled trial (RCT)—is the definitive method for establishing the cause and effectiveness of an intervention.[8] Yet, even theoretically, rationality itself is filled with many ambiguities: Heisenberg uncertainties, the prisoner's dilemma, the inability of all competitors to maximize their gains, the impossibility of Pareto optima, Godel's theorem, and others.[9] RCTs necessitate a number of important safeguards against research pitfalls: prospective experimentation to assure a complete sample and the integrity of the experimental variable; random selection from the population at risk to assure representativeness; random assignment to assure comparability between experimental and control groups; reliable and valid measurement of outcomes; and a variety of other methodological protections against bias, attrition, and the loss of data (censoring).

In the case of poverty research, an RCT implies a test in which a representative sample of people at risk of poverty is randomly selected and randomly assigned to either of at least two conditions: an experimental condition in which the presumed causal factors are present and a control condition in which those factors are absent. To assess the effectiveness

8. This position (see Burtless and Orr 1986; Fraker and Maynard 1987) conflicts with at least a portion of the current view that nonexperimental data may be just as good, especially in light of the failures of the social experiments to produce credible findings (Manski and Garfinkel 1992). This issue is handled in greater detail in the following chapters.

9. The literature on rationality and its contradictions is vast. See Nozick (1993) and Rorty (1991) as examples.

of any intervention—training programs, counseling, workfare, and the like—an experiment must then be conducted that compares the randomly selected subjects in the experimental group with those in the control group. In a similar way, the issue of whether genetic or environmental factors cause poverty would necessitate one of two experiments: the first in which people of varying genetic endowments are placed in similar situations and the second in which people of exactly similar genetic inheritance (identical twins) are placed in dissimilar environments.

True tests of causal relations discipline scientific scholarship. Reliable and valid tools are constructed to explore a field's defining problems, and hypotheses of causality are screened through preliminary tests leading to more systematic pilot tests, which are far less costly but still less rigorous than full-blown trials. Indeed, methodologies for these early tests, while mimicking RCTs, are often uncontrolled, imprecise, and unrepresentative. Failed ideas are weeded out; promising leads are refined. The tentative findings feed into the field's discussion of its own social and theoretical value. Finally, mature ideas with theoretical reach and social importance are put through definitive tests.

The research process may proceed gradually or through sudden paradigm shifts. It may be a social expression of cultural tastes or relatively free of political tastes. Nevertheless, the scholarship in a field with claims to rationality builds cumulatively toward decisive tests of its value.

The rigor of these tests define the contingencies of its truth and act as a sorting device both for the field's information and for its practitioners' rewards. In immature fields, the contingencies of the tests of causality are weak; in scientifically mature fields, the contingencies of truth conform with the rigors of RCTs.[10]

It is no wonder that rational information is rare and that even the most important strategic issues of social policy are undecided. RCTs are very expensive and frequently impractical except in clinical settings. Indeed, most deep social causes defy experimental verification. For example, no rational experiment can practically settle the issue of any macroeconomic policy: interest rates cannot be raised for a random sample of Americans and held steady for others. The only possible strategies involve before-and-after comparisons and other historical analyses; however, as social factors cannot be held steady so as to isolate the effects of the experimental concern, "before" conditions customarily de-

---

10. This still recognizes that some very mature scientific fields—such as astronomy and geology—are unable to apply RCTs. Still their predictive capacities are great. Quarks do not talk back, but the human sciences share a compelling need for randomized controls and a host of other protections against bias.

velop in unmeasured ways that contribute to the "after" conditions, apart from any influence of the experimental variable. As a consequence, the outcomes of quasi experiments, those without true controls, cannot reach any causal conclusion about their experimental variables.

The absence of good information is a customary springboard into social dialectics. Yet the absence of rational proofs deprives Glazer (1988), Lasch (1978), and Murray (1984), among many others, of rational grounds for indicting welfare arrangements as a cause of family breakdown. Indeed, given the weaknesses inherent in social science research, it seems especially unlikely that the relationship between the state in its totality and the institutions of civil society could be tested. Thus, the refutation of the "moral hazards" of welfare, curiously contained in Glazer (1988), eludes definitive verification:

> The uniqueness of the United States consists not only in the lateness and incompleteness of its social policy system, but also in the scale of its social problems. Are the two related? *It would appear so.* It can be argued that if there is too great an inequality in income distribution, it is because an insufficient amount is collected in taxes and redistributed as benefits on the basis of need. If there are large numbers of poor people, it is because insufficient funds are provided them to get out of poverty. If there are slums, it is because they are not cleared by government provision. If the poor live in inadequate housing, it is because they are not provided with subsidized housing. If they are unemployed or without jobs, it is because the system of education does not have enough funds, or the system of relating education to work or of retraining workers is inadequate. And if there is family breakup, juvenile delinquency, and crime, it is because of all of the above, not to mention other inadequacies. (Glazer 1988: 176–7, emphasis added)

In any event, the problem remains whether the *appearance* of a relationship, as well as other breaches of rationality, can establish sufficient or reasonable grounds to legitimize social policy. The assertion that the welfare state undermines civil society has a plausible elegance; so does its denial. Without the authority of empirical proof, the argument becomes frankly partisan. The social sciences become enmeshed in the play of power and not in the production of decisive tests of social reality.

RATIONALITY AND STATE INTERVENTION

Yet the ability to evaluate the state in its totality—its synergistic combination of bureaus, programs, regulations, traditions, capacities, and so forth—is circumscribed by the impossibility both legally and ethically of creating controlled tests. In similar ways, the issue of power—the relative influence of business hegemony (welfare capitalism), industrialization, national values, class, gender, and race (using Skocpol's [1992] categories) cannot be known except through their proximity to policy choices. For the same reasons, the influence of an autonomous state in designing and implementing social policy cannot be assessed rationally against alternative explanations. Indeed, even the proof of state autonomy itself, divorced from civic influence, appears to be a nearly impossible condition to prove except in the extremes of tyranny.

Thus, attempts to "bring the state back into" analyses of social welfare, as well as the general testing of social, political, and economic theories, are doomed as rational enterprises; their fundamental pitfall is the absolute inability to create definitive situations in which causation can be known with any sort of scientific credibility. The recent intense argument over the impact of state structures—government, parties, and the political process—on a variety of policy choices is irresolvable (Almond 1988; Orloff and Skocpol 1984; Quadagno 1984; Skocpol and Amenta 1985). Conditions prior to state structures themselves must be taken into account along with transcultural differences (for comparative analyses) and other environmental considerations, including the ambiguities of popular consent, industrialization, and tradition, to name a few. This is impossible except through the fumbling fingers of historical reconstructions with all their inherent limitations of incomplete and incompatible information and their inability to control for unknown possibilities through randomized control groups.

Thus, the intellectual search for knowledge of social welfare must make peace with the inability to know. These compromises are "middle-range generalizations [recalling Merton] about the roles of states in revolutions and reforms, about the social and economic policies pursued by states, and about the effects of states on political conflicts and agendas" (Evans, Rueschemeyer, and Skocpol 1985). Yet the compromises open wide the backdoor to political orderings of reality and the descent into dogma—however refined, detailed, and erudite—that the social sciences promised to transcend. Skocpol's call for "solidly grounded and analytically sharp understandings of the *causal* regularities that underlie the histories of states, social structures, and transactional relations in the modern world" can only be approximated. All that is possible is one or another form of satisfying surmise and varying levels of compatibility between theory and political convenience. This limitation exacts a price from the social sciences: the absence of true tests of causality creates an opening for bias that drains their authority. More important, imperfect analyses, subverting the rigors of rational proof, create discretion for the researcher to interpret and define causal relationships that reflect dominant social preferences instead of social reality. In the end, politically compatible social research becomes myth, presenting decisive social values in authoritative forms.

Causality for Skocpol as well as for the majority of social scientists who try to come to grips with welfare policy may be better understood as metaphor than as science itself. Cause as metaphor vests false scientific authority in some particular ideological system that justifies particular benefits and burdens. The authority of the scientific sense of causation masks an essentially literary use: scientific cause hiding a subjective, "convincing" causality. Yet contemporary policy analysis characteristically lacks proof of either initial or sustaining cause—the essence of rational social policymaking.

Nevertheless, at least in principle, the effects on identified social problems of particular interventions, particularly social services delivered in a clinical setting, can often be credibly verified. Thus, the underlying assertions of both the welfare state and the antiwelfare state positions are testable to the extent to which the outcomes of social welfare programs are evaluated and to the extent to which they can be taken together to evaluate the state itself.

However, rigorous tests of outcomes have rarely if ever been conducted. The few exceptions relative to issues of poverty and dependency, or better said the few rare candidates for scientifically credible prospective RCTs—the Negative Income Tax (NIT) experiments, Manpower Demonstration Research Corporation's (MDRC) work/welfare studies, Bouchard and colleagues' identical-twin investigations (Bouchard 1994; Bouchard et al. 1990), the study of family preservation programs in Illinois (Schuerman, Rzepnicki, and Littel 1994), and very few others—are scientifically controversial, violating many of the canons of research even while they conformed to the rules of randomization. Nevertheless, the common currency of the social welfare literature is composed of far less rigorous research than these few RCTs. As a result, little rational authority exists for social policymaking.

POWER AND TRUTH

Even while conceding noble motives to the social scientist, the infrequent application of credible evaluation to social welfare programs, especially in amenable settings, is one of the major reasons for the continuing intellectual immaturity of the social sciences. The social sciences have squirmed in the light of their own overstated promises to pursue rationality, compensating with practical substitutes for definitive experiments: microdata simulation, quasi experiments, case studies, and a large number of qualitative methods. All of these alternatives are seriously marred by their compromises with rationality, however.

An impaired ability to create rational data implies that the social scientist's role will be proportionately influenced by political interests. Indeed, the possible dominance of power over truth, to use Aaron's (1978) formulation for the tension between social preference and objective fact, has been the second major threat to the authority of the social scientist. The social scientist exists in an intensely partisan and ideological environment in which the contingencies of power are dominated by organized private interests, notably the business community and the government. The very human ambitions of social scientists for status, money, and influence are fulfilled in large part by the degree to which their research satisfies the needs of these constituencies. To the extent to which social scientists fail to conform with the canons of rationality while furthering factional ambitions, they become factional themselves, more priests, advocates, sorcerers, and shamans than arbiters of objective social reality. The barbered scholarship of biased social investigations testifies to the postmodern critique that the social sciences create narratives that exculpate dominant social interests. In this way, by failing to fulfill a neutral role in the production of objective social information, the social sciences invent the myths of culture, the decisive dramas of social existence that influence policy choices.

Over the years, the most troublesome party in these power relationships has been the government. Government may pursue objective data but frequently, for its own bureaucratic imperatives, needs "scientific" justification for its political role. The extensive use of contractual social science both in the academy as well as in private research firms is often bent to the narrow needs of public agencies for budget justifications. As deLeon (1988) points out, "The financial hardships visited upon the Urban Institute and Mathematica by the Reagan administration demonstrates that even the most prestigious of the 'think tanks' are no more safe havens for independent thinking than the medieval churches" (111).

The social sciences also have developed similar relations with a variety of commercial agents and private foundations, most of which are customarily committed to particular points of view. Reliance upon a process of mutual adjustment to inform public policy through the factional studies of competitive interests provides no protection for excluded stakeholders, however. The problem becomes pressing when the excluded interests are sizable or strategically positioned in the cycle of social problems.

Not surprisingly, social scientists, building their arguments on pillars of data and research created through government funding, often laud the benefits of publicly funded research for the policymaking process. Nathan (1988), drawing upon a variety of projects, notably including MDRC's study of GAIN and Supported Work, argued that public funding for the applied social sciences (the policy sciences) creates important information for policymaking through demonstration and evaluation research. DeLeon (1988) extends the argument to include the creation of important intellectual tools. The field is well aware that the auspices of research influence its independence and that, without the assurance of rationality, information is susceptible to the charge of propagandizing particular points of view.

THE POLICY ELITE AND DECISIONMAKING: THE ROLE OF THE POLICY EXPERT

Barr (1993) provides a common reconciliation of rational policy expertise and political bias:

> . . . the proper place of ideology is in the choice of aims, particularly the definition of social justice and its trade-off with economic efficiency; but once these aims have been agreed, the choice of method should be regarded as a *technical* issue, not an ideological one. Whether a commodity like health care is produced publicly or privately should be decided on the basis of which method more nearly achieves previously agreed aims. (Barr 1993:109)

This attempt to define a practice of limited rationality redeems the social sciences from a hopeless dependency on political favor by ennobling its capacity to provide scientifically credible advice. It accepts a political process that defines social goals but insists that once the normative criteria of social acceptability have been established, alternatives means to achieve them can be compared rationally. In this way, the social scientist can pragmatically sidestep a disqualifying utopianism by fulfilling an obligation to neutral and rational analyses while accommodating social preferences.

Thus hobbled by the problems of political preference, practicality, and theoretical ambiguity, a pure rationality may be impossible to achieve in the social sciences. The challenge for the policy sciences, then, is to develop this practice of limited rationality so as to produce definitive, useful information to guide social policymaking. Nevertheless, in spite of an interminable grind toward greater quantification, the social sciences may have failed to achieve a practice of limited rationality that withstands social pressures for comforting truths. The analytic pitfalls of research may create irresistible opportunities for political discretion to masquerade as scientifically credible authority. This occurs when the necessarily compromised rationality of the social sciences fails to distinguish itself from more frankly political forms of decisionmaking, or worse when its epistemological imperfections lead to misleading and harmful counsel. In these cases, the social sciences function largely as partisans in the play of power, although with a unique symbol of authority, a bishop's miter of rationality derived from the successes of technology and the natural sciences.

Having failed to establish a practice of limited rationality in the policy realm, the social sciences may be prematurely celebrating their autonomy, neutrality, and rationality. The intellectual life of the social sciences may fall far short of producing an independent policy community of experts that exerts autonomous influence over social policy. Blank offers one prominent but common example of the social sciences' exaggerated self-regard: "Recent major expansions of work-welfare programs and of tax supplements to work were politically possible because *the policy community became convinced* that these programs would satisfy both the work goal and the income goal" (in Danziger, Sandefur, and Weinberg 1994:169, emphasis added). However, this explanation for the popularity of workfare must contend with alternatives that draw inspiration from a growing political intemperance and from the failed and compromised research of a variety of welfare experiments.

The existence of an autonomous policy community is even less probable than an autonomous state; indeed, it would likely operate in tandem with the state. Judging from the current dependence of academic research, policy institutes, and contract research firms on government funding, the existence of an autonomous policy community seems highly unlikely. Through funded research and a variety of other rewards, intellectuals are susceptible, perhaps even unwittingly, to the temptations of the state and other stakeholders in society. Without a true scientific rigor, their convictions express the converging streams of subtle social interactions rather than any guardianship of the public interest realized through objective assessment. True, a few heroic intellectuals and iconoclasts seem persistently to defy orthodoxy, but the community of policy experts customarily, and perhaps even institutionally, acts on behalf of the state and dominant social interests, autonomous only in pursuing its own perceived interests. Skocpol's comment about the state is probably more applicable to the policy experts themselves: "autonomous state actions will regularly take forms that attempt to reinforce the authority, political longevity, and social control of the state organizations whose incumbents generated the relevant policies of policy ideas" (Evans, Rueschemeyer, and Skocpol 1985:14). Indeed, analysts are frequently advocates, if not of particular policies then at least of intervention itself.

WELFARE POLICY AS SOCIAL SYMBOLISM

The history of welfare for the poor whether written from the liberal or the conservative camp seems to describe weak interventions and ones that fail. Notwithstanding Katz's (1986) feeble justification and strong sentimentality for the War on Poverty, little credible evidence has accrued testifying to the success of any welfare (nonmarket) intervention. At the same time, the success of the market itself—its social consequences as well as its economic fairness—is in fierce dispute. Even if the modern economy could lift all boats, it still might fail to improve distributional justice, sustaining unequal relations and systematically leaving large numbers of people behind.

Public welfare programs, notably AFDC and Food Stamps, provide subsidies that are insufficient to raise the poor out of poverty while they (even taken together with other antipoverty programs) offer little opportunity for the poor to gain employment and few avenues through which to socialize the marginal. Job training and the other social services do not appear to be effective in spite of the many claims that they may alleviate social problems.[11]

The welfare scholarship has written many of the morality plays for the modern state, creating the myths of status, deservingness, rights, and obligations that reconcile social ambition with social reality. Welfare

---

11. Even the role of the social insurance programs is limited by their attachment to labor force participation. There is considerable evidence that the social insurance programs do provide at least a modicum of income and health security, but only to those who work or to those whose problems emerge in the work place. Even though they seem to remove 30 percent of the poor from poverty, these programs largely perpetuate social and economic inequalities even while their role in providing income security is limited. In any event, the social insurance programs certainly address few if any social problems aside from their narrow aims (health and income security). Social Security is a conservative approach to social problems that largely institutionalizes current social attitudes and perhaps current problems. The insurances as responses to social need are probably adequate only to the extent to which society has already achieved a just distribution of its wealth and income that can be carried proportionately into insured benefits. However, they provide no solution to, and may even exacerbate, problems when deep imperfections are imbedded in the culture itself: unjust inequalities, intolerance, bigotry, ignorance, isolation, social and psychological marginality. Moreover, the largest portion of money targeted at the poor, Medicaid, is spent increasingly on long-term care for groups that have exhausted their Medicare eligibility, groups that until that point were not poor.

scholarship, in spite of its quantification, is polemically committed. Each study and experiment contend for influence by extending their political and social symbols well beyond the rational authority of their own data and methods into the social dialectics that influence priorities for policy relief.

Without a true production function, social welfare programs become dominated by their ceremonial usefulness for social dialectics. The symbolic role is not simply ancillary to production but itself can be very powerful, providing the guiding language for the political play of power. The customary superficiality of public welfare interventions and their inability to achieve either narrow goals or more general ones, taken together with their timeless popularity, suggest that they may fulfill a symbolic political role that dominates their strict economic function.

The experience of the social sciences in the analysis of poverty and dependency reveals the role of social scientists in creating myth. Unfortunately, scientism conspires with social forces that seem to perpetuate many of the problems that the social sciences so vehemently claim to attack. This role is evident in the development and analysis of proposals for welfare reform itself.

2 The Assumptions of Welfare Reform

However vague, there may be broad national agreement over an ideal sense of society: an idyllic vision of man and community—inclusive, nurturing, egalitarian, neighborly, just—that reaches for ideological purity into the mythic American past and projects itself onto a destiny of chosen greatness. Yet, there is considerable factional dispute over transitional goals and how to achieve them.

Differences over the provision of welfare are expressed in the debate over what constitutes a social problem. For example, conservatives such as Herrnstein and Murray (1994) argue that the current distribution of income and wealth is an appropriate, even generous, reflection of cognitive inheritance; problems only arise when the less gifted and less motivated arrogate a right to greater economic and social rewards. In contrast, liberals see these same economic inequalities as a central social problem.

Defining certain conditions as problematic is a prerequisite for social policy. A limited number of strategies, involving a multitude of specific techniques and programs, exist to remedy social problems: change individuals, change social conditions, or both. Additionally, the decision not to intervene, either out of a sense of benign neglect—that intervention will only aggravate a situation—or because nonintervention is just and useful, is also an option. The intervention can be conducted by a public auspices or through private agencies. The intervention can be extensive or minimal, sustained or short term, procedural or substantive. Regulation implies changing the laws that govern society. Substantive interventions provide direct money transfers (such as payments from AFDC or OASDI), vouchers (Food Stamps), or social services. Personal social services cover an immense range in an infinitude of forms; supportive social services, such as day care, information and referral, case management, and tutoring, supplement the activities of life: childrearing, job search, recreation, and so forth; therapeutic social services, typically some form of psychotherapy, target deviant social behaviors, such as criminal delinquency, mental disease, emotional instability, and substance abuse.

Liberals and conservatives tend to differ over the wisdom of particular interventions and over the facts of their effectiveness. In general, conservatives view the market as the best source of social welfare and therefore prefer private auspices, short-term interventions, low expenditures, and few social services. In reaction to the threats of an unregulated market, liberals tend to argue for a large, relatively long-term or permanent role for the central government. Liberals place the source of social failure in the imperfections of social institutions—the economy and labor market, the family, educational and health systems, embedded social prejudices, and community—and therefore invoke a collective responsibility to repair social problems. Conservatives argue that individual character flaws (immorality, incompetence, and sybaritic irrationality) are often the result of deviant subcultures and cause social problems; on these grounds, the obligation of the state is minimal, principally to assure protection for the obedient citizen and a stern necessity for the miscreant.

The different ideologies are obviously attractive to different political constituencies that are in themselves rarely dominant. Therefore, the live discourse of politics infrequently contains disputes over issues in their pure form but rather softens the sharp edges of categorical commitment in Solomonian fashion to recruit uncommitted support for a governing plurality. Political debate reflects the immediate stakes of partisans in a process of accommodation and conflict.

THE PARTISANS AND REFORM

While the heated congressional debate in 1995 and 1996 concerning the reform of welfare seemed to focus on two proposals—the Republicans' Personal Responsibility Act and the administration's initial proposal— the actual differences between them were negligible. Both proposed cutoffs in eligibility, both insisted upon work while making only token provisions to secure it, both employed punitive sanctions especially for adolescent mothers, both restricted eligibility for benefits, both refused to increase benefits, and both refused to challenge the existing system of providing only minimal financial support. While there are some notable differences, particularly the Republican desire to gut federal responsibility through block grants to the states, the proposals largely reflect the exasperation of the American public with prolonged dependency, out-of-wedlock births, the size of the federal government, and the apparent growth of the American underclass. As a consequence, these proposals as well as most others in the public sector during the past two decades have followed American public opinion toward the right (Public Agenda 1996). Indeed, the welfare law that finally emerged from Congress and that was signed by the president—the Personal Responsibility and Work Opportunity Reconciliation Act of 1996—clearly capitulates to the Republican position.

The administration's proposals, despite undercutting the liberal promises of the 1930s and the hopes of 1960s, are still seen, to many eyes, as too committed to the welfare state, maintaining an irresponsible disregard for traditional American values. Thus, the right attacks the proposals as expensive and permissive, while the left is only occasionally heard to bemoan the reforms as inadequate.

Yet in spite of public policy's current rush for a safe haven on the right, liberal and conservative assumptions lead to proposals for very different social welfare policies. Even since 1980, the range of serious social welfare proposals measured in terms of their draw on public resources and consequently the size of the public role has been great. Moreover, the potential of the different proposals for social disruption is great: some proposals would vastly increase the amount of social and economic inequality while others would largely underwrite new relationships between the different social and economic classes.

|The liberal position pursues the programs enacted during the Progressive Era and 1930s and enhanced during the 1960s. In recent years liberal positions on welfare have focused on either increasing or maintaining a sizable public position in addressing need. The logic of this stance justifies a federal role in terms of the failures of the market and the success of programs already in place.|The range of liberal proposals includes minimalist arrangements—such as those enacted in the Family Support Act of 1988, which directly preceded the 1996 act—to maintain or slightly change the current system as well as major overhauls and expensive interventions, such as those contained in Haveman (1988).|

Conservative preferences for overhauling the liberal welfare state received an enormous boost with the election of Ronald Reagan in 1980 and the congressional landslide of 1994. The conservative proposals have all argued for reducing the public role, either supplanting it with private charity or gradually diminishing the level of public support. Invariably, the justifications are grounded in the failures of liberal programs to fulfill their goals—indeed, current conservative thought actually blames those programs for current problems—and some form of trickle-down theory based upon the promise that the American market place if liberated from government regulation would produce enough economic growth to lift all who would work out of poverty.

Conservatives frequently bolster their proposals with social Darwinist arguments that the American system already maximizes the natural capacities of its citizens. Therefore, any interference with natural economic forces will subvert the efficient use of resources and reduce overall productivity; the parallel assumption is that the gross domestic product is the principal measure of social well-being. Sharing the liberals' logic, conservatives also offer social scientific testimony to the value of their proposals, defending them on grounds that they have proven merit and avoiding implicit arguments based upon their self-evident value. However, along with attempts at rational proof, all of the partisans, liberal and conservative, rely on frankly implicit truths—exhortations, ideal types, and hypothetical thought experiments.

The debate over welfare would be complex enough simply on instrumental grounds, that is, over issues of what is effective in achieving consensual goals. The complexity of the policy debate is ratcheted up by differences over the goals of welfare and the fact that these goals are bound together in an iron triangle; achieving some of them implies giving up on others.[1] Incentives to work, adequate benefits, and modest costs cannot all be achieved. Moreover, Okun (1975) argued that programmatic effectiveness and economic efficiency, except under a strained definition of these concepts, cannot both be achieved unless the costs of the intervention, and therefore the need for taxes, are very low.

It seems an obligatory etiquette for any welfare proposal to claim that it is going to radically overhaul the hated current welfare system. Nonetheless, few if any proposals seem to contain the necessary mandates and resources to achieve a radical overhaul and even fewer aim to change the economic or social institutions of the United States that probably underpin the problems in the first place. Even the most lavish proposals—Bane and Ellwood (1994) and Haveman (1988) being two prominent examples—would do little more than close the poverty gap by an appreciable margin. They would not much alter the underlying social problems related to poverty itself. Neither, however, consider the social consequences of creating separate social classes based upon each class's relation to public welfare.

Except for a rare few, the budgetary differences among the various proposals are small when measured against the size of the federal budget,

1. The iron triangle of welfare analysis contains a guarantee (G), a benefit reduction rate (BRR), and a breakeven point (BEP). These three concerns define all transfer programs in terms of their guaranteed adequacy, the incentives they provide for work, and their cost. They are related in such a way that choices are available for only two of the variables: $G/BRR = BEP$. A fuller explanation is provided in the next chapter where the NIT is discussed.

against social need itself, or more important against the size of the A₁ can economy. While tens of billions of dollars may make a needed differ- ence for a small number of welfare recipients, the economic and social perturbations of the proposed interventions, however they are spent, would probably be minimal. Indeed, in important ways liberal proposals are simply a more generous version of conservative ones, with liberal pol- itics still refusing to offer deep redesigns of society or the economy.

The rare exceptions to minimalism and social efficiency are best ex- emplified by Tobin and Haveman (both in Danziger, Sandefur, and Wein- berg 1994) in their recognition that welfare interventions have produced little success. Haveman calls for a comprehensive strategy to address pov- erty that implies an amount of resources far beyond the current bound- aries of political feasibility but does nothing to restructure the customary institutions of American society. He seems to assume that a comprehen- sive intervention can succeed without a major cultural shift, despite the fact that contemporary society has steadfastly rejected this approach for decades.

THE CONSERVATIVE WELFARE PROPOSALS

Taken together conservative welfare proposals pursue social integration through the traditional if not the romanticized institutions of American society: work, community (frequently implying the church), and family. As their overarching goal, the proposals adhere to economic self-suffi- ciency—that is, independence from public welfare programs—for all able-bodied adults by creating a situation in which everyone who is not independently wealthy must work. The proposals also attempt to dis- courage family dissolution and illegitimacy among the poor by reducing any welfare provisions that might facilitate divorce or out-of-wedlock births. Conservative scholarship is largely devoted to convincing the American public that the able-bodied who do not work deserve a harsh rebuke, that economic self-sufficiency is socially desirable, and that less public provision is the most effective method to achieve it.

Conservative thought locates the causes for idleness, family dissolu- tion, illegitimacy, and social problems in failures of character resulting from dysfunctional subcultures and in the actual provisions of existing welfare programs. Conservatives argue that these provisions create in- ducements, "moral hazards" in Murray's words, that encourage people to choose welfare over work and then trap them in dependency. These moral hazards exist because AFDC, Food Stamps, Medicaid, housing subsidies, and the rest allow single parents to receive benefits, which are frequently above the wages that recipients could command by working.

They argue that these programs increase the prevalence of the very behaviors that society scorns.

The moral-hazards argument is at the center of the neoconservative critique. Detailed earlier by Lasch (1978), Glazer, who is one of the original editors of the *Public Interest*, expresses a general indictment of the welfare state:

> ... there is the simple reality that every piece of social policy
> substitutes for some traditional arrangement, whether good or bad,
> a new arrangement in which public authorities take over, at least
> in part, the role of the family, of ethnic and neighborhood groups,
> of voluntary associations. In doing so, social policy weakens the
> position of these traditional agents and further encourages needy
> people to depend on the government for help rather than on the
> traditional structures. (Glazer 1988:7)

The conservative policy wisdom hesitates to supplant traditional structures with new ones or to develop public policy that sustains "new versions of old traditions" (Glazer 1988:8). More specifically, the basic strategy of the conservative proposals is to reduce the attractiveness of welfare relative to work and the attractiveness of motherhood outside marriage. These goals are to be achieved by reducing welfare benefits and thereby increasing the likelihood of both work and marriage. Where protection is missing for obviously deserving people, conservatives such as Olasky (1992) prefer that private sector arrangements, frequently church auspices, rather than public entitlements meet the need.

The conservative position is not simply an argument to reform welfare but part of a broader attack on the role of central government in managing society. The moral-hazards argument carries over into an antipathy for the regulation of business on the assumption that the general welfare would be better served by an unfettered private enterprise. The broader regulatory role of government is at issue along with the desirability of redistributive policies—taxes and spending—necessary to support the welfare state's aims. By disparaging redistributive policies, conservatives tend to diminish the value of greater equality in achieving social integration.

Modern conservatives have embraced, in theory, the notions of equal opportunity and the role of the government in protecting these procedural rights. They tend to reject, however, current practices, such as affirmative action, along with any redistributive impulses to actually create equal starting lines. Instead, conservative welfare policies, mimicking Emerson's self-reliance and Theodore Roosevelt's rugged individualism, endorse an unforgiving moonscape of public relief to goad even the poorest citizen toward entrepreneurial independence.

The conservative vision presses for a private system of charity as opposed to a centralized publicly supported welfare state. A private, voluntary system of relief naturally supports the desires of the wealthier sectors of the nation, and the business community generally to retain profits and enhance their control of community institutions. The more that social welfare is reduced as a public obligation, the fewer taxes that need to be raised. Obviously, private discretion over private giving—charity—is much greater than over public budgets.

Yet the conservative position is not simply protective of the commercial sector, which constitutes the core of the modern Republican Party, for portions of the corporate elite share many of the values of liberal intellectuals. The business conservatism of the right has been augmented with the ideological impurities and considerable strength of populist reactions against contemporary culture—"anti-statism, anti-feminism, anti–New Dealism and just plain anti-ism" (Lind 1995). Thus, the conservative position on welfare—broadly conceived as a reduction of federal power—is managed by a coalition of the leading businesses and the new right reactionaries who blame a large central government—the welfare state—for their perceived loss of power, economic advantage, and social status.

The reactionary populism of the right has long been one of the most difficult conundrums of politics for liberals to explain. The very people who are the intended beneficiaries of a progressive social agenda—national income guarantees, progressive taxation, social services, and universal health insurance, as four examples—seem politically opposed to it. The Reagan presidency and particularly the 1994 congressional upheaval enjoyed large amounts of support among poor and working-class people, particularly in the South and West. The strength of antigovernment populism transcends racism and bigotry even while it is frequently associated with nativism and ethnic chauvinism. Indeed, in Mississippi, by far the poorest state in the nation, Trent Lott, a very conservative Republican U.S. senator, won reelection with perhaps as much as half of the black vote and an overwhelming percentage of the poor white vote.[2]

2. Blacks constitute about one-third of the Mississippi population. They probably turn out to vote in the same proportion as whites; the number of votes in Mississippi's largely black 2nd and 3rd congressional districts were about the same as in its largely white 1st congressional district. Equalization of the different congressional districts had been achieved on the basis of the 1990 census only shortly before the 1994 elections. The *New York Times* (November 10, 1994) reported that in the race for the U.S. Senate, Trent Lott, a conservative Republican, won 69 percent of the 596,719 votes that were cast; the

The social conservatism of the right, especially if it can be explained by status displacement, is a profound challenge to the notion of political interest driven by rational economic choices (Hixson 1992). As a consequence, prospects of liberal welfare policies become proportionately remote as the political actions of the working class and the poor themselves become propelled by their fears of upwardly mobile native populations and immigrant groups more than by the discomforts of their immediate economic deprivations. Economic security and competition among unskilled labor groups are not necessarily incompatible. However, the new right's competition for jobs through reactionary politics seems unlikely to secure for themselves any enduring solution even while it deprives the liberals of a sufficiently large constituency to attempt solutions to long-term economic insecurity.

The new right's preferences for an insular culture, tinged with religious fundamentalism and a millenarian discomfort with modernity, are not easily explained away by liberals as insubstantial emotion that hides an undiscovered but real craving for the core programs of the welfare state.[3] Rather, this rejection of the welfare state stands as a tough rebuke to the liberal nostalgia about what people need.[4] The modern conservative constituency may be making as informed a choice on the basis of their values (protecting their status) as liberals would have them make on the grounds of economic security. After all, it is not clear that liberal proposals or the current welfare state itself offer a sufficiently enticing vision of life to draw many lower status and poor people out of their fantasies

---

Democrat Ken Harper, a liberal at least by Mississippi standards, won 31 percent. Therefore, if 80 percent of the whites (constituting two-thirds of the electorate) voted for Lott—probably a high estimate—then nearly 50 percent of black votes also went to him. Still, blacks may constitute more than one-third of the Mississippi electorate and less than 80 percent of whites probably voted for Lott, thus raising even higher the proportion of blacks who voted for a candidate seemingly antagonistic to their interests.

3. Cook and Barrett (1992) are often cited in support of the belief that Americans support the welfare state. Yet they fail to provide scientifically credible data. Their evidence can be reinterpreted in light of their survey's many biases to reach antithetical conclusions. Public Agenda (1996) probably provides a far more accurate statement of the current electoral mood.

4. These sorts of populist reactions defeat the sentimental treacle about naive wisdom in a democracy. The voice of the poor and displaced—the grass roots, the masses, the "people"—often comes from a sullen and windowless hostility to any notion of social progress that threatens the tatters of their respectability. Indeed, the failures of social progress among the socially deprived are increasingly apparent in the journalism of social corruption documenting widespread failures of local control (in Newark, the South Bronx, and Ocean Hill–Brownsville), racism among the oppressed, the oppression of women by women, and so forth.

of individualism, self-worth, specialness, and value. The inducements of rational theory may simply be insufficient to displace the current culture of many new right conservatives and tempt them to break with the business community's cherished sense of freedom, equality, and achievement.

Murray (1984) proposes to scrap "the entire federal welfare and income-support structure for working-aged persons, including AFDC, Medicaid, Food Stamps, Unemployment Insurance, Worker's Compensation, subsidized housing, disability insurance, and the rest" (227–8). He argues that "there is no real question about whether" these changes would provide benefits since "a wide variety of persuasive evidence from our own culture and around the world, from experimental data and longitudinal studies, from theory and practice, prove that" his program would be effective (227). These studies also apparently identify the causes of dependency and promiscuity as emanating from a deviant subculture of the poor that is propped up by the liberal welfare state, which in turn provides "official sanction to reject personal responsibility for one's actions" (198).

Relying upon a variety of data, Murray (1984) concludes that the programs of the welfare state since the 1960s actually caused a deterioration in the social conditions of poor people: employment, wages, crime, and family structure (divorce, separation, abandonment, and illegitimacy). Indeed, in each of these areas, Murray reviews the social science literature to go past simple association between factors to "address the more difficult question of causes" (8). Murray insists that because of the social science data "we know much more than we knew twenty years ago about the real-life consequences of alternative social policies" (8). Indeed, he claims that a number of studies—notably the Negative Income Tax experiments of the 1960s and 1970s—have provided definitive answers to long-standing questions (in this instance of labor supply under conditions of income guarantees) to identify the causes of dependency and social failure. In most cases, Murray relies upon the outcome studies of the Great Society and War on Poverty programs.[5]

5. Liberals as well as conservatives rely frequently upon the extensive "fugitive," ephemeral welfare literature. An enormous amount of the so-called proofs of program effectiveness are contained in unrefereed, quasi-publications of consultant firms, foundations, public and private agencies, and universities. These publications have not gone through any sort of independent scrutiny, such as the peer review process of academic journals or the editorial reviews of less scholarly magazines. This fugitive literature is decidedly outside the quality control processes of the social sciences and therefore carries commensurately less authority than even the customary social science product. Nevertheless, while lacking scientific authority, the fugitive literature may accurately portray the factional desires of its authors and aegis.

Murray's 1984 position gained an even greater elegance with the publication of *The Bell Curve* (Herrnstein and Murray 1994). Both works went past the relatively unsophisticated blandishments of traditional conservative testimonies to rely upon systematic social science research for their authority. *The Bell Curve*'s considerable controversy resulted from a reliance upon genetic and cultural explanations for social failure. This insistence on genetic factors reinforced Murray's earlier preference for subcultural explanations. The seemingly immutable effects of genetic determination gave even greater weight to Murray's earlier assertions that the public sector should do little to relieve the economic insecurity of the poor. Any attempt to interfere with biologically determined behaviors was doomed from the outset.

The Bell Curve argues that contributions to society are made in proportion to cognitive ability and that cognitive ability is largely inherited. Unlike a number of previous works that embraced eugenic strategies to eliminate undesirable biological flaws in the population, Herrnstein and Murray stopped short of Shockley's (1965, 1966, 1970) position, although they relied heavily upon the scholarship of Jensen, Bouchard, and Lynn. Still, their proposals for addressing the problems of social failure, obligingly packaged as "A Place for Everyone," attacks the roots of the welfare state and endorses Murray's earlier desire to abandon those programs for the rigors of an unregulated market.

Their desire to dismantle the liberal welfare state is couched as a bleak warning. "The Way We Are Headed"—toward a totalitarian custodial state that embodies, in the terms of House Speaker Newt Gingrich, the decline of American civilization—argues that such policies will produce a growing underclass, the reemergence of racism, and a growing pool of the cognitively disadvantaged presided over by an ever more centralized and dissociated government:

> If we wish to avoid this prospect for the future, we cannot count
> on the natural course of events to make things come out right. Now
> is the time to think hard about how a society in which a cognitive
> elite dominates and in which below-average cognitive ability is
> increasingly a handicap can also be a society that makes good on the
> fundamental promise of the American tradition: the opportunity for
> everyone, not just the lucky ones, to live a satisfying life. (Herrnstein
> and Murray 1994:526)

Herrnstein and Murray (1994) are enthusiastic to restore a "traditional context" to American community in which "people found valued places for themselves, urban neighborhoods teemed with useful things to do" (537). Their laissez-faire approach to welfare reflects this yearning for an earlier, simpler age, which they feel can be largely recaptured by dismantling the liberal welfare state. The Earned Income Tax Credit (EITC) seems to be the only program they would continue since it rewards work not idleness, although even here they warn that it carries an inherent price, presumably the distortion of the true value of labor. Where relief is necessary they rely upon the private charitable sector to provide "neighborliness." Indeed, they fault the welfare state for removing the charity of the early nineteenth century from neighborhoods.

> . . . [C]ongress and presidents have deemed it necessary to remove more and more functions from the neighborhood. The entire social welfare system, services and cash payments alike, may be viewed in that light. Certain tasks—such as caring for the poor, for example— were deemed to be too difficult or too poorly performed by the spontaneous efforts of neighborhoods and voluntary organizations, and hence were transferred. . . . Whether federal and state policymakers were right to think that neighborhoods have failed and that the centralized government has done better is still a subject of debate, as is the net effect of the transfers, but the transfers did indeed occur and they stripped neighborhoods of traditional functions. (Herrnstein and Murray 1994:539)

Mead (1986, 1992) takes a fiercely subcultural and characterological view of dependency, rejecting both liberal and conservative economic theories that the poor make rational choices about work. In explaining the failure of the War on Poverty, Mead argues that,

> A better explanation [than rational choice] is that the programs failed to overcome poverty because they largely ignored behavioral problems among the poor. In particular, they did not tell their clients with any authority that they ought to behave differently. New benefits and services were given to the disadvantaged, but virtually no standards were set for how they should function in return. (Mead 1986:49)

Thus, Mead identifies permissiveness as the culprit, framing his argument against "the sociological approach," a series of assumptions by "elitist" intellectuals in the 1960s and 1970s—Galbraith, Clark, Lampman, Harrington, Cloward, Ohlin, and Moynihan—that transferred responsibility from the individual to the collective society. Solutions to poverty became located in government action, undercutting personal responsibility by ignoring personal failure:

> The emphasis of Great Society programs on social, as against individual, responsibility helps explain why they sometimes seemed to undermine the ability of recipients to cope rather than improve it. In this respect, the antipoverty and training programs had the most influence, even though they were smaller, in cost and caseloads, than the income programs. (Mead 1986:61)

Mead largely accepts the moral hazard implicit in providing cash benefits without exacting a work obligation arguing that "a benefit-oriented social policy might after a point produce *more* poverty rather than less, because of the behavioral changes it would induce" (Mead 1986:65). Mead reconciles this seeming rational-choice explanation for dependency with his avowed commitment to a subcultural analysis by pointing out that the "welfare mentality" among the poor (a phrase he attributes to Auletta [1982] in reference to a sense of entitlement to benefits) is the direct result of income guarantees.[6] In this way, Mead attributes poverty, joblessness, and dependency to cultural and psychological barriers in the poor themselves—their "human nature"—rather than to a lack of opportunity or jobs. Mandatory work thus becomes the remedy of choice.

More precisely, Mead (1992) argues that jobs, even at the lower end of the skills ladder, are plentiful and that the American system is open; discriminatory barriers have largely fallen. But the psychology of the poor, coddled by an imprudent public policy, prevents them from seeking out these jobs. The poor are incompetent insofar as they do not pursue "the best chances they can find to get ahead; . . . they are not excluded from the society; rather, they exclude themselves" (Mead 1992:156). The incompetence includes inappropriate values, such as the lack of a work ethic, hostility to authority, and defeatism. In this way, Mead (1992) rejects economic rationality, the notion that the poor maximize their economic self-interest: "the entire tradition of explaining poverty or dependency in terms of [economic] incentives is bankrupt" (Mead 1992:138). Instead, he embraces the inherent social deviance of the poor, their irrational, counterproductive reliance on inappropriate subcultural values.

Mead (1986) analyzes a variety of work programs, particularly the Work Incentive (WIN) program and the more coercive Community Work Experience Program (CWEP), commonly referred to as workfare,

---

6. Paradoxically, Auletta, while using similar concepts of personal responsibility, attributes the problems of poverty and dependency to structural impediments that he feels can be overcome only through extensive job training and therapeutic social services.

to demonstrate that their abrogated work tests defeat welfare reform; their lax enforcement allows recipients to avoid work. Mead wishes to strengthen these programs as common substitutes for all cash relief (AFDC, Food Stamps, unemployment insurance, and where possible, disability insurance.)

WIN was initially established to prod recipients to take jobs by providing a variety of services—child care, support services, job search, training, and placement—and a series of sanctions. Mead claims that its success was undermined by a legislative and administrative lack of resolve that weakened its ability to effectively apply its sanctions (particularly the loss of benefits). "While WIN has internal problems, its main difficulty is that its authority over its clients is still severely limited. Even under the mandatory registration rules, only 38 percent of adult recipients have to sign up for WIN (Mead 1986:124)."

Mead prefers workfare over the WIN training approach but complains that it too is largely voluntary. Therefore, his desire for the greater use of work tests—a substitution of workfare for WIN and a tightening of WIN's sanctioning abilities where it is implemented—as the principal mechanisms for providing welfare benefits is to be implemented by more extensive work registration, simpler and quicker adjudication of recipient complaints, and a strengthening of sanctions.

Mead's discussion of WIN and workfare are central to the conservative position. It embraces subcultural and characterological explanations of social failure to justify coercive and punitive approaches to social welfare that focus on decreasing the attractiveness of "nonwork" over work instead of increasing the attractiveness of work itself. While arguing that programs can be "affirming" of clients even while they are demanding, Mead focuses on a personal, frequently psychotherapeutic, social service approach to dependency rather than upon broad economic entitlements or measures to regulate the market place itself (for example, by raising minimum wages or by providing wage supplements).

The Mead analysis is curiously ambivalent about the utility of social science; empirical research appears to be useful to resolve issues of program effectiveness but inconvenient for examining goals. When it fits his position, Mead (1986) accepts social science, arguing for the viability of a work test on internal evidence: WIN succeeded better in registering and placing recipients in jobs when its regulations were stringent than when its sanctioning ability was compromised, thus commending a stringent work test for social policy. Augmenting this limited internal evidence, Mead (1992) later reviewed the influence of structural and transitory factors on program outcomes, concluding that the welfare system itself provides telling disincentives to work. Moreover, he took the position that in spite of unemployment work is plentiful though employers are reluctant to hire workers who are demanding, unreliable, and unskilled (Mead 1992:109):

> The Progressive debate about how to improve jobs or equalize rewards remains important. But social forces do not appear to explain the extent of nonwork now found at the bottom of society. . . . Few Americans are literally barred from work. . . . (Mead 1992:132)

In contrast with the use of social science to shore up his position on the availability of work and the viability of workfare, Mead ignores empirical evidence in selecting goals; the political and social desirability of his program to reduce permissiveness and increase civic responsibility is argued more broadly. Indeed, he justifies a coercive and punitive social welfare policy not in economic terms but in terms of achieving a popular ideal of civic conservatism. This civil ideal is based upon an implied contract between society and the recipient: social welfare as payment for civic virtue and work effort. However, while Mead's proofs of the programmatic effectiveness of his measures rest with their specific outcomes—essentially a question of social science fact—his justification for the stern means of achieving a civic ideal subtly shifts to political theory, philosophical argument, and the insights of the eighteenth-century American patriarchs. Through this curious rhetorical inconsistency, common to many conservatives as well as liberals, social science is recruited to an ideological banner.

Notwithstanding the Constitution and original intent, the value of a coercive work test to society's cohesiveness and civic institutions can also be made a question of fact and, at least in principle, amenable to social science analysis. Yet Mead diminishes the role of empirical argument in demonstrating the instrumental importance of his welfare goals, their actual ability to achieve specific elements of civic responsibility.

Olasky (1992) provides a history of social welfare grounded in a reconstructed empiricism that implicates flawed character in creating the problems of poverty and dependency. He concludes that these problems of the soul cannot be corrected by material means. Attempting to do so is the fatal flaw of the liberal welfare state, explaining its failure to solve the nation's problems. Instead, he proposes spiritual solutions for spiritual problems. Following Murray's argument that public provision has actually caused modern social problems, Olasky draws inspiration from the period in American history—1875 to 1905—that existed between the demise of outdoor relief and the rise of the social gospel. At this time, he argues that the central institution of charity was the urban religious mission, and Olasky together with the more recent religious right sees in its operation a model for current society.

Modern problems have arisen because the welfare state departed from the lean and accountable city mission. Modern welfare programs fail to place adequate demands upon service recipients. Rather than entitlement, recipients should be taught gratitude and required to fulfill certain social obligations. "Compassion fatigue," the crowding out of private giving, and programmatic ineffectiveness have become the moral hazards of universal entitlement. Only a return to the spiritual basis of social reform—affiliation, bonding, categorization, discernment, employment, freedom, and God—can assure effective outcomes. Reinvigorated charity organizations will become the cornerstone of social welfare effectiveness if the modern welfare state is aborted. Charitable societies will compensate for diminished public services, voluntarily collecting the tax dollars that have been freed up by abandoning the welfare state. Moreover, by providing work tests, categorization of deserving and undeserving poor, and the surveillance of welfare recipients through friendly visits, these private, religion-based organizations will better manage the charitable dollar.

Olasky would address illegitimacy and homelessness with programs that stress affiliation and bonding through personal counseling—pastoral in this case—and city mission activities, such as preaching and work for relief, that place demands upon service recipients. Accepting the premises of Alcoholics Anonymous, Olasky faults city shelters for "subsidizing addiction" by not requiring recipients to take responsibility for themselves. In this sense, personal responsibility implies the need for harsh penalties—a therapy of tough love—that exacts a high price for moral lapses and encourages miscreants to become good citizens.

Olasky's history is more than simply a narrative of social welfare provisions. Rather, he argues for the wisdom of private, sectarian charity using objective evidence of the success of those programs. Similar to Murray, Olasky also accepts the decisive logic of the social sciences in questions of program effectiveness, citing the successes of a large number of contemporary and historical programs that attest to his choice of program strategy.

In addition to its religious style, the Olasky argument recalls the promises of psychotherapy and other therapeutic social services designed to correct deviant behavior. Indeed, the processes of religious conversion and the psychotherapeutic epiphany may be the same cathartic experience. Both Olasky's religious revivalism and modern psychotherapy focus on nonmaterial, "spiritual" reformations that emphasize taking responsibility for one's own life; both employ a heavily personal mentoring intervention, locating the causes of deviance in the individual rather than social and economic structures; and both claim the capacity to correct socially undesirable behaviors. Moreover, both rely upon supposedly systematic, objective social science to prove their effectiveness. And it should not be missed that private charity, voluntary counseling, and city missions are as socially efficient—that is, inexpensive and socially compatible—as psychotherapy itself. The differences appear to be largely stylistic.

Blankenthorn (1995) and his Institute for American Values, a group characteristic of the numerous think tanks and policy institutes of conservative thought that compete for public as well as private research dollars, in addressing the problems of family structure (divorce, abandonment, and illegitimacy), advocate a classically conservative remedy of voluntary communal activities. Blankenthorn's project to restore the centrality of the family expresses a reformed relationship between the citizen and the state that prominently substitutes private initiatives for government programs:

> Fatherlessness is the most harmful demographic trend of this
> generation. It is the leading cause of declining child well-being in
> our society. It is also the engine driving our most urgent social
> problems, from crime to adolescent pregnancy to child sexual abuse
> to domestic violence against women. Yet, despite its scale and social
> consequences, fatherlessness is a problem that is frequently ignored
> or denied. Especially within our elite discourse, it remains largely
> a problem with no name. (Blankenthorn 1995:1)

Identifying fatherlessness as the cause of family dissolution and not simply as one of its indicators, Blankenthorn advocates "the recreation of fatherhood as a vital social role for men" (Blankenthorn 1995:223). Recalling the missionary characteristics of Olasky's program models, notably Alcoholics Anonymous, the twelve-plank Blankenthorn program contains a pledge of paternal responsibility from every man in the United States; an annual report from the president on the state of fatherhood; Fathers' Clubs in every hamlet and city; congressionally authorized "State Zones" that are "Enterprise Zones for male responsibility"; the transformation of public housing by increasing the ratio of two-parent families that live there; strengthening community life through fervent Alinsky-like community organizations; an interfaith council that would publicly advocate marriage; assessments of proposed legislation for its impact on family solidarity; the universal adoption of the Hennepin County (Wisconsin) resolution disapproving illegitimacy; regulated sperm banks; an athletes' campaign for responsible fatherhood; and a project to rewrite marriage and family manuals for high school students. *Fatherless America* makes Joshua's call to crusade against moral decline in the long tradition of voluntary, nongovernment, noncash responses to social need, notably President Reagan's "Just Say No to Drugs."

The debate over family policy is profitably illuminated by the contrast between Blankenthorn's moral explanations and Popenoe's (1988) more sociological understanding of the relationship between family change and social problems.[7] According to Popenoe,

> [The United States] is the only major industrialized nation, for example, that has no general allowance program for families with children and lacks a national insurance plan covering the medical expenses connected with childbirth. It is one of the few nations that does not provide maternity benefits to all mothers. Political attempts over the years to develop a national family policy have consistently failed. (Popenoe 1988:285)

> ... Thus American families ... are largely "thrown on their own devices." The problem is that strong families have always depended over the long run on strong communities, and the strength of both have declined. (Popenoe 1988:290)

Popenoe extends his observations, based upon comparative analyses of international differences, to lament the commensurate decline in America of the nuclear family and civic culture—the structures of community such as neighborhoods, churches, and voluntary associations—that mediate between the family and the state. Popenoe's yearning for the traditional nuclear family endorses the conservative position, even while his comparisons with Sweden implicitly suggest a powerful role for social policy and a large public sector in protecting family functions. Yet in the hands of a conservative such as Blankenthorn the need to restore

---

7. The unacknowledged spirit of George Gilder pervades Blankenthorn's analysis, conclusions, and recommendations. Providing one of the crudest subcultural explanations for poverty since the frankly racist manuscripts of the nineteenth and twentieth centuries (notably including Percy's 1973 *Lanterns on the Levy*), Gilder constructs an argument for punitive social policy that is characteristic of the conservative position on welfare. Although largely coextensive with Murray's conclusions—Murray has been referred to as a thinking man's Gilder—Gilder is frankly polemical, dismissing too many of the canons of empirical argumentation to be considered seriously in any analysis of the rational bases of policy except as an expression perhaps of the conservative mood. Still, Gilder has been influential, often cited in support of the conservative position. See Gilder (1971, 1981, 1986).

local mediating structures leads to a call for voluntary social movements; to pleas for religious renewal, more family time, parental leave, and tax relief; to arguments for changes in family law; and for "disaster relief from the impact of movies and television on family life" (Blankenthorn, Bayme, and Elshtain 1990:253). In contrast, the same longing to restore community in liberal hands leads to recommendations for supportive public policy, including social services. The two different sets of causal assumptions about the decline of families—moral decline versus policy insufficiency and structural failures—lead to very different recommendations about the role of policy in restoring families. In theory at least, the two strategies are empirically testable.

In the same manner that the tactics of civil disobedience have been appropriated from the civil rights movement by the anti-abortion religious right, conservatives such as Blankenthorn give increasing prominence to Saul Alinsky, a radical community organizer who achieved his greatest prominence in the 1960s. Alinsky appears to offer contemporary conservatives a method to achieve community renewal without centralized government supports or an expensive array of economic transfers and personal social services. Alinsky's emphasis on self-reliant organizations was frequently expressed as a refusal to accept funds and strings from central government. Alinsky's autarkic bravado has attracted notice among conservative organizers and theoreticians who have conveniently downplayed his antagonism to the traditional sources of American power (the power elite, the "haves," the establishment) and his strongly redistributive goals (Mead 1992). Conservatives also conveniently ignore Alinsky's own questionable successes.

Blankenthorn departs from traditional social science in developing an argument that is *tested* and not simply posed in reference to Weberian ideal types—hypothetical statements about fictional composites. While he invokes a variety of empirical sources to define the dimensions of the family problem—the association of fatherlessness with a number of other social problems—he largely argues for "The Good Family Man" on intuitive grounds. Nonetheless, he accepts the logic of empirical proof, at least formally, when offering solutions based on the evidence of objective effectiveness. Not only are his goals desirable but their feasibility, he claims, has been demonstrated by a variety of live programmatic successes.

The conservative position on welfare has come together in the proposal of the new Republican congressional majority—the Personal Responsibility Act (PRA) that was largely followed in the final 1996 legislation. Both transform AFDC and the Food Stamp program, changing, in Mead's sense, the civic relationship between poor people and their soci-

ety. Welfare is no longer a right; work at almost any level of remu
tion becomes an obligation. The 1996 act codifies Murray's desire f(
end to the welfare state and puts support for social failure more in
hands of the voluntary charitable sector. It takes Gilder's censorious attι-
tude to illegitimacy and family dissolution. Its unrestricted block-grant
strategy, by undercutting the desire of the original framers of social security to pursue national standards, is a step toward fulfilling Olasky's vision of localism and neighborhood responsibility. But most important
the 1996 act while not eliminating the entire welfare state symbolizes a
popular desire to reshape government more along conservative ideals.

The core of the conservative position is defended as an intuitive vision
of a simpler, more communal America, but more important its goals and
programs are justified rationally as a number of factual assertions about
the causes of and remedies for poverty and social failure: Welfare benefits undermine labor force participation; They promote—"facilitate" in
Murray's terms—marital dissolution and illegitimacy and retard family
formation; A variety of specific social services—mostly workfare and
counseling programs—have been successful in putting people back to
work and achieving important social goals. In other words, conservatives
claim that the authority of their position—their assertions about cause
and effect and their preferences for reform—is endorsed by credible social science research.

THE LIBERAL WELFARE PROPOSALS

The liberal proposals, like the conservative ones, represent a choice
among the adequacy of benefits, work incentives, economic independence, and cost. Reflecting popular political tastes, liberals have largely
accepted a mandate to encourage recipients to accept jobs. The liberal
proposals tend to combine three general types of reform measures in
varying degrees: proposals to change the conditions of cash and voucher
benefits; proposals to train and educate welfare recipients; and proposals
to arrange social services that provide work supports (such as day care)
and that seek to change recipients' antisocial or dysfunctional attitudes
usually through case management and counseling.

One of the central sources of liberal welfare thinking has been the
Institute for Research on Poverty (IRP) at the University of Wisconsin–Madison. IRP was initially funded in the 1960s by the Office of Economic Opportunity, the lead agency in the War on Poverty, and later by a
number of philanthropic foundations, notably the Ford Foundation, that
have aligned themselves with a liberal perspective. The IRP has produced
an immense number of policy analyses relating to poverty and social

welfare. The research is grounded in the contemporary policy sciences, notably econometrics and operations research. Indeed, its research is consistently among the best scholarship that the applied social sciences, especially economics, have produced.

Haveman (1987a), one of its leading economists, has pointed out that the current system of income transfers offers no long-term solution to poverty and inequality. Long-term gain is "possible only through programs that make it possible for individuals to acquire sufficient skills and training to become economically independent, and give them the incentives and hope to make the effort" (23). His proposals address the problem of economic and social inequality, particularly the needs of recently impoverished groups: minority youths, single mothers, and children living in one-parent homes.[8] Still, his general strategy is to create a universal program of entitlement that focuses on particular problems (Haveman 1988). His specific goals are to reduce inequality, especially the "new inequalities," by equalizing opportunities and assuring a social minimum of support. Moreover, Haveman argues that this can be done while also realizing a number of other cherished values: increasing individual accountability and responsibility, improving the flexibility and performance of the labor market, reducing disincentives for work, raising saving and personal initiative, and simplifying the administration of welfare programs (see Haveman 1987b, 1987c, 1988, 1992, 1994; Haveman and Wolfe 1984).[9]

The programmatic elements of Haveman's (1988) strategy include first a universal tax credit, modeled after the Negative Income Tax proposals of the 1970s, that will supplant most current welfare programs: AFDC, Food Stamps, Supplemental Security Income, housing supports, and perhaps others, but not Medicaid, unemployment insurance, and OASDHI. Haveman proposes to fix the guarantee at between one-half and two-thirds of the poverty line; he implies a benefit reduction rate of 50 percent. He argues that the universal tax credit would reduce income inequities while providing incentives for recipients to work. It would also greatly simplify program administration compared with the current system.

8. His proposals and analyses are contained in a very large body of work. As important samples, see the work cited throughout the chapters.

9. Paradoxically, Haveman acknowledges that "no strategy can achieve all of these objectives simultaneously; compromises must be made" (Haveman 1988:153). Yet it is not clear what compromises (between adequacy and labor force participation and between simplification and labor market rigidity) the proposals make, and therefore it is not certain that the starting objectives are truly pursued. But this may be a quibble.

The benefits of this refundable income tax credit would be great, according to Haveman. He states that it would obviously reduce the deepest poverty. Moreover, Haveman maintains,

> [his plan would] decrease the work disincentive created by the existing high-benefit reduction rates; strip away the complexity of the melange of current programs; eliminate much of the stigma associated with public assistance programs as we know them; and increase equity. In such an integrated structure, incomes are taxed and support provided in a simple, open, universal, and just manner. (Haveman 1988:158)

Second, Haveman proposes a standard retirement benefit paired with tax-favored private annuities. Haveman claims that these provisions would guarantee a retirement income above poverty for all workers while still encouraging them to save during their working years. In addition, focusing on the problems of poor children, disadvantaged workers, and youth, Haveman proposes three additional program elements: a universal child-support system, an employment subsidy for disadvantaged workers, and a universal capital account for youth. Haveman claims that these initiatives would reduce economic and social inequality for these groups and increase their employment.

Haveman argues that his proposals would largely eliminate current problems of poverty while preserving the value of work. He estimates that the net costs would entail a 1.5 percent increase in federal outlays (about $20 billion in 1988 dollars). This estimate, however, hides an immense amount of internal redistribution among program components and tax sources since the $100 billion in savings from social security are reallocated to other purposes. In any event, the program promises to do much without huge new expenditures.

At the core, Haveman identifies unequal opportunity as the cause of contemporary social problems, although he is less specific about the sources of the unequal starting lines:

> Although researchers have studied these questions for decades, the only clear conclusion is that inequality can neither be simply explained nor easily partitioned among its various sources. I will try to convey some of its primary causes. . . . (Haveman 1988:33)

Despite the caveat, though, Haveman comes to prefer the traditionally liberal explanations for these unequal opportunities: structural failures of the American society and economy, particularly racial discrimination and the differential opportunities offered to various socioeconomic classes. These structural differences result in an unequal distribution of resources that reduce access to education, training, and jobs.

Yet without the ability to ferret out the underlying factors that precipitate these inequalities, the causes of inequality Haveman (1988) does address may only pinpoint the transitional relationships—the intervening factors—that exist between unfavorable social and economic outcomes on the one hand and a variety of associated factors on the other. In this way, he argues at one point that community environment and peer group influences have "longstanding effects on ultimate economic success" (34). However, without controlled tests of cause, and he offers none in this case, the statement is more of an assumption than a credible statement of cause. For this reason, the central task to convey true cause is necessarily sidestepped as something ineffably complex . . . "I will try to convey some of its primary causes."

The actual focus of his effort—to identify the sustaining causes of inequality—is more practical than profound. Thus, existing inequalities in the access to resources are associated with unequal outcomes and assumed to be the sustaining causes of those outcomes, especially when evidence can be adduced that repairing the initial inequalities also repairs inequalities of outcome. Therefore, Haveman argues on the basis of enumerated research that there is a high rate of return on education and that this is sufficient proof to sustain a broad policy recommendation to invest in education. This practical approach is as good as the proofs: the empirical evidence basically assumes that the causes underlying the dysfunctions are adequately addressed and will not express themselves in other ways.

These sorts of practical arguments are inherently uninformed and unproven, however. They assume that underlying social pathologies can be cured by addressing the outcomes alone—treating the symptoms of a cold without attacking the virus. They fail to acknowledge alternative possibilities, in this case that subcultural factors may account for both educational attainment, whatever the educational environment, and labor market success. Indeed, if subcultural factors predominate, then any policy that ignores them is bound to fail and will simply defer or transfer the problem to new arenas. This sort of logic impelled both Moynihan (Office of Policy Planning and Research 1965) and Wilson (1987) to attend to subcultural influences as a necessary consideration in any structural change.

Nevertheless, the authority for Haveman's (1988) proposals resides in a large number of social science studies. In an impressive and comprehensive summary of the state of social science and poverty research, Haveman (1987a) lays out the social science evidence that endorses the wisdom of his proposals. He tests the value of the proposals in economic as well as social terms. Economic consequences are measured as work participation, savings, unemployment, and redistribution. Other effects are measured as they influence social mobility, status attainment, discrimination, and the concentration of poverty. Haveman is making the characteristic claim of the modern social scientist that the relationships among the labor market, social systems, and a variety of social inventions are rationally understood. Consequently, the outcomes of his proposals, the promise that they can achieve important social goals without debilitating social consequences, can be predicted with confidence.

This claim—that the social sciences have reached the level of reliable engineering—is typical of the modern liberal position. At least methodologically, it is shared increasingly by the conservatives who find that it frequently compliments their nostalgic visions. At its heart the liberal promise claims to identify the essential factors that influence social behavior and to develop programs that successfully short-circuit the many years of deprivation associated with human dysfunctions and social problems. The liberal position is built upon notions of social efficiency— that problems can be understood through some rational form of functional analysis and repaired relatively cheaply and with little disruption of customary social relations.

In this way, the Negative Income Tax experiments of the 1960s and 1970s, the Manpower Demonstration Research Corporation's experiments in "workfare," the systematic evaluations of programs for training, job placement, mental health, social supports, and education, as well as a great variety of demonstrations and experiments to reduce poverty, have created the scientific credibility—the fundamental authority— for welfare reform in the United States. Moreover, the pool of evaluative research, while concerned largely with program outcomes, comes to profound conclusions about the initial and sustaining causes of social problems. Programmatic success is not simply a description of the instrumental value of an intervention but usually proof that the nature of a social problem, its cause, is understood. By extension, this proof testifies to the social utility of the social sciences. Without the empirical testimony provided by the policy scientist, the different proposals are speculative and unfounded, no matter how elegant, subtle, inclusive, and sophisticated their fundamental theories. Implicitly, then, without an ability to test the social relevance of their theories, the social sciences lose their practical value and remain immature disciplines forever trapped in a ruminative intellectualism.

In 1994, based upon a summary of thirty years of antipoverty research and policies, IRP produced *Confronting Poverty* (Danziger, Sandefur, and Weinburg 1994), a more thoroughgoing evaluation of poverty in the United States than Haveman's earlier work. It concluded with a comprehensive series of policy recommendations that continues the assumptions and solutions of a structural perspective. The volume is one of the very few that calls for a comprehensive approach, recapitulating Haveman's earlier proposals and also suggesting an employment strategy, programs to address ghetto poverty, macroeconomic strategies for increasing growth, health care reform, creation of public sector jobs, provision of social services, education reform, immigration reform, and antidiscrimination policies:

> The changes prescribed here and in the rest of this volume are not out of the question—indeed, some are likely to take place. What is certain is that we cannot discover the full potential of our prescriptions for confronting poverty unless we take bold action. (Haveman in Danziger, Sandefur, and Weinberg 1994:448)

The authors do not estimate the price of their package although it is a fair guess that the price would imply far more than the 1.5 percent increase in federal budget outlays of Haveman's earlier package. Apart from the question of its political feasibility, the value of this comprehensive approach rests on the merits of its separate strategies as well as their synergistic effects. In characteristic fashion, each of *Confronting Poverty*'s authors presents a large body of social science research to prove that he or she has identified the causes of the problem and that the proposed solutions will be effective.

The Ellwood perspective (Bane and Ellwood 1994; Cottingham and Ellwood 1989; Ellwood 1988; as well as a variety of separate papers) traces its intellectual and social science lineage from the same structuralist roots as Haveman and IRP. It has had a large influence over contemporary policy proposals; the Clinton Administration's initial welfare reform package was drafted by Ellwood and Bane. While less costly and less comprehensive than *Confronting Poverty*, the Ellwood proposals share many of their social scientific commitments but also implicate many subcultural factors as causes of poverty. It is noteworthy that the Ellwood perspective speaks about poverty and dependency interchangeably. Haveman clearly identifies poverty as a social problem and dependency on public relief as an unwanted consequence of handling this problem—like morphine addiction that results from its use as a painkiller. Ellwood frequently elides the difference between poverty and dependency, however, subtly accepting the conservative assertion that the provision of public relief is a cause of the poverty it seeks to resolve. Yet

Ellwood also seems to suggest, as do conservatives, that dependency on public relief is a more compelling problem than the underlying social conditions that produce it.

Most important, the Ellwood perspective explicitly makes an intense and conscious effort to identify the factors that determine and sustain dependency, planting the authority of its program reforms in the value of causal insights. Bane and Ellwood (1994) posit three alternative explanations for dependency and attempt through a comprehensive review of the existing literature to evaluate the relative contribution of each in explaining welfare receipt, family structure (marriage, divorce, and childbearing), intergenerational welfare use, and a variety of associated social problems, interventions, administrative decisions, and program characteristics.

Rational-choice models explain dependency on the grounds of economic disadvantage: people make choices that maximize their economic returns; where education is low, work experience minimal, and welfare payments relatively high in comparison with earnings capacity, people will opt for welfare. In contrast, expectancy models, relying heavily upon psychological factors of motivation, explain behavior as a result of personal experience in attaining individual goals; people act according to their personal expectancies of success and failure. Thus, people's self-image, their learned expectations of what to expect from interactions with their culture, explains their behaviors. Finally, cultural models draw their explanations of failure from the assumption that people may be socialized to different subcultures which determine their goals, values, expectations, and behaviors; this model explains poverty and deviant behaviors as a consequence of a social underclass that produces its own aberrant subcultural norms. In a sense, all three models offer rational, that is, objective and logically coherent, explanations for social behavior but emphasize different factors: rational choice relies upon economic incentives; expectancy draws from psychology; and cultural models draw from sociology.

Each model implies different solutions, however. Obviously, if people are similar psychological and social beings, then their differences emerge from differential economic investments and opportunities, which can be equalized through policies, *pace* Haveman. Moreover, if economic rationality explains reliance upon welfare, then work needs to be made more attractive relative to welfare if the object is to have recipients look for jobs. This can be accomplished by either making work more attractive, welfare less attractive, or a combination of the two. If there are deviant subcultures, then solutions should be targeted to reduce their particular resultant behaviors—such as lawlessness and sloth. If psychological impediments create dysfunctional social attitudes, then appropriate expectancies can be produced through motivational interventions, such as counseling and psychotherapy that improve self-image.

It is important to note that Bane and Ellwood's causal constructions sidestep the more fundamental issue of structural causation since a number of their determining variables, particularly education and prior work experience, can be reinterpreted as the result of individual motivation: people who are appropriately industrious will acquire both an education and a work history. In this way, demonstrating the predictive power of any one of their theoretical bundles still does not necessitate any particular strategy of intervention. For example, the power of rational-choice models to anticipate welfare use—the differential effects of education and work history on earnings, and therefore on reliance upon welfare—still does not compel any sort of solution. It is as logical to rely upon motivational factors and cultural factors as it is to provide greater education and employment opportunities.

Bane and Ellwood (1994) acknowledge that their analysis of the competitive claims of the different explanations is limited by the quality of the existing literature as well as by the predictive clarity of the three theories themselves. Many of the theories are more moods of causation than specific hypotheses. Yet their commitment to social science, the linchpin in their claim to wise policy advice, means they must identify the causes of dependency in order to justify their proposals.

Their description of welfare use is compelling but still produces "an understanding" of welfare dynamics that cannot identify cause but only the factors associated with welfare use. More important, their analysis of the differential contributions of the three explanations of dependency, based upon a review of the social scientific evidence, necessarily suffers from the limitations of that literature. Frequently, the models make similar predictions, which seem to undercut the search for causal factors and the construction of differential theories:

> As the choice models predict, education, number of children, employment rates, and work experience all have an important influence on participation. Of course, some of these influences could be interpreted using the expectancy or culture theories as effects of confidence or ambition. (Bane and Ellwood 1994:84)

For these reasons they caution that

> [s]ome parts of dependency seem relatively easy to understand with existing paradigms and existing research. Other areas are poorly understood, but research is likely to shed further light on them. Still

other areas seem worthy of attention, but further research may
be unlikely to yield a great deal of new insight. (Bane and Ellwood
1994:121)

Notwithstanding the limitations of logic and data, Bane and Ellwood
(1994) derive a number of guiding causal principles from their analysis of
the literature. They observe that "every significant study of welfare participation has shown that economic variables are strong predictors of
who is working fully and who is on welfare" even while these factors
poorly explain variations in welfare over time, particularly the increased
fraction of single parents who began receiving welfare in the late 1960s
and 1970s (Bane and Ellwood 1994:84). Nevertheless, marital status
also seems to explain work behavior, with never-married women working less than women who have been married, even after taking other factors into account. Thus, they conclude that rational choice combined
with an expectancy model predicts the incidence and duration of welfare use quite well. In contrast, "cultural explanations do not seem to
explain the bulk of welfare use, but in areas of concentrated poverty such
as America's ghettos, they seem to offer insights" (Bane and Ellwood
1994:122).

Culture-of-poverty explanations seem barren for Bane and Ellwood
since the literature suggests that only a very small proportion of the poor
(perhaps no more than five million) live in areas of concentrated poverty
(ghettos). Moreover, they find only a modest intergenerational welfare
effect, warning that it is difficult to disentangle the relationship between
"cultural and attitudinal factors" on the one hand and "continuing disadvantage" on the other. Moreover, none of the existing theories seems
to explain changes in family structure, particularly illegitimacy.

Not surprisingly, the Ellwood enterprise, relying largely on the rational-choice model, comes to the conclusion that policy reform needs to
"make work pay" for both single-parent families as well as working families. This is elaborated in terms of structural solutions aimed entirely at
work, not poverty reduction directly. The current welfare system is to
be converted into a short-term system of transitional support providing
job training, job search assistance, and social services, including counseling. At the end of the transitional period, perhaps eighteen months,
minimum-wage jobs would be offered to people who could not find jobs
in the private sector. Work would pay more than welfare through an increase in the EITC, higher minimum wage, refundable child care tax
credit, and, for single mothers, a uniform child support assurance system. Moreover, everyone would be assured medical coverage. Unlike the
Haveman proposals, the Ellwood program does not include a negative

income tax, with its guaranteed minimum level of support. Ellwood (1988) is neither precise nor clear in estimating the total costs of his proposals. Presumably his estimate of between $20 and $30 billion in 1988 dollars covers additional costs over then current programs.

| The Ellwood proposals created the framework for the Clinton Administration's initial proposals for welfare reform (U.S. Department of Health and Human Services 1995). While certainly less generous than Ellwood's, the administration's package seemed better adjusted to the realities of contemporary American political tastes. Like Ellwood's, it included national health coverage, the termination of open-ended welfare and the incorporation of transitional services (to employment), the inclusion of two-parent families, and modest increases in the EITC. The Clinton proposals dropped, however, the notion of government as the employer of last recourse and provided only minimal amounts of money for job training; the measures recanted Bane and Ellwood's (1994) commitment to a national system of child support allowances, raises in the minimum wage, and a refundable child care tax credit. Moreover, the administration's national health care reform was killed by a suddenly conservative Congress. The costs of the administration's modest package were anticipated to reach a mere $6 billion over current program costs by 1999 (presumably in 1995 dollars).|

As with the Moynihan assumptions that produced the Family Support Act of 1988, the feasibility of the Ellwood proposals and those of the administration hinged on the ability of poor people to obtain jobs. In turn, employment was projected to result from the transmission of marketable skills to recipients—through transitional services—and their motivation to find work. It is notable that few planks in any liberal platform deal with structural reforms to produce jobs either through strong macroeconomic stimulation, massive investment in human capital, or the direct provision of public sector jobs paying competitive salaries. While Kaus (1992) directly addresses the availability of work, the liberal agenda in recent years has largely adopted a low-level skills training as a way to combat unemployment.

Nor should it be forgotten that, from another point of view, the success of the Ellwood proposals, including the Clinton Administration's initial package, relates as much to reducing poverty and economic equality as to reducing reliance upon welfare. Yet, the reduction of poverty has become increasingly peripheral to the public debate over welfare during the past two decades. The powerful shift in social attitudes, from a concern with poverty to a concern with dependency, also seems to explain the defeat of Clinton's health care reforms and the inexorable slide of the welfare debate toward more conservative policy interventions, a change in political tastes that was realized in the 1996 welfare legislation.

An emphasis on social equality (less poverty), central to Haveman but compromised by Ellwood's superordinate desire to reduce dependency, links welfare reform to the broader goal of a socially tranquil and satisfying culture. In this light, too, economic self-sufficiency is presumably important not simply to reduce public budgetary obligations but also because universal self-sufficiency is desirable as a binding national experience and a requirement of the American ethos. In this way, many liberals have come to share the conservatives' enthusiasm for work as the instrument for achieving greater social equality and as the central institution of socialization and even civic life in America. The force of this commitment to achieving social solidarity through the labor market recalls earlier generations' enthusiasm for personal redemption through work. Indeed, Kaus (1992) expresses the fury of the middle class's reaction to the poor in general and to the perceived degradation of its work ethos through welfare state programs. The work ethos validates "the rules the mainstream culture tries to live by, and they are the norms that are in danger of disappearing entirely in the culture" (Kaus 1992:257).

Kaus believes that the requirement of near-universal work is needed to destroy the culture of poverty, or at least the culture of welfare, and to repair the fractiousness in American society created by the welfare state. His terms of analysis are similar to Murray's: welfare programs have created an inequality that is destroying the shared culture of America. Giveaway welfare policies—AFDC, Food Stamps, housing subsidies, Medicaid—that pursue an equality of outcomes ("money liberalism") without insisting on an equality of contribution ("civic liberalism") reinforce ("enable") a culture of poverty and welfare dependency, which is at the root of American social problems. Kaus's goal is to transform "the welfare state into a work ethic state" by

> replacing AFDC and all other cash-like welfare programs that assist the able-bodied poor (including "general relief" and food stamps) with a single, simple offer from the government—an offer of employment for every American citizen over eighteen who wants it, in a useful public job at a wage slightly below the minimum wage for private sector work. The government would supplement the wages of all low-wage jobs, both public and private, to ensure that every American who works full-time has enough money to raise a normal-sized family with dignity, out of poverty. (Kaus 1992:125)

Specifically, Kaus proposes six million sub-minimum-wage "neo-

WPA" jobs, together with wage supplements through the EITC, to raise above the poverty line the incomes of those who are willing to work. These jobs would be open to everyone. Those who refuse to work, including all single heads of household, would not be eligible for any cash assistance, although they would be eligible for training and a variety of other services. The recalcitrant would necessarily fall back on private relief, such as soup kitchens and flop houses. Single welfare mothers would not be excluded from the work requirement but free day care would be available to them:

> The key welfare question left unresolved by the New Deal—do we
> expect single mothers with children to work?—would be resolved
> clearly in favor of work. The government would announce that after
> a certain date able-bodied single women who bear children would
> no longer qualify for cash payments. Young women contemplating
> single motherhood couldn't count on AFDC to sustain them. As
> mothers, they would have to work like everyone else. The prospect
> of juggling motherhood and a not-very-lucrative public job would
> make them think twice, just as with Murray's cold turkey solution.
> But the public jobs would (unlike Murray's plan) also offer both
> mothers and non-mothers a way out of poverty. (Kaus 1992:126)

Kaus would exclude mothers with children under two from the work test, providing them temporary one-time cash assistance for two years. This assistance would not be renewable for subsequent children, however.

Although many of Kaus's concepts recall the conservative argument, his solution certainly does not. He poses a very strong role for the central government and estimates the cost of his proposals at almost $60 billion a year *more* than 1992 expenditures.

Kaus's assumptions about the causes of poverty and how people would respond to changes in policy buttress his proposals for transforming the cultures of poverty and welfare through a WPA-style work program. His basic assumption, softened by a structuralist's recognition of the role of discrimination, is similar to the conservative perspective, placing the causes of both poverty and dependency in the attitudes and behaviors of the poor themselves and in the programs of the welfare state: "cash welfare plus prejudice" is the worldwide recipe for the under-class. He insists with the intensity of a conversion experience that a culture of dependency, created by the welfare state, reinforces the culture of poverty.

The value of Kaus's (1992) proposals rests on the ability of sub-minimum-wage jobs to enable the recipients "to participate in the larger working society with dignity" (127). Under the scheme, single mothers would be less willing to share their hard-earned paychecks (as opposed to unearned welfare checks) with a bum of a man who does not work; thus the unemployed male in Kaus's culture of poverty also would be strongly motivated to take a public job and become a responsible member of society. These two incomes, supplemented by EITC subsidies, would raise the family over poverty. Moreover, work would become the norm, creating greater social stability and providing appropriate role models for poor children. Kaus rejects the notion of child assurances, as proposed by both Haveman and Ellwood, because they would weaken these sorts of dynamics, providing women with a disincentive for marriage.

Work would serve as a deterrent to illegitimacy as well, especially in light of the two-year lifetime limit on welfare benefits. In this way, Kaus utilizes a rational-choice perspective as a strategy to attack the cultural perspective. For Kaus, people seem to make rational choices about subcultural norms.

Kaus minimizes a number of potential problems with his proposals, most notably their potentially adverse effects on working-class incomes and social stability. An army of the underpaid may put downward pressure on the wages of near-minimum-wage workers, creating not only work disincentives but a turmoil of social displacement and competition among a large portion of workers. While theoretically raising the status of the very poor, Kaus's proposals may threaten the status of working people. All of the proposals, not just Kaus's, increase the labor pool through their work proposals and are likely to dampen wages. While Kaus proposes sub-minimum-wage jobs, none of the current reform packages proposes a broad labor strategy to raise wages by creating a large number of competitive jobs to employ the structurally unemployed. The ghost of inflation still hovers in the debate over public expenditures, the budget deficit, and economic growth.

It is worth noting that Kaus goes beyond his cited literature to perform thought experiments, similar to Murray's (1984) famous discussion of Harold and Phyllis, that postulate motives and outcomes as a method to validate his assumptions. While the social science literature figures prominently in Kaus's writing, a variety of common-sensical assumptions about the dynamics of dependency perfuse his arguments. Where choice theory encourages Kaus to offer jobs and cut AFDC payments, it becomes "bribe theory" when it fails to explain illegitimacy and thus certifies alternative assumptions about subcultural causation. These sorts of useful journalistic devices (Kaus is after all a journalist) commonly fill in the lapses of social science logic. But the potential efficacy of the proposals and the accuracy of their underlying theories depend upon proof and fact, even while their goals may rest upon questions of value.

| Jencks (1992) supports the current liberal position of child supports and job training for low-income mothers along with an enhanced EITC program, tax credits for child care, and higher minimum wages for all poor families. Jencks, however, makes no provision for increasing jobs while endorsing the desirability of pressuring single mothers into the labor force: "if a mother does not have a God-given right to stay home with her children, if paying her to do so does not make economic sense, and if it does not do her children much good, the case for welfare collapses" (Jencks 1992:229).

Jencks tries to finesse the problem of an overarching cause for social problems—structure versus subculture versus genetics—by taking a case-by-case approach that resonates with America's faith in pragmaticism. He does not need to affiliate with any camp if social problems can be handled as they arise and if no single causal constellation, no transcendent causal force such as discrimination or class, can explain the emergence of social problems:

> If we want to understand what is happening to those at the bottom of American society, we need to examine their problems one at a time, asking how each has changed and what has caused the change. Instead of assuming that the problems are closely linked to one another, we need to treat their interrelationships as a matter for empirical investigations. When we do that, the relationships are seldom as strong as class stereotypes lead us to expect. . . . Portraying poverty, joblessness, illiteracy, violence, unwed motherhood, and drug abuse as symptoms of a large meta-problem, such as the underclass, encourages people to look for meta-solutions. We are frequently told, for example, that piecemeal reform is pointless and that we need a comprehensive approach to the problems of the underclass. (Jencks 1992:202)

Jenck's practicality is in frontal opposition to the strategy of IRP's *Confronting Poverty,* which implies both structural causation and the need for a comprehensive approach to social and economic failure. Still, Jencks clearly accepts the coherence of social science in framing the problem and its solutions. Indeed, he follows the logic closely in deriving his own focused solutions from proofs of isolated cause. Both the Jencks and the IRP positions take heart from the weaknesses of each other, seeming to acknowledge prior programmatic failures to address social problems along with the difficulties of comprehensive approaches. However, decisive proof of their separate value still rests with central social scientific issues—cause and programmatic effectiveness—related to work participation, adequacy of program benefits, social cohesion, equality, equity, and family structure.

Funiciello (1993), Rank (1994), and Reimer (1992) reject any hint of a distinct culture of poverty. The poor are largely like the nonpoor, except that they suffer more of the nation's structural economic failures (usually a lack of jobs), the iniquities of the welfare system, and the Roseanne syndrome of bad luck, an unjust social system (discrimination), and a belated personal maturity.

Funiciello (1993) in particular, provides a scathing indictment of privatized services, notably food pantries and shelters, for the poor. Funiciello and Rank are no more grounded in empirical proof than Kaus; indeed, the serious, basic flaws in their data are not simply reasonable differences with the established points of view. They reject the culture-of-poverty viewpoint largely on the basis of their own personal witness, arguing that the poor are as responsible as any other group in society and should be fully empowered to make their own decisions by cashing out all vouchers and in-kind support. Both endorse the IRP proposals, although both resemble Kaus's money liberals, hinting that an equality of outcomes is necessary to secure greater equality of opportunity in the future.

In an extreme preference for work, Reimer (1992) proposes to eliminate poverty entirely through the labor market. Except for the elderly and the physically and mentally disabled, he argues that all the poor can be brought above the poverty line through public sector employment, augmented by a more generous EITC, health insurance, and day care. Rejecting income guarantees (except for the disabled and the elderly) and allowing demogrants (entitlements for a demographic group) solely for children, he estimates that his jobs program would entail only $10 billion more in annual appropriations over what is currently spent:

> In fact, while a more highly motivated, better educated and trained, and less discriminated-against poor population that can afford day care and health insurance would certainly be a good thing, modifying the internal and external obstacles that affect the poor will never get them out of poverty as long as the U.S. job market remains what it is today. . . . The primary cause of poverty in the United States is precisely [the] shortage of employment and prevalence of low-wage employment. America's poor will never get out of poverty, in the foreseeable future, until these deficiencies in the American job market are corrected. (Reimer 1992:182)

While his proposals lack the subtle distinctions and tailored programs of Haveman and Ellwood, they are unusual, at least in the current political climate, for proposing the creation of jobs through the public sector as opposed to the more customary route of training welfare recipients for jobs in the private sector. In this way, Reimer directly contradicts the Mead (1986) assumption that jobs naturally expand to take advantage of those skills available in the labor force. Yet Reimer still fails to address "the tradeoff between generating useful jobs that pose a threat to existing public workers and creating make-work jobs that yield little experience or taxpayer support" (Lerman 1990).[10]

In a concise statement of faith and practice, Caplow (1994) also endorses the basic position of the IRP. He identifies a narrow problem of poverty and welfare—poor, female-headed families—and locates the sustaining cause of this problem in the self-defeating provisions of welfare programs themselves along with "the professionals who operate the systems" (147):

> The most promising way of reducing the number of such families
> is to remove the marginal taxes that make it unprofitable for poor
> women to marry, take jobs or save. But this cannot be done in
> the existing system without allowing welfare clients to have higher
> incomes than those of the working poor. The only way out of the box
> is to abandon Aid to Families with Dependent Children altogether
> and substitute a universal family allowance. (Caplow 1994:146)

It is obvious in this formulation that Caplow accepts structural arguments, even extending economic-choice theory to explain illegitimacy. Indeed, he insists that these proposals result from a sophisticated understanding of social need and public policy, a human technology that the social sciences have produced. Caplow's (1994) explicit reliance on the value of social science in producing a technology of human behavior and attendant social policy is characteristic of the social policy debate.

Caplow justifies his centrist policy reforms as rationally superior to alternatives at either extreme. On the one side, the conservative alternatives aim at cutting the responsibility of the state to provide economic security. On the other side, expansive liberal alternatives embrace proposals that would deeply affect the working class by increasing wages, providing support services, and providing jobs. Caplow argues the middle ground not simply as a necessary political compromise but as the result of the

10. A program to provide jobs at higher skill levels, advocated by Harvey (1989), would cost more than the Reimer proposal. Harvey makes the case for a guarantee of full employment through the provision of federally sponsored public works and training programs.

science of human technology. This faith in rational policy development explicit in Caplow and implicit throughout the social policy debate honors the social sciences for having already achieved a proficiency at social engineering. Caplow argues,

> Effective reform projects respect the basic principles of social technology. They identify core problems and root causes, specify precise objectives, accept incurred costs, monitor results, provide for continuous attention to incentives, and anticipate midcourse corrections. (Caplow 1994:145)

THE SOCIAL SERVICE EMPHASIS

Many of the proposals, conservative as well as liberal, contain provisions for personal social services—frequently therapeutic services, case management, counseling, day care, and job training—that focus on a clientele of the poor and dependent, and frequently the most needy. The administration's initial proposals as well as the 1996 act specifically target unwed teenage mothers for case services, pregnancy prevention programs, parenting activities, and supervised living arrangements. The PRA allows funding for similar "programs to reduce out-of-wedlock pregnancies." Other government grant programs, notably Title XX and the social service components of child welfare, frequently support counseling targeted on employability. Moreover, social skills training, self-image counseling, and other counseling interventions are often included in training programs for the unskilled unemployed and long-term welfare recipients. These kinds of services have been part of Supported Work, many of the MDRC training programs, WIN and WIN-DEMO programs, as well as a host of experimental and demonstration programs to increase economic self-sufficiency.

Counseling to change deviant behaviors has long been central to strategies for reducing poverty and dependency. As distinct from supportive social services, such as day care and job training that derive from structural assumptions about the causes of poverty, therapeutic social services frequently assume that the individual's deviant behavior—emerging from a deviant subculture, character flaws, or both—impede economic self-sufficiency.

Counseling has been used to decrease truancy and improve school performance; to treat drug and alcohol addiction; to rehabilitate criminals and juvenile delinquents; to handle problems of mental health and social maladjustment; to reduce teenaged pregnancy; and to motivate the lazy and careworn. All of these behaviors have been implicated as causes of poverty and dependency. Counseling strategies explicitly claim that they are effective and that their effectiveness has been demonstrated rationally. A substantial portion of the social science literature, particularly in psychology and social work, has been devoted to these kinds of programs.

The PRA and the final 1996 act, but notably the Clinton Administration's initial proposals, mandate counseling and case management for many "hard" cases, usually the long-term welfare recipient and single teenaged parents. Indeed, a modest amount of supportive and personal social services appears to be the liberal's political compromise between the hardships imposed by conservative strategies and the very costly structural approaches of some liberal plans. Riding the rail between personal reformation and social engineering, the liberal's pragmatic use of social services adopts a Solomonian strategy of funding self-insight: a commitment to a traditional notion of responsibility with a bit of help from the government. Yet, the funding of these services is so superficial as to suggest their use as political symbolism—a bow to both the human potential movement and the fiscal-restraint forces.

AN ISSUE OF AUTHORITY

Liberal and conservative visions of social welfare differ over long-term goals as well as the methods for achieving those goals. Yet, the distinction between goals and methods frequently elide. Propositions are usually evaluated instrumentally as impacts on important social indicators, such as crime and delinquency, family structure, employment and work effort, and so forth. Thus, the value of work is assessed against its ability to achieve more fundamental goals, such as social cohesion, civic participation, and economic growth. Similarly, the value of greater equality, a goal that can be measured as the relative level of adequacy that welfare programs provide, is assessed as a method: its impact on social harmony and economic productivity. The notion of intrinsic, fundamental value is approached very gingerly.

While the conservative vision relies frequently on the self-evident truths of a fictive past—the force of an imagined tradition—both visions insist upon rational procedures, at least the middle-range theories of the social sciences, to identify cause and evaluate interventions. Nevertheless, the current range of alternatives and the long-standing welfare programs themselves testify that both nostalgia and functional analysis are in service to notions of social efficiency—inexpensive and orthodox solutions for social problems. Only rare reform proposals approach the need for deep and costly change.

Over the years, discussion of welfare's ability to achieve antipoverty goals has tended to focus narrowly on issues of work, adequacy, and cost and broadly on those of fairness, equity, social harmony, and economic efficiency. Yet the contemporary concern with welfare has come down to work alone, a desire to reduce dependency on public welfare regardless of the poverty effects. Specific propositions in the reform proposals relate to the effect of welfare on work effort and economic efficiency; the effect of training and education on wages and income; the effect of programs and programmatic rules (such as Head Start, Supported Work, benefit reduction rates, counseling) on family structure and work participation. Moreover, recent legislative bills as well as most outside proposals to reform welfare are infused with notions of social efficiency, insisting that their relatively inexpensive and noninvasive interventions are capable of delivering profound benefits.

Conservatives contend that state intrusions are too costly to warrant their benefits while liberals argue that neglect carries an even higher social and economic price. These differences are amenable to decisive tests of program outcomes, that would also evaluate the evidence upon which a variety of political communities base their authority for social leadership. Yet, each side has failed to apply empirical tests evenly to welfare's complex social and economic interactions.

In the end, the politics of welfare have left a large residuum of unanswered social need, failing to resolve the problems of insufficiency or dependency. At worst, critics claim that current welfare programs actually exacerbate the problems, creating perverse incentives that keep people on the welfare rolls by discouraging work and tolerating antisocial behaviors, such as illegitimacy. At best, welfare provides a meager sustenance. These deficits of current policy are not surprising considering its superficiality.

The desire for welfare reform is near universal; perhaps more accurately, dissatisfaction with the current system is near universal. Unfortunately, the social science literature provides little authoritative support for either the current system or any of the proposed alternatives. Instead, the symbolism of welfare dominates the policy debate.

3 Welfare and Work

Hardly anyone likes welfare the way it is. Liberals and conservatives differ over whether welfare programs are too generous, maintain poverty, and threaten family stability. Even apart from disputes over these specific effects, conservatives argue that relieving an able-bodied portion of the population from the obligation to work tears at national purpose and solidarity. In contrast, liberals argue that welfare is a necessary civic contribution, providing a protection against scientists' own failures.

Yet perhaps the greatest impediment to welfare reform is the large political divergence over its goals. "The hodgepodge of uncoordinated but interacting programs, each written for diverse motives, each written without regard for most of the others" is not the result of mindless social policy (Aaron 1978). Rather, the fragmentation of social policy reflects the fragmentation of social motives, with different political constituencies gaining incremental advantages in separate programs. A deep divide separates those who see welfare as an income maintenance program and those who view it as instrumental in either promoting or retarding basic social goals.

Income maintenance need not be the critical reason for providing cash assistance to the poor. The cash and security it provides can also induce recipients to function in particular ways (such as restrict fertility or forgo leisure for work) or can further another goal, such as social equality. Yet for the past few decades at least, the debate over welfare has returned to a traditionally narrow focus on the labor force participation of recipients and whether welfare promotes certain social ills, such as family dissolution, illegitimacy, and personal irresponsibility.

Family dissolution has been condemned more as a determinant of welfare dependency than as a social problem in its own right. In turn, the reduction of dependency on public provision has largely replaced the reduction of economic disparity as the goal of public policy. Work under any condition and at any wage has become politically preferable to de-

74

pendency. Perhaps reflecting the slow growth of the American economy and the desire for federal deficit reduction, the popular assumption that life in the United States would be better if welfare rolls were smaller and more people worked has dominated the contemporary assumptions behind welfare reform.

This may simply be wrong. While welfare apparently reduces poverty and perhaps income disparities, its deeper value, and indeed its very justification, lies in the attainment of broader societal goals, namely socialization and social cohesion. Presumably, in the face of deep failures to socialize the population, adequate income will be insufficient to prevent social problems.

The implicit assumption in encouraging work is not that society will save money but that near-universal employment among the adult population provides an important shared experience that promotes social cohesion. But greater work participation may not save public money if low-paying jobs in the absence of proper socialization produce the resentments that lead to costly social disruptions and other problems or that cause more social damage than life on welfare. The same logic applies to single parenthood; family dissolution is not simply undesirable in itself but also because it seems to lead to more serious social consequences. In this sense, the critical value of welfare lies in its ability to achieve some social tranquility, perhaps evidenced as satisfying relationships among different groups and between the individual and society.

Therefore, the provision of welfare needs to be measured not simply against promoting work participation and stable families but also against whether these goals contribute to greater social parity, lower crime rates, better psychological and social adjustment, better educational attainment, more harmony among ethnic, racial, and income groups, and even perhaps whether they promote improved economic performance—particularly, efficiency and growth. The decision to provide welfare itself may be an important commitment to social repair apart from its putative value in achieving intermediary social goals, such as work and particular family arrangements.

The following discussion explores how AFDC, Food Stamps, and Medicaid, both separately and jointly, affect the incentives to work. It evaluates the logic of welfare reform in light of the quality of the available information—whether the common understanding of poverty and social problems is justified by the general summaries and the primary research that they rely upon. It also asks whether the causal factors that seem to have been identified are valid and therefore whether the reform strategies they inspire are reasonable.

WORK INCENTIVES AND WELFARE

"The central policy issue is whether there is a causal link between welfare and poverty" (Gottschalk, McLanahan, and Sandefur in Danziger, Sandefur, and Weinberg 1994:97). The moral-hazards proposition that welfare is the empty-headed effusion of naive do-gooders and actually contributes to poverty lies at the heart of the conservative critique of welfare. It is an important instance of the broader conservative attack on the scope of government, the notion that the general good is degraded by public interference in the market place. The liberal intellectual community has accepted these same terms—welfare and the general good—differing from the conservative argument only in the predicted outcomes, namely that welfare relieves poverty and that its provision is an important improvement on the unregulated market.

The moral-hazards argument and its liberal refutation have materialized as a number of specific researchable propositions. For example, if welfare causes poverty, then the incomes of those on welfare will fall either directly by inducing workers to give up their low-paying jobs for a guarantee of welfare income or indirectly by trapping them in idleness and thus reducing their long-term earnings potential. Moreover, welfare may sustain poverty to the extent to which it imperils the family as the critical economic unit, encouraging divorce, desertion, and illegitimacy, all of which reduce earnings capacity.

If the moral-hazards argument is true, then welfare provision needs to be restricted or changed. If not—if welfare plays a negligible role in retarding important social behaviors and if the benefits of welfare are greater than its costs—then "a reformed and more generous welfare system could reduce poverty" (Gottschalk, McLanahan, and Sandefur in Danziger, Sandefur, and Weinberg 1994:99). It is worth stressing, however, that both the liberal and conservative formulations of the problem accept the same logic, namely that money poverty is at the root of social distress and that a reduction in money poverty produces, pari passu, a reduction in social problems. The conservatives simply offer the ironic codicil that the provision of welfare actually increases poverty. This agreement between the two forces holds up even as policy symbolism: progress against money poverty is a sign of society's willingness to handle broader social problems, and political success in reducing poverty implies the ascendancy of concern for the poor that stretches to other instances of social distress.

A number of influential summaries of the primary research—in particular Moffitt (1992) and Danziger, Haveman, and Plotnick (1981)—have been widely cited by both sides. The most basic assumption of these summaries is that their evidence, the "substantial literature" (Gottschalk, McLanahan, and Sandefur in Danziger, Sandefur, and Weinberg 1994:5) upon which they rely, is scientifically credible and therefore embues policy discussions with a special authority. At a minimum, scientific credibility implies representative samples and reliable measures of outcomes; where causality is claimed, it also means randomized controls. Obviously, as the research becomes friable due to methodological and analytical imperfections, the central rational arguments for and against welfare fall apart along with their policy recommendations.

Danziger, Haveman, and Plotnick (1981) argue that *modest* changes in the iron triangle of welfare analysis—particularly small changes in either the income guarantee or the benefit reduction rates—failed to produce large changes in either recipients' work behavior or aggregate labor supply. Raising the annual guarantee by $500 raised the aggregate employment of female heads of households by only 1.7 to 5.8 percent; similarly raising the benefit reduction rate by 10 percent lowered this group's employment by only 1.4 to 2.1 percent. However, changes in benefit reduction rates also produce unexpected balancing effects. While increasing the benefit reduction rate discourages work among some recipients, it also encourages others to leave the program, presumably because it puts a ceiling on their earnings. Similarly, decreasing the benefit reduction rate encourages current recipients to work but increases program costs proportionately by increasing the breakeven point at which it "mechanically" provides benefits to more people. These effects were later corroborated by Moffitt (1986a) and others. While most of the research covered in Danziger, Haveman, and Plotnick (1981) reports that higher guarantees depress recipients' labor efforts, there is disagreement over the size of the effect and seems to be a great dispute over the impact of changes in the benefit reduction rate. Indeed, two respected researchers differed by a factor of thirty-seven, even though they analyzed the same data set (Hausman 1981 versus Moffitt 1980).

Because of the many methodological problems in their base of studies, Danziger, Haveman, and Plotnick (1981) reach a cautious conclusion that the then-current AFDC program, which operated with a benefit reduction rate of two-thirds, reduced recipients' work participation by 600 hours a year. They estimated that Food Stamps reduced recipients' work by about 300 hours a year. These reductions of almost one-half-year of work are what Moffitt (1992) concedes to be "nontrivial" disincentives, underpinning some arguments for *major* reductions in welfare benefits. Yet, overall, these disincentives reduced the total hours worked by all workers by less than 1 percent.

The methodological problems of the research would seem to undercut any conclusion, however. Many of the studies employed aggregate data; "relied on statutory instead of effective tax rates"; often ignored unearned non-AFDC income and local labor market conditions; and employed inadequate measures of the critical outcome variables. Few of the studies handled selectivity bias, while most made a number of analytic errors. Almost all of the conclusions were derived from nonexperimental descriptive studies. Moreover, none of the studies attempted to estimate the impact of the reported changes in income and labor force participation on the wider considerations that affect social problems. Most important, no study handled the Edin problem (discussed below), namely that the estimates of total income (derived from a variety of surveys) may be very inaccurate.

The methodological problems of the research led Danziger, Haveman, and Plotnick (1981) to remark that "the net change in hours worked, earnings, and incomes for the entire population is thus theoretically indeterminate" (1015). Nevertheless, they go on to accept "a clear message" on the basis of simulations of the Negative Income Tax experiments in Seattle and Denver (SIME/DIME) that supports the structuralist position:

> [F]airly major reforms and extensions of current transfer programs can be undertaken without larger additional adverse impacts on aggregate labor supply. The studies generally find declines in work hours [of the total group of female headed households] of under one percent. With some reform options, especially those which include a public employment component, total work effort increases. (1018)

Moffitt (1992), reviewing similar studies, tended to support Danziger, Haveman, and Plotnick (1981) using a superior base of research that is routinely applauded by economists. Nevertheless, in contrast with Danziger, Haveman, and Plotnick's sense of indeterminacy, Moffitt concludes that the literature supports a number of clear conclusions: "unequivocal effects on labor supply, participation in the welfare system, and on some aspects of family structure" (56). Still, he points to some of the limitations on the importance of these effects. First, the work reduction caused by welfare, although statistically significant, is small and incapable of explaining the extent of poverty among AFDC women, many of whom would still be poor in the absence of the program. Second, changes in AFDC benefit reduction rates have not been associated with changes in the overall labor supply of females who head households, which appears relatively stable and inelastic.

In relation to labor supply, Moffitt (1992) largely relies upon the Danziger, Haveman, and Plotnick (1981) review, although giving it an "unequivocal" standing that the authors did not. Moffitt goes on to demonstrate, however, the enormous range of estimates of labor supply reported in those studies "for reasons difficult to explain," and "as a consequence there is still considerable uncertainty regarding the magnitude of the effect" (16). Indeed, the variation is of a magnitude that makes the findings useless for policy purposes. Under a variety of different assumptions of income elasticity and benefit reduction rates (varying between 100 percent and 25 percent), work reduction is estimated to vary from as little as one-third of an hour per week to more than seven hours per week. These numbers estimate the loss for all female heads of households. However, adjusting the findings for the fraction of female heads who may be on AFDC (about half of all female heads) and for the even smaller number who reportedly work (about 20 percent), the effects become quite large for the minority of female heads who are reportedly oriented to the work force. Danziger, Haveman, and Plotnick (1981) had estimated a similarly large range of plausible losses in labor force participation, from one to about ten hours a week. Still, Moffitt (1992) draws the conclusion that "the work disincentives of the program have little effect on the size of the caseload itself," and therefore "the problem of welfare dependency (i.e., participation in AFDC) cannot be ascribed to the work disincentives of the program" (17). The labor supply of female heads appears to be relatively inelastic, and changes in the generosity of the program have little effect on their work efforts. Unfortunately, the NIT experiments, designed to reduce this ambiguity and included in these reviews, only added to the confusion.

The attention to labor supply, valuable in itself, is a contributing explanation to the more critical concern with welfare participation—dependency. Following Killingsworth's (1983) categories, Moffitt's (1992) review of welfare participation relied upon three types of studies (many of which also estimate labor supply effects): static models of welfare that analyze data from a single point in time; dynamic studies that collect data from different points in time and are able to estimate changes among particular individuals; and experimental data that manipulate independent variables to estimate their impact on welfare. The static evidence leads to the conclusion regarding participation in AFDC and work effort that "the results across the studies are remarkably uniform. Almost universally, guarantee effects are positive and significant and benefit reduction rate effects are negative and significant" (Moffitt 1992:19).

Moreover, the dynamic studies of welfare corroborate these findings: "virtually all studies have found the level of the benefit to be negatively and significantly related to the probability of leaving AFDC and, when estimated, positively and significantly related to the probability of entry

onto the AFDC rolls" (Moffitt 1992:24). These general conclusions from
the Moffitt review underscore the contemporary orthodoxy: welfare reduces work since participation in the welfare program and therefore welfare dependency increase with the generosity of benefits; conversely, increases in benefit reduction rates seem to create clear disincentives for
work. One problem, however, is that the disincentives appear to be
small—in spite of Danziger, Haveman, and Plotnick's (1981) findings—
and ambiguous.

Implicitly, these beliefs endorse changes in the current system that promote greater reliance upon the market place. By themselves, the conclusions do not support any particular welfare-to-work strategy, except perhaps to illuminate the possibility of fixed barriers to work, such as
racism, the presence of small children together with the absence of af-
fordable day care, and inadequate vocational preparation. It would seem
to make as much sense to reduce the guaranteed benefit and minimize
program costs as it would to reduce the benefit reduction rate and increase the costs of the program.

Nevertheless, liberals have adopted the Moffitt (1992) review, thus
refuting the moral-hazards position in favor of expanded welfare: "We
conclude that welfare does have disincentive effects. These effects are
not large enough, however, to support assertions that increases in welfare
benefits increase the number of families in poverty" (Gottschalk, Mc-
Lanahan, and Sandefur in Danziger, Sandefur, and Weinburg 1994:98).

THE STATIC MODELS

A number of static studies predict the conditions of welfare participation.
Each of them suffers, however, from debilitating methodological problems that undercut their scientific credibility. Thus, in spite of their impressive quantitative sophistication, their insistence on valuable policy
conclusions actually signals their shallow ideological meaning. Barr and
Hall (1981) drive toward a conclusion that endorses the structural view
of poverty: "family responses to AFDC accord strongly with economic
rationality," which "implies that it is not a waste of effort to design income support schemes with incentive issues in mind" (120). On the
strength of their findings, they recommend a series of policy changes that
ignore the possibility of subcultural or personal determinants of welfare
use in favor of increased incentives derived from their structural assumptions: wage subsidies, low marginal tax rates, increased education, and
the provision of day care. Yet their research cannot sustain these conclusions, and certainly not the recommendations.

First, their research is neither prospective nor longitudinal. Comparisons among states make the working assumption that the variation among their benefit packages constitutes a natural experiment. While this assumption creates an interesting analytic device, the assumption of a natural experiment is incorrect given the wide differences in subcultures, histories, caseloads, and public attitudes that determine the characteristics of the states' separate welfare programs.

Second, Barr and Hall's (1981) use of imputed wages is valuable only to the extent to which the simple modeling assumptions—education, age, and so forth—capture the true situation of recipients. These assumptions may be incorrect in light of the enormous variation within the welfare population that can bias the research; certain groups may more readily participate in the research than others, masking the true amount of heterogeneity among welfare recipients. Indeed, the wage imputation procedures along with other adjustments that extend the findings to non-respondents (Heckman 1979; Manski and Lerman 1977) rely upon powerful assumptions of equivalence between the two groups. However, without refuting the probability of large personal differences in the pre-dispositions between welfare recipients in the samples and those who are not, perhaps reflecting subcultural differences, those assumptions are suspect.

Furthermore, Barr and Hall's (1981) data on unearned income, one of their critical variables, were probably grossly inaccurate. Their conclusion that only 10 percent of recipient families—"an important minority"—have earnings in addition to their benefits is in stark contrast with more likely estimates of the true incomes and work participation of welfare recipients—the Edin effect. Indeed, the likelihood that a large portion of the welfare caseload works recommends a labor market solution—higher wages and more generous jobs from a liberal perspective and lower welfare guarantees from a conservative point of view—as a solution to poverty.

Their analysis of demographic characteristics seems to show that race, education, age, health, and the presence of children and other adults explain a surprisingly small amount of the dependence upon welfare. The difference between having fewer than eight years of education and having at least a high school diploma accounts for a difference of only 14 percent in total dependence. These findings would seem to contradict a structuralist view of dependence, suggesting that the provision of more day care and education will have only small effects on dependency and, further, that other factors—perhaps individual attitudes and responses to stigma (Moffitt 1983) that points to variation within the welfare population—are more important.

Barr and Hall's (1981) comparison of income guarantees and benefit reduction rates across nine cities creates the largest threat to their claims that the behaviors of AFDC recipients are economically rational. With monthly benefits varying from $101 to $253 and benefit reduction rates varying from 18 percent to as much as 72 percent, total dependence rates varied only eight percentage points from 76 percent to 84 percent. Apparently, the incentives explain only a small difference in total dependence. Increasing the guarantee by two-thirds increased total dependence by only seven percentage points, from 77 percent to 84 percent. In other words, providing greater protection against poverty provided slight work disincentives. From a different perspective, this would seem to recommend generosity.

Low guarantees and, in a number of cases, the small penalties for working would seem to predict a far greater amount of variation in dependence. Indeed, these findings if true would argue against incentives to change dependency behavior and for a subcultural or personal approach. Still, the range of variation in average welfare benefits, amounting to about $1,800 a year, may simply be too small to motivate recipients to cross any threshold of behavior. The limited variation may also be tied to the possibility of higher incomes due to unreported income. Moreover, their cumulative findings are very minimal, leaving a large amount of unexplained variation.

On their own terms, the results of so-called economic rationality (the degree to which benefit reduction rates and income guarantees predict work and welfare) are very ambiguous, explaining only a small amount of recipients' behavior. Some people are discouraged from work, others are impelled to leave welfare. In the study's own terms, "the vector of unobserved characteristics of the family" is large. Again, this would seem to call for subcultural and personal solutions, not structural and economic ones.

Moffitt (1983) estimates the degree to which stigma accounts for welfare dependency and work participation. He defines stigma as the sociological residuum after economic reasons for participating in AFDC have been taken into account. In this way, it includes all inhibitions to join the program, including personal as well as social attitudes, in excess of financial utility. Moffitt concludes that "the decision to not participate in a welfare program despite a positive potential benefit can be successfully modeled as a utility-maximizing decision resulting from stigma" (1033). Stigma is offered in explanation for the low participation rates in AFDC, estimated to be 69 percent of eligible persons in 1970 (Michel 1980). However, others have reported higher participation rates in recent years, about 80 percent in the later 1980s (Blank and Ruggles 1993; Giannarelli and Clark 1992). Moffitt's simulation model, estimating changes in welfare participation and work as a function of changes in both the AFDC program as well as prevailing economic conditions, makes a series of orthodox assumptions about cause but fails to account for changes in the stigma itself. The simulation suggests that independent changes in program parameters—minimum guarantees and benefit reduction rates—are sufficient to predict changes in participation and work. This assumption lies at the heart of the literature in the field (Giannarelli and Clark 1992).

Yet Moffitt's (1983) conclusions draw causal inferences from nonexperimental, cross-sectional data, creating a muddle of causal propositions. For example, Moffitt (1983) concludes that increased age and increased education have important effects on welfare participation and work. Yet the groups that provide the basis for this assertion were not observed over time to demonstrate the impact of individual changes brought about by enhanced education or maturity. These typically structural conclusions leading to recommendations for increased education and maturity fail to account for the likelihood of important qualitative differences among successful and unsuccessful groups and not simply the absence of a common commodity, education. Additional education may not be an easy task of instruction alone; other emotional and institutional supports may be needed to achieve the next level of education. Similarly, raising wages (or lowering AFDC benefits) may not produce the same amount of labor supply among the AFDC clientele as it would among nonparticipants. It is noteworthy in evaluating the quality of his simulation that Moffitt's (1983) estimated participation rate of 38.3 percent for those eligible for AFDC in 1976 is only about one-half the actual figure estimated by Giannarelli and Clark (1992) for 1981, a similar year.

For a variety of personal and sociological reasons, many among the poor may not "age" in the same way as either the nonpoor or those who decide not to rely upon welfare. In short, those who respond to stigma and avoid welfare may have quite different histories and attitudes than those who use welfare. In essence, Moffitt's simulation subtly assumes unproven structural causes for poverty and dependency without appropriate tests of those relationships. Unaddressed subcultural factors, subsumed within his residual definition of stigma, may be more important determinants of both dependency and work. Perhaps participation in welfare programs might more profitably be explored as a function of social attitudes and individual responses. In any event, the findings are further weakened by the likely unreliability of the data—the Edin problem—for one of his critical dependent variables, hours of work.

Interestingly, Moffitt's analysis of stigma itself, in his analysis an attitude powerful enough to modify important economic motivations, draws additional attention to the probable dissimilarities between participants and nonparticipants, whose labor force participation rates may vary at any given level of wage, family characteristic, guarantee, or benefit reduction rate. By extension this suggests that any correction for sampling bias cannot assume equivalence between those in the sample and those left out or, in the case of surveys, between respondents and nonrespondents. Other static studies make similar errors.

The static literature generally agrees that all welfare programs provide disincentives for work and incentives for participation in welfare, although the effects are generally weak. In contradiction with the conventional wisdom, the Medicaid program seems not to affect work participation except insofar as a notch problem exists, that is, those who receive Medicaid are much better off than those who are just above the eligibility cut-off point. Yet these findings are all weakened by a common underlying design problem—reliance on the observation of a sample at a single point in time as well as other serious methodological flaws.[1] By

1. The following prominent studies are not discussed in the body of the chapter. Hosek (1980) estimates the determinants of participation in the AFDC-UP program, a very small program designed for families with dependent children in which both parents are unemployed. He claims that his model, containing the customary economic variables—AFDC-UP benefits, external income, wages, education, and so forth—"performs well in describing the AFDC-UP participation decision." However, the explanatory power of his separate variables is tiny. Curiously, his study is based upon a survey of AFDC-UP recipients yet he provides no information about procedures, response rates, and reliability.

Winkler (1989) largely corroborates Blank (1989b) and also extends Blank's analysis to estimate Medicaid's impact on work:

> Medicaid is found to have a generally significant but small negative impact on an average female head's probability of being employed. But contrary to expectations, Medicaid is found to have an insignificant impact on hours worked. (310)

Both studies measure the disincentive effect of Medicaid generosity—variation in the insurance value of Medicaid across states—but not participation in the Medicaid program itself. The notch problem still exists in that any small increase in potential wages that makes a recipient ineligible for Medicaid is likely to act as a large deterrent to work. Moreover, the findings on work are obviously limited by Winkler's reliance on the data from the Current Population Survey.

Finally, Fraker and Moffitt (1988) estimate the disincentive effects of both the AFDC and the Food Stamp program using data from the Panel Study of Income Dynamics. They find that these welfare programs reduce labor supply in the total female-headed population by about 9 percent, which represents an average of about 1.1 hours a week for the whole female-headed population and something more than two hours for the average welfare recipient. However, none of their variables was significant at conventional levels; the authors utilized cut-offs of .2 and .1. Their estimates annualize to a small work disincentive of about 125 hours of work loss for the average recipient; these estimates are enormously different from Danziger, Haveman, and Plotnick's estimate of 900 hours of work loss—almost one-half year of work—attributable to the AFDC and Food Stamp program for a

following cohorts through time, the dynamic studies provide more credible findings.

THE DYNAMIC MODELS

The research that measures welfare utilization over time improves upon the cross-sectional studies, being able to describe the impact of changing conditions on entries and exits from welfare. Dynamic research comes closer to conforming with the methodological requirements for establishing cause while better describing the long-term characteristics of welfare use. Nevertheless, dynamic research still fails to create prospective conditions of experimentation. True experimental manipulation does not exist while problems of selectivity bias persist in spite of adjustments. Moreover, the same problems of data unreliability that undermine the static research also constrain the dynamic studies.

Hutchens (1981) provides some weak, and usually statistically insignificant, support for the proposition that higher AFDC benefits and breakeven points encourage dependency by encouraging entry and discouraging exits. He further concludes that nonemployment income and a recipient's potential wage are directly related to the probability of leaving welfare. In spite of a number of anomalous results, he found that the size of the guarantee increased the probability of reliance on welfare while decreasing the exit probabilities. However, neither the breakeven point nor the actual payment level (the guarantee plus the set-aside) seems to explain a substantial portion of entries or exits. Still, the impacts of these two variables although not statistically significant, are in the expected direction three out of four times.

Hutchens's findings, buttressing the structural perspective, suggest that conditions in the market place, particularly wage rates, have the greatest ability to predict AFDC participation. Given the effects of wage rates on exits and entries, he concludes that "the results presented here lend support to efforts at reducing welfare dependency through programs that raise wages" (235). His simulation suggests, however, that raising the wage rate by 10 percent has only a minimal impact on welfare use, decreasing the entry probability by 2.7 percentage points and increasing the exit probability by 2.0 percentage points. This would appear to contradict the common understanding that the level of AFDC benefits

---

similar population. The difference may be due to reliance upon a 1968 panel of respondents and the general acknowledgment that social attitudes toward welfare participation have changed since then, becoming less stigmatizing.

relative to prevailing work possibilities—the assumption behind "less eligibility" being that welfare provided at levels below the lowest market wage discourages entry—is a powerful predictor of welfare use; the Hutchens findings suggest that the effect is actually quite small.

Curiously, the differences between the guaranteed benefit and a second corrected variable that also measures benefits (and that increases the guarantee by a few hundred dollars at most) should not be great; yet they are.[2] It is also surprising that the relationship between the guarantee and exits is so small and that nonwage income seems to explain so little of it. Hutchens (1981) offers the strained explanation that "although no definitive conclusions can be drawn on the reason for these anomalies, there are grounds for hypothesizing that unobserved variables are responsible" (232). But this is always true and in the light of routinely insignificant and small effects, perhaps the utility analyses of economic rationality need to be augmented with other considerations. Moreover, there is little comfort in the notion that the unexplained variation in exits and entries is random or that "nondeterministic" models are needed to explain welfare behavior. Both undercut fundamental assumptions of rationality and deny the value of the social sciences and of any systematic understanding of social behavior. If only a small portion of social behavior is explainable, why bother with rationality at all? Given prevailing economic assumptions—that welfare dependency is explained by welfare benefits and program characteristics—Hutchens's findings are surprisingly weak and inconclusive.

Moreover, the accuracy of Hutchens's findings is seriously constrained by limitations on the research. He only correlated two years of experience; he did not conduct prospective research. The sample was overly weighted for dependency implying a selectivity bias, namely that his model predicts dependency among a population largely composed of the poor, especially those who are predisposed to utilize welfare, and not among the general population. Consequently, it is difficult to extend the findings to the whole population affected by welfare programs. Moreover, his analysis depends greatly upon accurate reports of both wage and nonwage income, which is highly suspect in the PSID surveys; the Edin (1991) demurrer remains a serious challenge. Other dynamic models are similarly flawed.[3]

2. The anomalous sign of PAY2 might be accounted for by a consistent relationship between the presence of the set-aside (and hence work) and exits. But this is very speculative. It may be more likely that the data are masking many errors in addition to inaccurate wage reports.

3. Plotnick (1983) conducted an analysis, covering four years of AFDC turnover, of the control group from the Denver Income Maintenance Experiment. Because the sample

None of the research—static, dynamic, and experimental—does more than locate its definitions of cause in the proximal events preceding welfare. The issue of subcultural and structural causation, and therefore the long-term and underlying determinants of poverty and welfare use, is not

---

overrepresented the poor (and therefore a likely group of AFDC recipients), he employed standard adjustments. Commenting on the contradictory findings in previous research (particularly studies that conflict with Hutchens's [1981] findings), Plotnick (1983) notes that they used different time periods in which to account for exits and entries. The artificial time periods imposed upon their analyses may bias the findings. Employing an annual as opposed to a monthly accounting period and a measure of welfare use that assumes dependency throughout the accounting period for any report of welfare income will produce different estimates of welfare duration. Moreover, artificial cut-off points, leading to problems of censored data, underestimate the lengths of welfare spells. His event history analysis attempted to correct for censoring problems.

Plotnick (1983) found that a few important variables had statistically significant relationships with AFDC exits and entries. As anticipated, increased age and higher AFDC guarantees increased entry and reduced exits, while increases in the imputed wage rate decreased dependency on AFDC. At all imputed wages, raising the guarantee by a factor of three (from $150 to $450 a month) doubled the duration of time on AFDC and reduced the duration between spells by more than 50 percent. These are substantial differences that imply great changes in the cost of the program. Moreover, in distinction to previous work, once a woman accepts AFDC, her level of education does not appear to affect her stay although it does seem to affect the length of time between spells of dependency.

The importance of Plotnick's (1983) findings are limited by a number of factors. He did not employ an experimental design and therefore cannot assume that changes in the guarantee will have the estimated effects. Indeed, the sample is self-selected by their very behavior. All of his estimates depend upon accurate reports of income, which in the NIT studies (discussed below) were probably grossly underreported in both the experimental and control samples. In the light of the enormous heterogeneity of the low-income population, the issue of selection bias is particularly relevant; it is not certain that the corrections for selectivity bias or the procedures for imputing wages account for this heterogeneity. Finally, his sample was restricted to one location, Denver.

Blank (1989a), in correcting for the use of annual aggregate accounting periods in the Panel Study of Income Dynamics, employs monthly reports across six years on the controls from the Seattle and Denver Income Maintenance Experiments. Her results "indicate that the welfare population is exceptionally diverse . . . with some women leaving welfare quickly, while others have few non-welfare opportunities" (272). However, time on welfare itself does not appear to affect dependency. Her estimates of welfare duration differ from previous research (notably Bane and Ellwood 1983). In contrast with Plotnick's (1983) conclusions about the importance of income, age, and prevailing wages, Blank (1989a) reports that change in marriage status "causes" both movement onto and off of welfare even acknowledging that changes in household status are presumably related to financial need (257). Yet here too the report of changed household status as well as income may be mere accommodations to welfare eligibility (hiding both the presence of partners and additional income) and not true reflections of living conditions or income.

Yet even accepting for the moment the accuracy of her findings, the independent variables she identifies, as well as the conditions that the other researchers identify in similar

decided. In this way, Blank's (1989a) observation that divorce and desertion seem to "cause" welfare dependency ignores the probability that family dissolution (however imperfectly counted in her study) is probably related to other more enduring sociological, psychological, and economic factors that cannot be addressed by welfare use itself. Solutions to welfare dependency must address those base factors if families are to be made self-sufficient and functional or at least to be prevented from becoming dependent.

Blank (1989a) provides no insight into the determinants of family dissolution and therefore no valuable insight into solutions for the problem. Solutions that focus narrowly on formal changes in AFDC and Food Stamps that may promote remarriage rates by enforcing a work test— perhaps by lowering guarantees and by increasing benefit reduction rates, making remarriage more attractive or separation less so—do not address the issue of cause. Moreover, if program elements are to be accepted as remedies for the sustaining causes of dependency, they still need to be validated experimentally.

In a broader context, a full evaluation of the benefits of prolonged but unhappy marriage and of forced remarriage (and, presumably, independence from welfare) need to be balanced against their social costs, including the impact on all family members. The tight focus on welfare dynamics—the effect of the iron triangle of welfare analysis on labor supply and dependency—as a substitute for concern about more general

---

analytic procedures, cannot be taken as true causes of dependency. While the causes may be logically connected to dependency and occur in appropriate temporal sequence before the events they are to explain, they may only be intervening variables between the true causes of dependency and the events of welfare utilization. They may also simply be correlates.

Fitzgerald (1991) analyzed the Survey of Income and Program Participation to assess "the determinants" of exits from AFDC. His findings largely corroborate Blank's (1989a) site-specific findings as well as the now conventional understanding of welfare dynamics discussed above:

> All studies conclude that marriage and earnings increases are the primary routes off of AFDC. Overall, they find that blacks are less likely than whites to leave AFDC by marriage, yet the rate of exit by earnings increase is not significantly different for blacks and whites. These results imply that the lower overall rates of exit by blacks is due to their lower propensity to marry. (Fitzgerald 1991:547)

However, Fitzgerald (1991) finds that benefit levels account for only a small although statistically significant portion of exits. In contrast with Wilson and Neckerman (1986), Fitzgerald's findings also suggest that the marriage prospects of blacks are not important reasons for their dependency on welfare. Wilson and Neckerman (1986; Wilson 1987) implicate the low wages of black males, which they conclude to be a consequence of racial discrimination, in the unfavorable marriage market available to black women.

social problems is a consistent failure of the literature. But in any event, the limitations of Blank's (1989a) research, repeating the failures of the rest of the literature, invalidate it on methodological grounds. For many reasons—different data sets, different data manipulations, and different coding procedures—the results of different studies are customarily not directly comparable.

Characteristically, Fitzgerald (1991) discusses the research on welfare as if the search for cause had succeeded, applauding the recent dynamic studies for finding dependency's structural determinants, such as education and the prevailing wage. Yet, neither the methodologies nor the theoretical foundations of the arguments allow for such causal interpretations, and analytic and data problems further circumscribe the wisdom of accepting these proximate associations as true causal estimates. Without deciding the debate between structural and subcultural causation and then testing the value of interventions inspired by these theories, no true cause can be identified.

If education and higher prevailing wages were the true paths to economic independence, then the findings suggest that training would be an appropriate intervention. Similarly, Wilson and Neckerman (1986) imply that raising the wages of black men would produce less dependency among black women. However, these simplistic conclusions avoid the possibility that poor educational attainment and the ability to secure attractive wages are the result of embedded characterological deficits and oppositional subcultures on the one hand and the actual provision of welfare on the other (the moral-hazards argument). The structural arguments have not refuted these possibilities. Indeed, the near-universal findings of the analyses distinguish between those who rely upon welfare for a short period and those who are long-term dependents. As a consequence, subcultural explanations of dependency remain as tractable as structural ones, while the possible unintended consequences of the interventions are unevaluated. In this light, raising the market skills of the least well off, as one example, might *contribute* to impoverishment by increasing the supply of unskilled labor without increasing the supply of jobs while maliciously requiring newly displaced workers to spend down to become eligible for welfare. In essence, increasing skills without increasing jobs may force underemployment or job-sharing among a larger pool of impoverished workers.

Moreover, simulating the results for policy projections in the narrow terms of the debate (ignoring the broader wage impact of increasing labor supply) repeats the causal errors of the analysis. Such simulations falsely suggest that investments in the problem population will secure benefits proportionate to the assumptions of equivalence between the AFDC dependent and the AFDC independent, between the short-stayers and the long-stayers, between the never-married mothers and the once-married ones, between blacks and whites. The simulations fail to account for system impacts, unintended but possible harms, and unanticipated consequences. In short, they are not studies of interventions but limited descriptions of dependency under largely unknown precipitating conditions.

THE NEGATIVE INCOME TAX EXPERIMENTS

The NIT experiments of the 1960s and 1970s promised to remove the design impediments and to isolate the sustaining causes of welfare dependency. These immensely expensive research demonstrations were justified as sources of authoritative policy information on whether to implement a universal alternative to the categorical system of relief.

A NIT is an instance of the iron triangle of welfare analysis (guarantee/benefit reduction rate = breakeven point) assuring a guarantee and a specific benefit reduction rate. Together they define a breakeven point below which people are subsidized and above which they begin to pay taxes. The guarantee is related to the notion of sufficiency, defining the maximum benefit for a recipient who cannot or does not work. The benefit reduction rate presumably creates a work incentive by defining the rate at which the guarantee is reduced for each dollar of earnings; the lower the benefit reduction rate, the greater the incentive to work. The breakeven point establishes the potential cost of the program as well as a point of equity. There is obviously a trade-off between these values. A high guarantee and a great incentive to work would create a massively expensive program providing subsidies to many people. So, if the guarantee were set close to the poverty line for a family of three, say $10,000 a year, in order to provide a decent floor for those who cannot work, and the benefit reduction rate was set at 25 percent so as to encourage the able-bodied to work, then eligibles would receive subsidies until they earn $40,000 a year. This politically unacceptable result dictates raising the benefit reduction rate or lowering the guarantee. However, holding the line on costs reduces the ability to provide a decent safety net or to provide reasonable incentives to work.

Alternatively, a NIT could be restricted to particular eligibles, such as single heads of households with children. This decision reinstitutes categorical welfare, however, and the NIT was commended as a substitute for the categorical system. A NIT would seem to provide a solution to poverty across the board while reducing the abuses of discretion and the costs of maintaining fifty separate state welfare programs. It would also appear to eliminate incentives to family dissolution and provide a national standard.

Both for liberals pursuing adequacy and fairness and for conservatives seeking lower costs, the NIT seemed to offer a solution to the problems of the categorical welfare programs, notably AFDC. Yet, for both groups, the desirability then as now of any welfare scheme hinges upon the degree to which it subverts cherished social norms, particularly work and family stability. The experiments were conducted largely to test the degree to which labor supply, and secondarily family structure, would be affected by a universal NIT. The design characteristics of the experiments—notably, randomized controls—were to allow analysts to attribute specific changes in labor supply to specific elements of a NIT program.

Four studies were conducted beginning in the late 1960s and cost more than $450 million in 1983 dollars (Haveman 1986c). The New Jersey experiment drew a sample of low-income urban families, offering benefit reduction rates of 30 percent, 50 percent, and 70 percent together with guarantees from 50 percent to 125 percent of the poverty line. The Rural Income Maintenance Experiment enrolled rural families in North Carolina and Iowa and provided program conditions similar to those in New Jersey. The Gary Income Maintenance Program oversampled black, female-headed families in an urban ghetto and also studied their utilization of social services and education; it also provided day care subsidies.

The fourth experiment, the Seattle-Denver Income Maintenance Experiment (SIME/DIME), was the largest and most sophisticated of the four. In addition to labor force participation, it measured family stability and the effects of inexpensive manpower programs and training subsidies on the work behavior of enrolled families. It also provided declining benefit reduction rates as well as the customary fixed rates of the other three studies. In all, the SIME/DIME experiment contained eleven different NIT packages, and subjects were enrolled for different periods of time—three, five, and twenty years.

The New Jersey and the rural experiments reported small reductions in the work efforts of male heads of families. Few of the differences were statistically significant. The Gary experiments also produced modest declines in work participation, but high reductions, near 30 percent, were reported for female heads of household.

SIME/DIME corrected some of the debilitating methodological problems of the other studies but contradicted their results, consistently reporting large labor supply reductions: work effort declined 5.4 percent for husbands, 22.0 percent for wives, and 11.2 percent for female heads of household. Higher guarantees and lower tax rates generally produced even greater work reductions.

Moreover, the reported rates of marital dissolution were generally higher in the experimental groups than among controls. The NIT appeared to raise divorce rates by 40 percent and sometimes by as much as 60 percent, perhaps because it allowed women to become financially independent of their husbands.

Murray (1984) made much of the results, offering them as testimony to the moral hazards of welfare:

> The key question was whether a negative income tax reduced work effort. The answer was yes. The reduction was not the trivial one that NIT sponsors had been prepared to accept, but substantial. In the SIME/DIME studies (which produced neither the largest nor the smallest changes, but probably the most accurately measured ones), the NIT was found to reduce "desired hours of work" by 9 percent for husbands and by 20 percent for wives. (Murray 1984:151)

Murray (1984) goes on to argue that the work losses were concentrated among wives and males who were not yet heads of families, "precisely the ones who were in a position to cause the most long-term damage to the goals of reducing poverty" (151).

A slew of technical critics (see Brasilevsky and Hum 1984; Hausman and Wise 1985; Killingsworth 1983; Metcalf 1973, 1974; Palmer and Pechman 1978) have pointed out the design problems in the NIT— breeches of randomization, truncated samples, attrition, misreporting, and demonstration effects. The conservative critics, notably Anderson (1978), argue that the design flaws, particularly its temporary experimental nature and truncated sampling, probably produced underestimates of the true labor effects; in a permanent NIT, more people would opt out of work.

The problem of misreporting was considerable in all of the sites. Greenberg, Moffitt, and Friedmann (1981) and also Greenberg and Halsey (1983) estimate that subjects systematically underreported their true incomes: for example, in the Gary experiment husbands underreported income by approximately 30 percent (28 percent for control husbands), while wives underreported income by up to 49 percent (37 percent for control wives). Moreover, these are apparently only estimates for legal income and do not include money derived from illegal work in the underground economy.[4] In contrast, Greenberg, Moffitt, and Friedman (1981) argue that the underreporting of income mitigates the labor supply loss. The work effort of participants was not reduced as much as the studies report, it was simply hidden. But this shift of income—probably induced by the experiment's high marginal tax rates (benefit reduction rates), from reported to unreported sources of income and possibly to underground, illegal work—provides little comfort that a NIT would improve civic culture.

The criticisms of the NIT experiments start with their basic data problems; the outcome data are not reliable and therefore neither the estimates of their impact on labor supply nor their analyses of the determinants of these impacts are credible. While Killingsworth (1983) acknowledges that the data problem is an important "caveat," he paradoxically holds that "the experimental studies have been fairly successful in providing measures of the impacts of the experiments they were designed to evaluate" (407). He acknowledges, however, the difficulty of estimating the causes of the wage and income effects on labor supply. His summaries of the labor supply elasticities from the different sites and from different studies of the same sites are too variant to recommend any particular interpretation of the outcomes. Ashenfelter (in Palmer and Pechman 1978) argues that the function of the experiments was to define the structural determinants of the outcomes as well as the outcomes themselves, that is, to estimate the changes in labor supply as well as the influence of the guarantees and the benefit reduction rates. The studies did neither credibly.

In addition to the problems of data reliability, other pitfalls of the NIT research invalidate any conclusion, supporting Ashenfelter's skepticism. Selectivity bias was a considerable problem: samples were truncated at relatively low incomes and true estimates of the impact of a NIT on relatively poor but excluded populations were impeded. In addition, randomization was breached in assignment to the various experimental conditions, and Killingsworth (1983:381) argues that attrition, a considerable problem, was probably not random. Corrections for these biases, discussed above, are only as good as the assumptions that the participants and nonparticipants are largely similar. Furthermore, the tem-

---

4. It is curious that in his subsequent papers Moffitt is so oblivious to the data problem that he identifies here. Hardly any of his subsequent studies either acknowledge directly or attempt to correct for the enormous inaccuracies of officially reported income and work effort, the central dependent variables of the labor supply literature. This problem is discussed below.

porary duration of the study created conditions that could not anticipate the reactions of participants in a permanent program.

In addition to their imperfect measurement of a impacts of a NIT on work and marriage, the experiments failed to measure their broader impacts on social cohesion and socialization. The political climate of the time may have justified these narrow choices, but judging by the subsequent reaction to the research the choices do not seem to have been wise or prescient. The issues of work and marriage hardly settle concern over social isolation and divisions created by relieving a huge population from work while providing perverse incentives for misreporting income and participating in the underground economy. These unexplored possibilities are far greater threats to the civic culture and social tranquility than any dispute over a few tens of billions of dollars.

THE EDIN CHALLENGE

The accuracy of the data is a fundamental problem in all of the research. Between 1988 and 1990, Edin (1991; Jencks and Edin in Jencks 1992) surveyed a convenience sample of fifty AFDC mothers in Chicago. All of the women reported that their welfare benefits were inadequate to support their families and that they augmented their incomes with unreported financial assistance from families, friends, boyfriends, absent fathers, and, most notably, work. The mean amount of their AFDC and Food Stamp benefits was $521 a month. The mean amount of their unreported income, $376 a month, added another 72 percent to their total income; unreported work accounted for $166 dollars of that, or 44 percent of the total additional income. In great contrast to Edin's study, the Current Population Survey (CPS) and AFDC Characteristic Survey for 1982, conducted only seven years before Edin's study, report that AFDC recipients received only $6.30 a month outside their legal benefits (Moffitt 1986:428). Similarly, SIME/DIME control respondents reported only $28.78 in nonwelfare income each month, while estimates of underreporting in the Gary experiment are between 30 percent and 50 percent. (Even these estimates may be underreports since they do not probe income from underground activities.)

By themselves, the very large benefit reduction rates of the AFDC program—100 percent after 1981 and before 1967 and 67 percent for the intervening years—and the NIT experiments provided enormous incentives for recipients to hide wage and unearned income. In the face of confiscatory tax rates, welfare recipients apparently underreport nonwelfare income and increasingly join the underground work force (Lemieux, Fortin, and Frechette 1994). As Greenberg, Moffitt, and Friedmann

(1981) speculate, however, their total work effort may not change much. Then again, this conclusion is neither precise nor particularly objective.

Edin (1991) uses her findings to argue that welfare "pays too little to entice recipients into a life of passive dependence" (Edin 1991:462). She goes on to point out that her evidence largely refutes the moral-hazards argument since it "challenges the validity of three widely accepted stereotypes about welfare recipients: they do not work, they do not want to work, and their behaviors reflect values different from mainstream society" (Edin 1991:472).

However, the weakness of her methods undermine these broader conclusions, while her narrower conclusions are also suspect. It is questionable whether her sample is representative of either Chicago recipients or the national pool of recipients. Her findings report only marginal work attachment, an average perhaps of only thirty-one hours a month (using Edin's report that they averaged $5 an hour), and hardly constitute firm grounds for concluding that recipients' values fit into the mainstream; to the contrary, being placed in a situation in which illegal activities are necessary may foster oppositional attitudes and a rebellious subculture. But Edin's apparent desire to deny the plausibility of subcultural differences may have blunted her enthusiasm to scrutinize the participation of her respondents in illegal work. Moreover, it is not certain that she obtained an accurate accounting of work and income; her reports of patently illegal work account for only $38 a month.

Still, welfare recipients are obviously receiving additional income. In low-benefit states, such as Mississippi which provides a maximum AFDC benefit of $120 a month and about $200 in Food Stamps, without additional income, reports of starvation and homelessness would be widespread. The great value of Edin (1991) lies in its challenge to the accuracy of income estimates in virtually all of the reported research. The challenge is substantial since Edin's estimates of unreported income, which themselves may be underestimates, are such a large fraction, even multiple, of reported welfare payments. Following Mattera's (1985) observations, the underreporting may be still larger since reports of expenditures are customarily more accurate than reports of income. In addition, the estimates of unreported income, which imply a considerable amount of work activity, challenge all of the reported predictions of labor force participation. If the Edin surmise is correct, the entire literature describing the behaviors of welfare recipients may be grossly inaccurate, providing relatively meaningless estimates while distorting the work participation and willingness to work of welfare recipients.

The Edin (1991) challenge, in spite of its overinterpretations and methodological limitations, remains particularly damaging for the microdata sources of the basic studies of welfare behavior: the CPS, the PSID, the Survey of Income and Program Participation (SIPP), and others. The income and assets questions are longstanding problems. Legal as well as illegal income is customarily underreported in these surveys as well as to the Internal Revenue Service (IRS). Validating the surveys against each other or IRS data is therefore pointless.[5]

The problem of unreported income is made more complex and problematic by the presence of a large and possibly increasing underground economy (Mattera 1985). Very little if any of this money is reported to official surveys. Presumably many welfare recipients are encouraged by the lack of accounting to participate in a variety of illegal jobs: drugs, gambling, sweat shops, child labor, moonlighting, illegal buying and selling, and so forth. Without accounting for either legal or illegal work, the literature on the work behavior of the poor and of welfare recipients is missing crucial information.

CAUSE AND ECONOMIC RATIONALITY

Apart from the ambiguities created by inaccurate data, none of the research has established the causes of dependency nor the effects of work incentives on welfare use. Static analysis of welfare are inadequate because they do not consider behavior over time. Dynamic studies lack both true controls and prospective manipulations of the independent variables, acknowledged in Danziger, Haveman, and Plotnick (1981) as the problem of estimating behavior in the absence of transfers. Finally, true experimental designs are particularly relevant for transfer programs,

5. In this regard, the problems of the SIPP are illustrative. Citro and Kalton (1993) report that the CPS experiences routine nonresponse rates to income questions of about 20 percent; SIPP nonresponse rates are less but still substantial in many important areas, particularly the amount of income. A number of their measures, notably related to participation in welfare programs, are subject "to appreciable error" (Citro and Kalton 1993: 48). For example, the SIPP reported only 76 percent of the true amount of AFDC income in 1983 (erroneous reports in SIPP data are also suggested by Blank and Ruggles 1994). Curiously, Harris (1993) estimates work participation rates of AFDC mothers based upon PSID data that are considerably above the official numbers, further suggesting a great amount of underreporting. In addition, the problems of longitudinal studies are exacerbated by attrition, with the PSID losing substantial numbers of participants over the years.

The customary adjustment for nonresponse in the research based upon these data sets has been to impute the missing information. However, the imputation procedures—whether to adjust for income, selectivity bias, or potential wage rates—assume similarity among certain types of respondents or samples on the one hand and nonrespondents or populations on the other in order to derive their corrections. This remains a remarkably shaky premise.

but the NIT studies, for one, were deeply flawed. At best, the research has identified some of the proximate correlates of welfare usage but not causes, and causal inferences based upon faulty methods may well mislead policymaking.

The practice of simulating policy decisions on the basis of research findings, while academically interesting, slyly imputes an undue level of causal influence to the so-called independent variables. Moreover, the fact that many of the models produce statistically significant results does not mean that the models explain much. To the contrary, they customarily explain very little, which heightens skepticism toward their policy pretenses. Technique has come to mask ignorance.

Thus, the common conclusion that higher education, greater work skills, and more day care would diminish dependence on welfare is not based on fact but on correlational studies that *relate* deficits in education, work skills, and day care to long stays on welfare. Other factors, perhaps subcultural (lacking mainstream values) or structural ("a future of lousy jobs"), may account for both the deficits and the dependency (Burtless 1990). Simply filling the deficits by providing social services may not produce a work-ready population, while the effects of expanding the low-income work force is routinely ignored. The narrow preference in the research for a set of proximate, and largely economic, independent variables blocks out a broader consideration of the social effects of changes in welfare policy.

The literature subscribes to a dubious causal assumption: if the long-term dependent population, the short-term dependent population, and the nondependent population share the same limited range of demographic characteristics (age, number of children, education, access to day care, and so forth), then they would exhibit the same work characteristics. This dubious assumption produces a curious circularity, justifying corrections for sampling bias of one sort or another that in turn reaffirm the value of the research itself. The corrections are necessary, but to apply the corrections it must be assumed that the sampled groups closely resemble the unsampled groups. Yet, the available evidence seems to argue more for an enormous underlying variation within the welfare population than for a well-defined set of stereotypical behaviors. This false assumption of similarity then leads to inaccurately adjusted conclusions and simulations that reinforce the appearance of similarity. As Haveman (1987a) observes,

> . . . at their core, all of the [correction] techniques rely on some set
> of assumptions about the shape of the distribution of the underlying
> data. These assumptions typically involve normality or symmetry and

are both strong and arbitrary; if they do in fact not hold, the
estimated results may be at least as biased as making no correction
for selectivity. (Haveman 1987:211)

Moreover, the corrections themselves, essentially forecasts, need to be
empirically validated. This has rarely been done.

Moffitt (1986b) provides perhaps the largest estimate of the degree to
which economic rationality accounts for dependency. Yet all of his economic variables—the level of income guarantee, the benefit reduction
rates, the prevailing hourly wage, other income, education, race, number
of children, prevailing unemployment, and so forth—only explain about
three-fifths of the variation in a single dependent variable, hours worked,
that itself has only a tenuous relation to broad social problems (407).
This is one of the more successful economic models described in the literature and notwithstanding its many methodological limitations, it still
leaves a great amount of unexplained variation while failing to establish
causal relations in the variation it does predict or the extended meaning
of the dependent variable itself.

Similarly, Bane and Ellwood (1994), Murray (1984), Kaus (1992),
and others fail in their extensive literature reviews to estimate the influence of different factors in explaining dependency. Rational choice-
models (the preference of economists) remain as tenuous and unsatisfying as expectancy and cultural models in identifying any of the causes
of dependency. In the end, they all fail to provide a compelling causal
justification for their policy recommendations.

The problem of causality is also affected by the arbitrary point at
which the phenomena of poverty and dependency is studied. In an in-
finite regression, the determinants of each proximate event can be
pressed back to its own antecedents. Thus, the demonstration of subcultural differences, such as attitudes toward work, does not deny predisposing structural factors, such as discrimination or structural unemployment, which in turn fail to preclude the possibility of prior subcultural
differences that precipitated the discrimination or differential work behavior, and so on and so on. In a similar way, economic factors (rational-
choice models) may imply certain subcultural characteristics as well as
personal expectancies. The issue of cause thus becomes an arbitrary decision about where to cut into the historical chain, a decision related to
predisposing ideology.

The ability to arbitrate among underlying causes may thus be ren-
dered impossible by definitional ambiguities and political predispositions
even if experimental verification of proximate causes was more practical.
Still, neither the practical impediments nor the theoretical ones have been

overcome in the literature. The fairest and most obvious conclusion is that no cause of dependency has been identified, notwithstanding the occasional assurance that cause is obvious—"it seems *ludicrous* to argue that motivation and self-worth are not linked closely to behavior; especially behavior on welfare" (Bane and Ellwood 1994:118, emphasis added).[6]

The concern with cause focuses most powerfully on the effects of interventions—their ability to achieve specified goals. Yet Moffitt's (1992) observation, commonly repeated (see Haveman 1987a and Killingsworth 1983), that the literature is in a methodological infancy and that even its sophisticated studies are groping and unsuccessful stabs at cause, is certainly accurate given the nearly universal methodological pitfalls. Unfortunately, these deep shortcomings have not constrained the intellectual hubris that boosts policy recommendations as economically rational, let alone rational in any other guise.

Still, "economic rationality" dominates the evaluation of welfare policies, despite the fact that the decision to tolerate a 35 percent level of program inefficiency in welfare transfers is largely cultural. The evaluation of welfare policy in terms of economic determinacy constrains the language of the debate to efficacy measures at the expense of other considerations, notably the extent to which general social dissatisfaction and the prevalence of deviance (such as addiction, violent crime, and mental disease) may pose greater threats to society than poverty and low work effort. To the extent to which poverty and work effort (together with their ties to welfare programs) are unrelated to deeper concerns over the domestic tranquility, the analysis of social problems in these terms is irrelevant. The literature cannot hide behind the moral-hazards question in this regard since by accepting its terms—that welfare decreases work and thus promotes idleness or that its provision is unconscionably inefficient—it also accepts its centrality for the broader policy debate. As such the primary base of studies fails to certify the relevance of economic rationality.

It may be true that definitive research is impossible, thus highlighting the political nature of decisionmaking, especially over welfare. Indeed, the absence of credible welfare research provides a residual proof of Lindblom's great formulation. When reduced to partisan analyses, the studies of welfare participation, however elegant and sophisticated, may

6. Perhaps it is not ludicrous to point out that many people with low self-esteem avoid welfare. Moreover, the theory of marginality, including psychological marginality, has been related to enormous work effort, counterintuitively recommending low self-esteem as the great motivator. See the psychohistories in Lasch (1965) as well as Marcuse (1964).

simply create political symbols in the play of power. Perhaps it is not surprising that without adequate empirical support for any position, the debate over welfare is so virulent.

A PREMATURE FORMALISM

The base of research, with a near unanimity, attempts to explain the effects of welfare in the rational terms of economics. Two formulations—the iron triangle of welfare analysis and Okun's (1975) "leaky bucket"—are its foundation. However, both are inadequate for decisionmaking. The iron triangle fails to predict welfare participation well and focuses narrowly on the trade-offs between income adequacy, work, and equity (and cost). Cultural concerns, which may be more important, are neglected, and the literature seems oblivious to the long-term and unintended effects of its various proposals.

Okun's (1975) famous metaphor likens the extent to which the impact of the public welfare dollar, the bucket, is diminished by losses to work, leaks. So, for example, Danziger, Haveman, and Plotnick (1981) estimate that the leak for all transfer programs is approximately 23 cents for each dollar transferred (1020). To the extent that welfare itself affects work, the leak for AFDC and Food Stamps is even larger; with higher estimates of work loss, the leak becomes larger still. Yet measuring the desirability of transfer schemes by Okun's efficiency argument ignores the direct benefits that could be purchased by the transfers themselves—better child care and greater economic security for the work force—and the more extended social impacts of reducing the labor pool among the unskilled and maintaining a safety net for the poor. Furthermore, from the perspective of a modern society, the lost work may be desirable. Toil at the bottom of the economic ladder is not customarily ennobling, and perhaps other chores might be found for those people to increase their contribution to themselves and to the society. The issue may be less a fair wage than a livable income.[7]

Work for some people may not be a productive activity from a social perspective, and their diminished capacity for steady, fruitful employment needs to be appreciated against the puritanical desire to exact toil from all public dependents. From a structural perspective, a social incapacity that is perhaps induced by the failures of the culture itself needs to

7. The labor pool at the bottom is rapidly ballooning with an ever-increasing supply of unskilled and semiskilled workers (Burtless 1990). Increasing this pool even further places downward pressure on wages, distributing a limited number of jobs among a larger number of workers, thus capriciously requiring relatively poor workers to spend down their meager assets during periods of unemployment in order to become eligible for welfare.

be factored into the welfare decision. Of course, with an antithetical set of subcultural assumptions, work failure becomes characterological and work a method of moral reform, while long-term welfare use may isolate a portion of the culture. Yet, in either event, the efficiency of transfers fails to capture the principal issues of welfare. It is not axiomatic that the cost of providing the benefits should be measured as transfer efficiency. Economically efficient programs may be socially ineffective.

In the end, any estimate of Okun's bucket is caught yet again on the unreliability of the data since labor supply, measured as hours worked or as income, may be grossly misreported. In fact, it is quite conceivable that welfare has little effect on work itself; its guarantee may simply raise income while its high benefit reduction rates discourage recipients from mainstream work and recruit them into the underground economy (Lemieux, Fortin, and Frechette 1994). If this speculation has merit, then the United States may have gone far to eradicate economic poverty (at least by official measures), but at the same time allowed social problems to increase greatly, suggesting that the focus on work is an inadequate answer to the society's broader challenges. The true cost of welfare may not be its economic efficiency but its divisive impact on society, created by criminalizing and disparaging a large portion of the poor population and by isolating them from the dominant culture.

Unfortunately, welfare policy may have become prematurely formalized in terms of economic rationality. In a broader social sense, the guarantee of adequacy is a social contract, implying the conditions of citizenship that constitute minimal cultural security, including cash transfers but also education, vocational preparation, family protection, personal and community security, access to fruitful social participation, resources for retirement, and so forth. Benefit reduction rates are a single instance of the incentives to participate responsibly in society. While these program tax rates figure prominently, other kinds of incentives are probably also important: fairness and nondiscrimination in civic life, social respect, the chances through work to achieve participation in common cultural institutions (stable families, secure communities, and so forth). Finally, the equity and costs of these provisions cannot be measured by the number of people covered multiplied by average outlays but also need to account more broadly for the benefits they confer on society. Therefore, Okun's efficiency formula needs to be expanded from an expression of transferred dollars and dollars lost to one that compares social costs with social benefits.

With its quick leap to quantification, economics may not be the culprit but rather an accomplice in the premature reduction of the welfare debate to a limited ledger of accounts. The broader social debate has resisted consideration of the longer-term impact of its policies. Instead, the culture has long set its mind on the notion that work redeems and that more work is the solution to dependency and poverty. Whatever the reality of jobs and wages, for the past few decades America has profoundly ignored any facts but those of increasing public expenditures.

Work participation and welfare dependency (even fleshed out with considerations of family structure) are inadequate measures of social cohesion and the social good. By accepting the narrow terms of the current policy debate with its near-total exclusion of wider considerations, social scientists, particularly economists, are serving a short-term policy constituency (and their own institutional ambitions) at the expense of a more thoughtful and well-considered policy debate. Policy analysis is not the same as critical analysis.

The base of primary research that informs welfare policy—the static, dynamic, and experimental research reviewed in Danziger, Haveman, and Plotnick (1981) and Moffitt (1992) as well as the body of subsequent research—falls into crippling methodological and analytic errors that invalidate any but their most general observations. In addition to the issue of cause, most of those studies also have perhaps unmanageable problems with selectivity bias and the accuracy of their raw data.

The imperfections of the NIT studies unleashed a large controversy over the value of social experimentation, with some arguing that good-time series data, giving up the possibility of experimental manipulation, may provide more reliable estimates. Heckman (in Manski and Garfinkel 1992) even suggests the possibility of a "randomization bias" that may be intractable. In the end, all of the labor supply research addressing issues of poverty and dependency evidences serious pitfalls that invalidate its scientific credibility and therefore its conclusions. This failure of theory and practice create a true epistemic fix presenting the nettlesome possibility that definitive empirical research may not be possible, a conclusion that is all the more vexing in light of the sophistication of the body of research upon which it is based.

CONCLUSION

The shortcomings of the literature do not sustain Haveman's comforting conclusions that welfare dependency and use are understood:

> Economists responded to concern over the labor-supply effects of income transfers with an outpouring of empirical research. These studies, employing a variety of data and methods, were all designed to evaluate the impact of transfer programs on the work effort of

recipients and potential recipients. They found that transfer benefits can, and generally do, induce recipients to work less than they would otherwise. In response to transfer benefits, some recipients reduce the number of hours they work; others withdraw from the labor force completely. Less labor supply leads to less production for the market. (Haveman 1987a:247)

Instead, the methodological problems of the research—particularly its uncertain measures of the critical variables, sampling biases, and porous designs—prevent any sort of conclusion.

The labor supply research in the welfare arena, and more generally in economics, is among the most advanced in the social sciences. Indeed the development of technique may be its principal disciplinarian function at the present time (Haveman 1987a; Moffitt 1992). Its many methodological imperfections greatly reduce its scientific credibility, however, and therefore restrict its findings to the narrow confines of its assumptions and methods. The basic scruple of scientific inquiry to stay within the credibility of the research is not respected by either the broader policy debate nor by the very authors of the research. With the complicity of the researchers themselves who clearly write to an audience of policymakers, the word of the research is taken far beyond its scientific limits.

The summaries of the research acknowledge the conventional wisdom: welfare distorts labor supply in "nontrivial" ways through its guarantees and benefit reduction rates. In tandem with these conclusions, the summaries acknowledge anomalous and conflicting findings, wide variations, imperfect methods, and so forth, leading to the complementary observation that the findings are uncertain, that much of the variation in the dependent variables still needs to be explained, that the discipline is still developing. The findings are offered as central to policymaking but the cautions vitiate their importance. Having selected the topic for study and honed its researchable importance on the stone of politics, the researcher is fully conscious of its broader meaning and, judging by the concluding remarks of many studies, often play openly for policymakers' affections.[8]

8. Indeed, given its obvious attention to the contemporary political implications of its findings, the authors and their journals could certainly make a greater effort to reduce the obscurity of their papers in providing easier access to their meaning. The literature does not appear to be forthcoming. Even when written for initiates, too many problems of clarity remain: dense, almost impenetrable prose, missing definitions, convoluted presentations, incomplete data presentations, and the persistent reliance upon social science's ephemeral (fugitive) research. This inaccessibility might be more tolerable if the underlying quality of the research itself was more substantial. However, its profound methodological

Moreover, the literature is too narrowly concerned with the incentive issue, rushing to operationalize and quantify variables without first establishing their connection with the underlying social problems that justify the research in the first place. Work does not stand adequately for the social good. But even on this score the studies are indeterminate about the causes of work participation.

Even accepting for the moment that welfare may greatly interfere with labor force participation, it is impossible on the grounds of the research to adjudicate between those who claim welfare is too generous and those who are not bothered by the work losses without a broader evaluation of welfare's longer-term social and economic consequences. The reduction of work may be as much a moral hazard of welfare—sloth encouraged by entitlement—as a result of poor job markets, discrimination, failed schools, and so forth. Moreover, in the face of the Edin challenge, the research has not credibly supported the conventional wisdom that welfare interferes with work. If Edin is correct, people on welfare continue to work although in the underground economy.

The value of the findings is further restricted by the fact that welfare has over the years offered only a narrow range of relatively weak interventions. Welfare has never provided more than a fraction of a very meager poverty line. Its benefit reduction rates are usually confiscatory, providing great incentives to hide additional income. Even the NIT experiments offered little variation in guarantee and benefit reduction rates; all of its benefit reduction rates created large incentives for underreporting income while its guarantees, inadequate for health and decency, maintained incentives for additional income. Therefore, in addition to its many methodological deficiencies, the findings are confined to a very limited range of experiences. There is little if any authority to extend this constrained knowledge to novel situations.

The research may simply reflect the fact that welfare has little effect on work behaviors or on the larger problems of socialization and social cohesion. As recipients continue to work illegally while receiving benefits, welfare may do little more than raise their incomes. The greater harm

---

shortcomings raise the question of intentional obscurity taking the privilege of genius, a desire to hide its shortcomings in a priestly mysticism of the rarefied and ineffable. The literature appears to be so self-congratulatory and introverted as to raise the issue of its cliquishness, the tendency to avoid criticizing colleagues. Much of the research on work participation appears to be created by a small group of people tied into similar streams of funding—the Institute for Research on Poverty and the National Science Foundation. NSF seems quite proud of the fact that their grant recipients read like the Who's Who of American economics, which perhaps explains why their funding procedures assure a club decision discouraging applications from the Who's Not.

may come from inducing illegal activity and reducing respect for law than from discouraging work.

The contemporary policy discourse over welfare has become obsessed with work as the principal measure of social contribution. The assumption that greater work participation determines the social good has reduced the policy issue to a trade-off between welfare and work, cheapening the conceptual value of the literature even apart from its methodological problems.

The research on welfare and work fails to establish a rational authority for policymaking. The scientific credibility of the individual studies does not sustain the general conclusions that Moffitt (1992) and Danziger, Haveman, and Plotnick (1981) reach in support of their structural explanations for welfare participation; much of the data, and the large amount of unexplained variation, can be reinterpreted to support subcultural and individual explanations for welfare use. At the same time, the research provides little support for those who argue that welfare creates moral hazards. The impact of work on welfare is indeterminate. Therefore policy recommendations carry little authority beyond a common, intuitive appreciation for the fact that welfare *might* discourage work, at least reported work.

An extraordinary review of the literature (Moffitt 1986b) depicts the depth of its inconsistency, although this may not have been the author's principal intention. The paper set out to reconcile conflicts among the studies that measured the impact on work of the 1967 and 1981 programmatic changes in AFDC—eligibility, benefit levels, and benefit reduction rates. The traditional understanding—that benefit reduction rates and benefit levels vary inversely with both labor supply and work participation among current recipients—had been contradicted by the times-series evidence that Moffitt (1986b) presented (in his Table 3) and by two summaries of studies suggesting that the increased tax rates of the 1981 legislation had no effect on labor supply (Hutchens 1981; Moffitt 1985). These conflicts threatened the basic credibility of the field's research and consequently its authority to comment on welfare policy.

Moffitt (1986b) also cited contradictory evidence from the NIT experiments in relation to these anomalous findings: those "experiments provided tax rate effects that were often weak and mixed in sign" in predicting labor supply (395). It is notable that these anomalies relate to the total labor supply for each group and not the labor supply of current recipients, which seemingly follows orthodox expectations, although weakly. The general effect, however, is crucial for policy considerations since it anticipates the broader impacts of changes in program design— higher breakeven points, and hence expanded eligibilities and costs, that would result from any combination of higher guarantees and lower benefit reduction rates.

Moffitt's (1986b) own attempt to reconcile the differences concluded that the relationship—"the sign of the partial correlation"—between the labor supply of female heads of household and the benefit reduction rate of welfare "is indeed negative, at least at current tax rates and guarantee levels" (423). This conclusion supports his earlier simulations; perverse effects do occur, but the predicted directions of the critical relationships are largely accurate, thus preserving the underlying rationality of the argument and the value of the field's research. Moreover,

> As part of the exploration of this question, evidence was also adduced (albeit with much less certainty) indicating that the 1967 Social Security amendments [that lowered benefit reduction rates] increased work incentives and the 1981 OBRA legislation [that increased benefit reduction rates] reduced work incentives of female heads. (Moffitt 1986b:423)

These findings are not necessarily a comfort to the liberal. In order to minimize work disincentives when setting the benefit reduction rates for married couples, Moffitt's (1986b) analysis implies that the "rate for men should not be reduced below about 50 percent and that the [benefit reduction] rate for women should probably be set at 100 percent" (423). At the same time, these proposals provide an enormous incentive to underreport income and, following the conservative logic, presumably increase pressure for family dissolution.[9]

---

9. The literature has also offered the possibility of an ambiguity, a "perverse tax rate effect"; the labor supply of a number of groups was depressed by both high- and low-benefit reduction rates but increased by moderate rates. Moffitt's (1986b) own simulations corroborate this anomaly, suggesting that under various assumptions of labor supply elasticity and benefit reduction rates varying from 25 percent to 100 percent, the labor supply of many groups, particularly some men and married women, did not follow consistent patterns. The anomaly was reconciled because:

> Eventually a tax rate reduction lowers labor supply, simply because the upward movement in the break-even level eventually reaches into the thick part of the . . . income distribution, thereby drawing proportionately more [people] into the program relative to the number who are already on it. (Moffitt 1986b:393)

Moffitt (1986b) explained that female heads of families are not affected by this anomaly seemingly because so many of them are so poor to begin with; therefore increasing the breakeven point by lowering benefit reduction rates captures a relatively small number of potential beneficiaries. These findings lead, however, to categorical, not universal, policy recommendations and tend to maintain incentives that are inimical to family structure. But the more important point is that the base of research and consequently the simulations lack rational authority.

The conclusions of this unusually comprehensive and incisive work of scholarship are based upon an analysis of "signs," which are analogous to "trends" in sociology, and lack the dignity and authority of statistically significant findings. Most important, none of the benefit reduction rate estimators was significant in predicting hours worked, although benefit reduction rates were significant in predicting participation in AFDC. This latter conclusion would seem to be a mechanical result of the increased eligibility created by lower benefit reduction rates.[10] In addition, Moffitt (1986b) drew data from both the CPS and the AFDC Characteristics Survey, despite their inaccuracies in reporting sensitive information, particularly income. Moreover, his design was not experimental, and his conclusions relative to causal inferences could not be substantiated, even if they were statistically significant. Recognizing many of these problems, Moffitt (1986b) heroically attempts to support his weak findings with a secondary series of ex post facto analyses, ruminations, and reconsiderations. However, his "spadework" in addressing the ambiguities of the data—a wonder of scholarship, ingenuity, and erudition—leaves a reality of weak and unconvincing findings.

Moffitt's (1986b) literature review also includes a devastating methodological critique of most prior studies. Politely but pointedly, he undercuts the existing body of research for its lack of experimental designs and true controls, inappropriate analyses, inappropriate measures (for example, formal instead of actual benefit reduction rates), faulty assumptions, missing data, and selective and truncated sampling. He might also have pointed to the Edin problem, especially in light of his own earlier research (Greenberg, Moffitt, and Friedmann 1981).

In the end, his review largely discredits the literature and endorses, however implicitly, alternative conclusions: the literature is contradictory, frequently weak, and methodologically suspect; even studies that employ the same data sets often reach paradoxical conclusions; none, including the NIT studies, is able to isolate causal variables with any confidence and hence the assumptions of their policy models cannot be validated. Moreover, all of Moffitt's concentrated summaries of the literature are diluted by the possibility that convergent findings when they exist are the result of methodological ambiguities and consistently biased assumptions, analyses, and data produced by a homogeneous and powerfully centralized culture. A critical test of the reality of labor supply remains elusive and resistant to any imagined weight of evidence.

---

10. In reporting the results of wage rates, Moffitt (1986b) points out, "Neither the coefficient on the age rate nor on other income is of the expected sign, but neither is significant" (408). Here apparently the sign does not count.

In short, Moffitt's notable summary suffers many of the same pitfalls as the research he criticizes. The relationship between welfare and work remains very ambiguous, and the dispute between structural and subcultural perspectives must remain unresolved. Dependency on welfare has not been explained in terms of program characteristics, labor force characteristics, client characteristics, or any interaction among them. It is not clear that guarantees and benefit reduction rates at any level reduce work; they may simply shift work to the underground economy and affect the accuracy of reporting. It is not clear that changes in employment rates affect dependency greatly, and so welfare recipients may not return to work in an improved economy. It is not clear that subcultural predispositions or personal failings of character are either relevant or irrelevant. Consequently, it is not clear that welfare dependency among a large portion of the caseload can be affected by changes in the current structure of welfare or by any of the proposals for welfare change, including the more ambitious ones.

Even more problematic, it is not clear that any of the proposed changes are desirable. Failing to estimate the social impact of changes in recipients' work participation—the effects on recipients, their families, and the civic culture—the literature is blindly insulated from the effects of work on socialization and social cohesion, the broader goals that have justified attention to poverty and welfare dependency in the first place. Furthermore, the literature fails to estimate the possible effects of increased work participation (particularly in the absence of increased jobs) on low-wage workers. As a result, the literature offers no telling insights for policy nor does it define the uncomfortable dilemma that popular distaste for welfare will continue to impede policy. Policy decisions based upon the "substantial" labor supply literature are perilous. Its wisdom hardly surpasses the common understanding that something provided for free may affect subsequent behavior.

Seemingly conservatives and liberals support the agenda of current reform efforts, including the 1996 welfare reform calling for higher labor force participation rates through a combination of time-limited eligibility, reduced guarantees, and curtailed social services (such as child day care, intensive social casework, and vocational training); that agenda carries little rational backing from the research on labor supply. It is not certain that any of the proposed changes will create greater work participation or that increased work effort among the target populations is socially desirable.

Similarly, the more conservative reforms based upon strategies of public neglect—such as Murray's call for dismantling almost all public provisions, Olasky's reliance on the religious sector, and the 1996 act it-self—are not supported by any evidence that welfare creates much of a moral hazard. At the same time, the effects of a negative income tax, and any other universal income support system, are poorly understood; its social harms in isolating the poor may outweigh its benefits. There may be greater evils than stigma.

Curiously, if adjusted for gross underreporting, the current welfare system may already operate, however imperfectly, to guarantee child support and encourage work, although illegally in the underground econ-omy. It may have blundered into becoming the system that Ellwood and others proposed (Ellwood 1988; Garfinkel 1992; Garfinkel and McLana-han 1986; National Commission on Children 1991). People may accept the welfare guarantee in the spirit of a child support allowance and then supplement the obvious inadequacies of their welfare checks with additional unreported work in order to avoid confiscatory taxes. In the face of increasing social problems, the possibility that economic depri-vation—money poverty—may have been reduced far more than official counts suggest further indicates that welfare by itself has little ability to redress the problems of socialization and social cohesion.

The proposals for welfare reform on the legislative table will also probably fail to change welfare as we know it or, to the extent to which they lower the basic guarantees of AFDC and Food Stamps, will rend the safety net, producing more hungry children and a greater amount of frank deprivation. People on welfare may already be working to the ex-tent to which they are socially and psychologically capable. Indeed, solu-tions to the labor participation component of dependency may have to face the unsettling possibility that large numbers of people cannot or will not, even under conditions of duress, accept the values of the dominant culture. Welfare may offer little to resolve the problem of oppositional subcultures and social antagonisms.

With few exceptions, the current proposals tinker with dependency and poverty. Something still undiscovered or at least unproved is proba-bly going on deep within the culture, producing the enormous rates of failure and the enormous amount of dependency that is unexplained by economic rationality. The current research, so taken with labor supply effects, ignores the search for these factors, refusing to address the cur-rent level of social need and social disrepair. The social sciences have conspired in this failure of will with a rococo literature notable for its or-namentation rather than its substance. Any consensus in the policy com-munity results more from the centrifuge of its own political dynamics than from the rationality of its scholarship.

The research attempts precise statements. Yet, limited by its many procedural and substantive faults, those statements become evocative—poems, metaphors, hopeful leads, tentative support—in the play of power and partisan conflicts. Work, especially for the welfare dependent, is a powerful political symbol. However, the voice of economic rationality has failed to provide credible advice to adjudicate between competitive policy proposals, and the suspicion remains that the layered complexity of the literature masks important disciplinarian and ideological stakes. In a similar way, the policy sciences have also failed to resolve the ancillary issues of welfare's effects on family structure—marriage, divorce, illegitimacy—and the closely allied issue of intergenerational poverty.

4 Welfare, Family Structure, and Intergenerational Dependency

As the nation's tolerance of premarital sexual behavior and nontraditional families increases, American society seems less concerned with the impact of welfare on family structure than with the very central notion of work and independence from public support. Nevertheless, family stability remains at the core of a political rhetoric convinced that the design and generosity of welfare policy affect marriage and remarriage, separation, divorce, and out-of-wedlock births.

Family dissolution and nonmarital births account for a large amount of the reliance upon AFDC and of poverty in general. Forty-two percent of all new spells on AFDC are associated with divorce and separation, while 39 percent are associated with an unmarried mother becoming a head of a household (Bane and Ellwood 1994). The feminization of poverty, resulting from the growth of female-headed families, has placed an increasing population at risk.

Conservatives implicate welfare itself for providing disincentives for family stability and for "enabling" illegitimacy, particularly among adolescents. They further argue that welfare creates an intergenerational underclass through which welfare-dependent parents pass on their own dysfunctional behaviors to their children. For their part, liberals are reluctant to acknowledge that welfare plays much of a role in contemporary problems of family instability, preferring instead to implicate the imperfections of the labor market in explaining family dissolution.

Yet both liberals and conservatives seem to agree with a "new institutionalism," the assumption that family structure is largely a rational response to economic realities, principally defined as financial incentives: social "institutions are assumed to evolve in the direction dictated by rational individual responses to changed conditions" (Becker 1991:15). Becker goes on to "bring the state back in" to the argument:

> Families are much less closely knit and perform far fewer functions
> in the twentieth century than in earlier centuries primarily because

111

market and government mechanisms have evolved to train and
educate young people, and to protect against the hazards of old
age, illness, premature death, prolonged unemployment, and other
economic disasters. These new institutions have reduced the value
of relying on families for these purposes. . . . Families changed at the
most rapid pace ever during the past few decades primarily because
earnings and employment opportunities of women improved greatly,
and the welfare state grew rapidly. (Becker 1991:15)

Becker's laureate theory is very direct in its assessment of welfare itself. Citing Bernstam and Swan (1986), in particular, he concludes that
"welfare may well have contributed to the propensity of poor women to
remain single and become mothers even though real welfare payments
per family fell" (Becker 1991:16).

Similarly, Hernandez (1993) argues that the shift away from farm-
ing after the Second World War contributed to increased separation, divorce, and mother-only families. The employment of mothers became
feasible and necessary to maintain family income. Moreover, for both
mothers and fathers employment reduced

face-to-face interaction with their families during much of the day
and [provided] them with increasing opportunities for extramarital
relationships—especially since behavior could no longer be inhibited
or controlled by rural and small-town censorship. The more recent
rise in mothers' labor-force participation contributed further to the
rise in divorce and mother-only families by providing mothers . . .
with income that made it feasible for them to live away from their
husbands. (Hernandez 1993:14)

Conservatives have taken heart from the economic rationality of the
theoretical literature, particularly Becker, to argue that reduced welfare
will encourage family solidarity. Liberals on the other hand argue that
improving the market position of the poor will protect families. The controversy has come to hinge on the causal influence of welfare on family
structure and intergenerational dependency. Both sides rest their cases on
empirical proof, referring back to a sophisticated literature that purports
to measure the impact of welfare on family formation and intergenerational poverty.

The empirical literature, however, documents only a small effect of
welfare on family structure, even smaller than its effect on work, and the
research is routinely limited, uncertain, and overgeneralized. The causes
of family dissolution, notably the role of the state's welfare policies, still
have not been credibly identified. In the end, the social science wisdom

neither endorses the therapeutic neglect of the conservatives nor the liberal faith in socially efficient solutions. As a consequence, the limited range of proposed reforms carries little rational authority, and the argument remains stubbornly ideological.

The current system of welfare and most of the proposed reforms maintain a tradition of relatively superficial and weak interventions. In addition to its sizable methodological imperfections and its vulnerability to political concerns, the literature fails to consider more thoroughgoing reforms that might change embedded dysfunctional behaviors.

THE CURRENT ORTHODOXY

Moffitt's (1992) review establishes the general social science orthodoxy of the impact of welfare on family structure. Before the 1980s, research found no consistent pattern of effect. More recent research indicates that welfare has a consistent, although small, effect on female headship and remarriage, an effect on living patterns (the formation of independent families as opposed to subfamilies), and perhaps some effect on illegitimacy. "Although the studies of the 1980s show slightly stronger effects than the earlier studies, the effects are still generally small in magnitude" (Moffitt 1992:31). In this regard, none of the studies can account for the increase in female-headed households before 1970. Indeed, "the failure to find strong benefit effects is the most notable characteristic of this literature" (Moffitt 1992:31).

Moffitt's (1992) summary relies heavily on Ellwood and Bane (1984, 1985). This often cited and comprehensive analysis grounded the dispute over welfare and family structure in 1970 and 1975 data from the Survey of Income and Education. Their initial controlled comparison of maximum AFDC payment levels by state produced "perverse" relationships with various measures of family structure, suggesting that higher benefit levels were associated with *more* favorable family outcomes—lower divorce and illegitimacy rates and a lower incidence of female-headed families. These findings were not only significant but large: a $100 increase each month in the maximum AFDC benefit level was associated with a 9 percent drop in the percentage of female-headed families, with a 42 percent decline in the divorce rate, and a 24 percent decline in the illegitimacy rate.

Ellwood and Bane (1985) rejected these results on a priori grounds of economic rationality arguing that "the theoretical impact of the AFDC program is unambiguous" and that important state characteristics were probably masking the true disincentive effects of welfare. "Unmeasured and largely unmeasurable differences in attitudes, preferences, and expectations are probably the largest influence on family structure" (Ellwood and Bane 1995:145). In the context of these regional, subcultural influences, the authors insist that welfare *must* provide incentives for family dissolution and illegitimacy since payments are only available to single parents, the overwhelming proportion of whom are mothers. Thus, welfare confers a financial advantage on separated, divorced, and unmarried mothers that in turn should translate into greater rates of family dissolution and illegitimacy as welfare payments increase, all (cultural) things being equal.

Ellwood and Bane (1985) set out to isolate the true disincentive effect of welfare on family structure. In their most important analysis, they controlled for these fixed state conditions by comparing those who were likely to receive welfare with those who were unlikely to receive welfare. They justified this logic on grounds that "many groups will be influenced by unmeasurable state differences in attitudes and norms, but only those who are likely to collect welfare are also likely to be influenced by benefit levels." In this way, the family structure behaviors of the "unlikely" group served as a control for the behavior of the group that was likely to collect welfare. In high-benefit states, the differences in behavior between the "likely" and the "unlikely" groups are expected to be greater than in low-benefit states.

The results of the analysis provided little support for the moral-hazards argument. The impact of a large increase in AFDC benefits appeared to be minimal. Increases of $100 a month in maximum AFDC benefits produced a sizable effect on living arrangements only and notably just for very young mothers (under twenty years of age)—a 30 percent decrease in the number of subfamilies (mothers with children living at a relative's home) and between 50 percent and 100 percent increase in the number of young single mothers living independently. The $100 monthly increase was associated with only a 10 percent rise in the number of divorced and separated mothers, but a 50 percent increase in the number of very young divorced and separated mothers, a 5 percent increase in single mothers, and a 15 percent increase in female heads of households. There was no significant impact on births to unmarried women.

While the percentage increase in family dissolution among very young mothers is large, the absolute number is very small and therefore the aggregate impact is also small. For example, the $100 increase was associated with 100 percent increase in the probability that a very young mother would become an independent head of household. However, their initial probability of being independent was only 3 percent. In summary, Ellwood and Bane (1985) found that the impact of increased welfare declined precipitously as the importance of the family behavior increased. Thus, increased welfare seemed to have its greatest impact on the living arrangements of young single mothers, modest impact on divorce and separation, and no impact on the decision to have an illegitimate child.

While comforting for the liberal position and largely corroborating the findings of serious social science research, the study is deeply flawed and misleading. In the first instance, all of its conclusions about causal influence are derived from cross-sectional data. With this limitation, the research's explanatory factors (AFDC levels) appear contemporaneously with their presumed effects. However, causes must precede their effects, and the study's assumption that contemporaneous data can stand proxy for cause is highly suspect. Prior levels of welfare, as well as expectations of future levels of support, influence current behavior but the study makes no adjustment for these lags. Instead, it finesses the problem through its likely/unlikely comparisons without explicitly studying changes within states (or better, within SMSAs) over time.

Second, and more important, the author's rejection of their initial "perverse" findings on the basis of "unambiguous" economic theory may not hold up. Countertheoretical relationships appear routinely in the literature, providing a variety of discomforts for the researchers (Honig 1976; Minarik and Goldfarb 1994; Plotnick 1990). Such rebellious findings point toward a profound alternative to the disincentive theory of welfare's impact on the family.

Low AFDC benefit levels are generally associated with poorer states, ones that record both higher poverty rates and a commensurate incapacity to address those needs. Poverty itself and all that it implies about economic and cultural deprivation may be associated with family dissolution and illegitimacy. States with less poverty may also contain fewer of the problems that threaten family solidarity and offer more of the conditions under which young single women defer childbearing until marriage. Thus, higher AFDC benefits may truly be associated with more favorable measures of family structure while the actual causes of family dissolution, perhaps poverty, may depress state welfare levels.

Furthermore, Ellwood and Bane's (1985) measure of AFDC benefits (the maximum monthly AFDC payment for a family of four) may be a proxy for the state's civic generosity. States that offer high AFDC benefits may also provide good schools, safe neighborhoods, other supportive social services, and, even more germane, a nurturing public consciousness. Moreover, the state may contain a population of people with relatively few received problems and a tradition of social institutions and attitudes that nourishes strong families. To the extent that this is true, higher welfare is reasonably connected to fewer problems of family structure. Taking the customary license to impute cause to correlation, welfare generosity may actually create the conditions necessary for family solidarity. In this sense, then, the alleged disincentives of welfare need to be balanced off against the benefits (and thus the incentives) they provide for stable families. Simple financial utility, the bedrock of economic rationality, seems a poor and ambiguous explanatory assumption.

Third, Ellwood and Bane's (1985) fundamental comparison of likely and unlikely recipients rests on the very suspect assumption that the two groups are similar to each other except in their probability of welfare receipt. Quite to the contrary, these groups may diverge sharply from each other (and even from the region's dominant culture). As a result, selection bias remains a large and unanswered threat to the credibility of the study. Likely and unlikely welfare recipients probably differ in their prior experiences as well as in their receptivity to the norms of the dominant culture. Their behavior relative to marriage, divorce, illegitimacy, and independence may reflect those differences, with prior experience being a more reasonable explanation for family dissolution than the level of welfare. Yet without a true control the influence of welfare on family structure cannot be assessed. In other words, the study's unlikely group constitutes a very unlikely control. Finally, Ellwood and Bane (1985) acknowledge a number of problems with the survey's reliability. Family status may not be accurately reported if the Edin problem exists, probably distorting reports of family income.

In the end, the Ellwood and Bane (1985) study, widely used to refute the moral-hazards argument, fails to provide any credible information on the relationship between welfare and family structure. Its findings can be taken to support the position that higher welfare poses some modest threat to family structure. The findings can also be taken as some encouragement for the contrary position that higher welfare, acting perhaps through a more nurturing civic culture, actually protects traditional family values. However, in light of its debilitating methodological problems, the study might more judiciously be discarded in favor of the position that the influence of welfare on family structure is indeterminate. The other research in the field does little to challenge this conclusion.

OUT-OF-WEDLOCK BIRTHS

Out-of-wedlock birth affronts American sensibilities. Children born outside marriage, particularly to adolescent mothers, suggest for many a promiscuous disregard for both convention and social responsibility, indicating the breakdown of family authority and legitimate social control. Less than 30 percent of children who received AFDC in 1969 were born out-of-wedlock; in 1992 they accounted for over 50 percent of the AFDC caseload. At any point in time, fully 55 percent of AFDC recipients were never married. Although unmarried adolescent mothers probably account for under 8 percent of new cases, their lengths of stay tend to be very long, and over time they have come to dominate the AFDC rolls (Bane and Ellwood 1994:44). Apparently, much of the problem of welfare dependency concerns illegitimacy, particularly for adolescent mothers.

Moreover, the conventional antipathy toward teenage motherhood appears well advised by their children's impaired physiological and social development:

> Unsupported adolescent pregnancy carries a high risk of adverse consequences, both short and long term, for mother, child, and family. These consequences result from interaction between a number of biological and socio-environmental factors. . . . Of greatest concern are: (1) the increased frequency of low infant birthweight and its associated risks of mortality and neurological and/or intellectual impairment; (2) early repeat pregnancy; and (3) inadequate parenting, with its limiting effect on the physical and socioemotional development of the child, leading in many instances to the repetition of the adolescent pregnancy cycle. (Hardy et al. in Scott, Field, and Robertson 1981:281)

Nevertheless, in a rebuke to cross-sectional studies, Geronimus and Korenman (1992) concluded that teen childbearing itself, as distinct from the mothers' socioeconomic background, may be overstated as a cause of mothers' poverty or their children's risks.[1]

Still, both race and class appear to be associated with out-of-wedlock childbearing (Bennett, Bloom, and Craig 1989; Farber 1990). The enormous rise in the percentage of children born out-of-wedlock also reflects the general decline in births to married mothers relative to unmarried ones, again more marked for blacks than whites. Indeed, in 1991 the birth rate for married black women was below that for married white women. Thus, while serious, the problem of illegitimacy may be over-

---

1. Bennett, Bloom, and Miller (1995), using cross-sectional data, "suggest a link between out-of-wedlock childbearing and an increased likelihood of subsequent poverty." However, they fail to respond adequately to Geronimus and Korenman's (1992) findings that this link is considerably diminished by within-family comparisons.

stated, even for adolescents. The adolescent birth rate has been decreasing since 1955, but the percent of those births to unmarried mothers has increased dramatically. Between 1970 and 1989, the proportion of teenage births to unmarried mothers had risen from about 30 percent to more than 65 percent. For blacks, about 80 percent of teenage births were out-of-wedlock, although this is noticeably due to the general decline in the number of teenage marriages more than to a large increase in the illegitimacy rate itself. Indeed, the total illegitimacy rate for blacks has remained constant for the past thirty years, with the adolescent rate per thousand increasing from 90.3 in 1969 to 108.5 in 1991 and the rate for older black women decreasing. Nevertheless, the number of births to unmarried women, unadjusted for population, has increased thirteen-fold since 1940, standing at 1.2 million in 1991 (U.S. National Center for Health Statistics 1995). A cumulative result that Murray (1984) pointedly comments on is the fortyfold increase in the total number of illegitimate children, again unadjusted for population, in the United States between 1920 and 1990 (179).

While acknowledging some role for family background, Murray has identified cognitive ability as the main cause of illegitimacy (1984, 1992, 1993; Herrnstein and Murray 1994). He indicts welfare for providing a moral hazard that "enables" the cognitively impaired to have children out-of-wedlock. "The welfare check (and the collateral goods and services that are part of the welfare system) enables women to do something that many young women might naturally like to do anyway: bear children" (Herrnstein and Murray 1994:186).

Murray's addition of a cognitive substrate simply gives greater weight to his earlier argument that financial incentives explain births to unmarried women. "Poor people play with fewer chips and cannot wait as long for results" (Murray 1984:155). Thus, a young single woman who is pregnant and faces the choice between marriage to the impoverished father of the baby or welfare will make an economically rational choice based upon a financial calculus between welfare and marriage. Since welfare frequently pays enough to sustain the woman and her family (at least according to Murray), she will opt for welfare and single parenthood when her earnings ability and that of her mate are low. In a similar manner, welfare relieves young women of the obligation to accommodate to a permanent spouse and thus undermines the family itself by promoting illegitimacy, weakening the work ethic, and penalizing marriage. Thus, this theory of relative risk commends a policy of reduced welfare in order to discourage nonmarital births (Hopkins in Hopkins 1987).

In addition to the possible impact of welfare on family formation, Hayes (1987) offers many other nonfinancial explanations for unmarried teenage motherhood in the United States. Social norms are changing regarding single parenthood and work. Sexual activity is occurring earlier among unmarried teenagers. Parental authority and responsibility are declining. Access to abortion services are becoming more limited. Increasingly limited job prospects limit marriage opportunities for those with low market skills. And youthful hedonism and disillusionment, perhaps reflecting institutional failures, notably of the family, to socialize children has increased.

Teenage illegitimacy has been extensively researched. At a minimum, the social science literature seems to have refuted Murray's moral-hazards position. The weight of evidence suggests that welfare generosity (usually measured as the level of AFDC payments) may not affect illegitimacy rates. In summarizing the survey literature, Haveman and Wolfe (1994) conclude that an important subcultural or neighborhood effect reflects an "important independent role" for race:

> Similarly, a variety of parental choices or circumstances (such as whether the girl grew up in a disrupted family, whether she had parents with little education, and whether or not she had a parent or sibling who was an unmarried childbearer) were significantly related to the probability that she would give birth out of wedlock, as were the availability and accessibility of contraceptive and abortion services (for whites). (Haveman and Wolfe 1994:192)

However, the literature is so extensively circumscribed by its lack of analytic credibility that no conclusion of cause seems warranted except that the factors explaining single teenage motherhood are still obscure. As a result, none of the many recommended interventions seems tractable unless we accept Sherlock Holmes's famous approach to truth through the elimination of untruths as a basis for social policy. Unfortunately, the elimination of welfare's causal effects on teenage illegitimacy does not leave any alternative. Each possible explanation seems to enjoy only tenuous explanatory powers, while an explanation based upon random factors is intellectually unsettling. As a result, the many suggestions for intervention—from limiting welfare to offering high school diplomas and parenting classes—carry little authority. These timid responses to illegitimacy seem futile.

Haveman and Wolfe (1994) analyzed twenty-one years (1968–1988) of PSID data describing 1,705 children. The obvious strengths of these data over previous research—continuous information on a large panel of children—need to be compared with their weaknesses: 40 percent attrition (in addition to natural mortality) and questionably reliable responses, especially relative to sensitive issues such as income.[2] Their analysis largely rejects Murray's enabling theory, concluding that welfare plays an insignificant role in teenage nonmarital births. Rather, they find that cultural factors, particularly the mother's level of education, religiosity, and other social factors, such as poverty, play the principal roles in explaining teenage illegitimacy.

The authors then suggest through their simulations that

> Increasing the educational attainment of parents has the largest effect in reducing the prevalence of teenage out-of-wedlock births. We estimate that if all mothers of teenage girls had completed high school, the probability their daughters would have a teenage out-of-wedlock birth would be reduced by nearly one-half [suggesting] important payoffs to increasing education, beyond those of market productivity and wages. . . . [Moreover] the estimated results of eliminating poverty among the families in which the daughters grow up . . . reduces the probability of both teenage out-of-wedlock births and the receipt of welfare benefits conditional on such a birth. (Haveman and Wolfe 1994:207–8)

These kinds of simulations and proofs justify the core of the liberal impulse to provide higher welfare incomes, greater education, and more social services (Burden and Klerman 1984; Moore and Caldwell 1977; Ross and Sawhill 1975). Still, the simulations are only as good as the quality of the prior research that tests causal relations among a variety of variables and teenage illegitimacy. Haveman and Wolfe's research, typical of the field's efforts, fails to conform with the methodological requirements necessary to sustain the causal implications of their conclusions.

Haveman and Wolfe's (1994) conclusions about education assume that but for a high school degree those at high risk of out-of-wedlock birth and those with relatively low risk are the same; therefore increasing educational attainment among the high-illegitimacy population will *cause* a drop in the number of their out-of-wedlock births. Following this

2. Still, of all the surveys, the PSID data may be the most accurate (Abraham and Haltiwanger 1995). In an impressive and thorough study of attrition in the PSID, Fitzgerald, Gottschalk, and Moffitt (1996), detect some attrition bias. Still, the analysis is not based upon definitive comparisons with the missing respondents; this is after all impossible.

logic, a variety of relatively inexpensive programs are recommended to provide high school diplomas (or GEDs) for teenage mothers or to prevent school dropouts among high-risk teenagers. However, this sort of argument confuses symptom and disease, the rash with the microbe. Both educational failure and teenage pregnancy are perhaps more reasonably the results of profound underlying social deprivations. Simply increasing the amount of education without addressing homelife, community, personal prospects, and attitudes will have little if any impact on teenage pregnancy.

While panel data are greatly superior to cross-sectional data in describing changes over time, they do not permit cause to be credibly tested. In order to test causal relations, equivalent groups need to be randomly assigned to different conditions, in this case implying that some children are assigned to mothers with high school diplomas and others are assigned to high school dropouts. Obviously, this experiment cannot be conducted. As a consequence, outcomes can always be attributed to unknown and "unmeasured factors that explain the level of education attained by mothers" (Haveman and Wolfe 1994:207). Moreover, a variety of plausible selectivity biases greatly reduce the credibility of the research. Corrections for these biases, assuming similarity among the different groups, the very fact that is suspect, are not plausible.

Therefore, in contrast to Haveman and Wolfe's relatively comforting surmises, alternative conclusions, possibly more tenable than theirs, remain unchallenged. Without fully replicating the conditions under which a high school diploma is achieved (the unmeasured social and familial conditions), it is quite doubtful that the high school degree itself (especially if it is only a GED) will confer much economic advantage or motivation. In addition, it is startling the small degree to which Haveman and Wolfe estimate that the elimination of poverty per se will affect behavioral outcomes of children. Increasing the average ratio of income to the poverty line for poor children between the ages of six and fifteen decreases out-of-wedlock births by only 10 percent. Indeed, the failure of their own findings to explain out-of-wedlock births among young women seems to allow for the possibility that social equality itself, and not the parity of income or simple educational attainment especially when measured crudely by the presence or absence of a high school diploma, is a more powerful cause of conforming behavior. People with similar social experiences act in similar ways. But equivalent educational attainment is only a synecdoche for true social equality. It is misleading, therefore, to maintain that education alone will solve the problem of illegitimacy.

Duncan and Hoffman (1990a) tested whether welfare itself or poor economic opportunities explain out-of-wedlock births among black teenage girls. They concluded that

> Like the earlier work of Ellwood and Bane, but in contrast to assertions regularly heard in the popular press, we find only weak support for the proposition that the generosity of AFDC benefits plays a role in promoting out-of-wedlock births. What we do find, however, is stronger support for the alternative view that decisions about such births are influenced by likely future marital and career opportunities. Women with the least to lose are most likely to have children during their teen years. (Duncan and Hoffman 1990a:532)

They then go on to recommend increased economic opportunity as a strategy to reduce illegitimacy among young black women. They are careful, however, to point out that their research does not indicate how opportunity is created and thus "we are unable to add to the lively debate on the relative importance of cultural and structural explanations of inequality" (Duncan and Hoffman 1990a:533). But this is the whole point of the research. Without some notion of causal direction, their policy recommendations are meaningless in the same way as Haveman and Wolfe's (1994) call for education.

Furthermore, Duncan and Hoffman's (1990a) fundamental assumption is highly suspect: the economic situation of twenty-six-year-olds "who did not have an AFDC-related-out-of-wedlock birth . . . were in other respects—for example family background—similar to women who did have an out-of-wedlock birth" (523). This would indicate great selection bias—two self-selected groups that differ in important yet unmeasured ways. Their extensive controls for family background (area of the country, parental receipt of AFDC, mother's education, family income, father's education, income of siblings, and so forth) still fail to provide measures of homelife, personal attitudes, quality of relations within the family, the effect of peer relations, participation in civic activities, and other sociopsychological events that would seem to be important predictors of teenage illegitimacy. As a result, their statistical controls explain very little of the variation in the income of twenty-six-year-olds, while their research fails to test for the influence of AFDC.

Raising the issue of premature quantification and the use of inappropriate operationalization, Murray (1993) addresses Duncan and Hoffman (1990a) specifically:

> For example, Duncan and Hoffman's procedure for constructing a variable estimating the alternative to welfare in the form of

expected income at age 26 is both sophisticated and ingenious from
a statistical standpoint. It seems fair to say as well that it remains
an open question whether the variable they constructed bears any
resemblance to the way a teenage girl from the inner city thinks
about her future economic opportunities—but the assumption that
it bears not only a resemblance but indeed is a quantitatively accurate
representation of the perceptions of a teenage girl from the inner
city is the linchpin for the analyses and conclusions that follow.
(Murray 1993:S241)

Unfortunately, Murray (1993) fails to apply this skepticism systematically to the research supporting his own preference for cutting all welfare
provisions. This portion of his argument could be extended to support
more thoroughgoing social provisions. For example, to reduce illegitimacy rates in the inner city, social policy might profitably take on the task
of assuring experiences for inner-city youth that more closely resemble
those of their peers in the suburbs.

In pursuing subcultural explanations for social deviance, Murray
(1993) claims to have shown that liberal welfare benefits abet the tendency of the "proximate culture" to promote illegitimacy. In particular, he notes the strong relationship between the density of blacks in a
state and its illegitimacy rate. Still, he ignores the Wilson (1987) argument that the rise in the number of single black women reflects the deteriorating economic plight of black men. Repeating the problems of Ellwood and Bane (1985), Murray consistently misinterprets state-level
data. While he cautiously refers only to "suggestive" relationships, his
analysis and conclusions are tendentious, failing to refute alternative explanations of his findings—that social conditions are different for blacks
and whites and that strong social institutions promote strong two-parent
families. This failure to pursue in an evenhanded manner the causes of
teenage illegitimacy undermines his thirst for a smaller welfare state.

Murray's (1984) antiwelfare position is given empirical support by
Bernstam and Swan (1986). Their analysis of state-level data between
1960 and 1980 accepts the economic causation that "illegitimacy is wel-
fareability," broadly conceived to include wages, welfare, and other financial benefits. They found that "the supply of teenage females without
marriage prospects increases as the earning capacity of young males is reduced by full or partial unemployment" (6). Employment, in turn, is affected by prevailing wages and alternatives to employment, notably welfare. Recalling Ellwood and Bane's (1985) initial correlations, they also
point out that illegitimacy is high in states that provide high welfare
benefits. Thus out-of-wedlock children are encouraged by a welfare sys-

tem "which requires the production of fatherless children as the entry condition" (Bernstam and Swan 1986). They conclude that lowering both welfare payments and the minimum wage will increase employment and the capacity to marry, thus serving to reduce out-of-wedlock births, especially among adolescents.

These notions are tributes to economic determinism, paying special homage to Becker's (1991) theory of family formation. However, Bernstam and Swan (1986) repeat many of Ellwood and Bane's (1984) methodological errors with the state-level data. But even apart from considerable data problems, their failure to credibly identify cause undermines their simulations. The conservative assumption that cultural change will pursue economic incentives is no more credible than its mirror-image liberal assumption that greater social equality is a necessary prerequisite for increased economic parity. But, in any event, the interventions that are routinely discussed and analyzed are probably too weak to produce any substantial change in family formation, especially when it involves births outside marriage.

The rational discourse over cause may not be the central concern, however. Bernstam and Swan (1986) along with their liberal adversaries knowingly reach beyond the authority of both their data and their methodologies to enter into the social dialectics over minimum wages and the responsibility of the state for the support of its social failures. For example, on the force of Bernstam and Swan's (1986) own research, it is as plausible to conclude that greater labor force participation produced by greater education and other social investments are as tractable as the coercive force of lower minimum wages and more restrictive welfare policies.

In another conflict with the standard liberal orthodoxy (see Duncan and Hoffman 1990a; Ellwood and Bane 1984; Moore 1980, Moore and Caldwell 1977), Plotnick (1990) finds that higher welfare benefits were related to "out-of-wedlock childbearing by black and white adolescents during the early 1980's" (744). He reconciles his research with previous studies that did not find an impact of welfare on illegitimacy, particularly among whites, by suggesting that attitudes toward illegitimacy had shifted. But even if this were true, welfare would not necessarily stand in a causal relation to illegitimacy. Instead, higher benefits could simply be mediating social attitudes, reprising the problems with Ellwood and Bane's (1985) reinterpretations. Explanations that pay more attention to "differences in sample, variable construction, and estimation method" as well as biases in the data themselves seem equally likely candidates to explain Plotnick's findings (Plotnick 1990:743). Moreover, Plotnick's (1990) very mixed results were not robust.

In the end, welfare has not been proven to affect the decision by young women to bear children outside marriage. Ellwood and Bane (1985) may be correct that the influence of welfare declines as the long-term consequences of any decision increases, and childbearing has very long-term consequences. Nonetheless, the proposition has not been rigorously tested—it may be impossible to do so—while the causes of out-of-wedlock births, particularly among teenagers, remain intuitive and scientifically indeterminate.[3]

FAMILY DISSOLUTION

In addition to illegitimacy, family dissolution (death of a spouse, divorce, abandonment, and separation) is the second avenue to female headship. A growing proportion of all female-headed families have come to rely upon AFDC: 36 percent in 1967 and 42 percent in 1987 (Moffitt 1992). Moreover, probably upward of 80 percent of the female-headed households that are eligible for AFDC participate in the program (Giannarelli and Clark 1992). Divorce, separation, and widowhood account for almost 50 percent of first-time AFDC recipients and may represent more than 40 percent of all AFDC recipients at any point in time (Bane and Ellwood 1994).[4]

As the number of female-headed households increases, so apparently does dependency on welfare. Legislatively, only single parents (customarily mothers) are eligible for AFDC. (The AFDC-UP program is very small and greatly limited by eligibility restrictions.) Therefore, in theory at least, by providing income security against family dissolution, welfare also provides incentives that increase family dissolution.

A considerable literature has accumulated that explicitly tests the relationship between welfare and family dissolution. The more recent studies have found that welfare has a greater impact on headship than earlier studies, largely conducted in the 1970s and summed up by Groeneveld, Hannan, and Tuma (1983). Moffitt (1992) reviews the recent experience,

---

3. Efforts to identify causes other than welfare are just as tortured as these. See, for example, Wu and Martinson (1993) and Rank (1989).

4. However, based upon the 1993 AFDC Recipient Characteristic Study (U.S. Department of Health and Human Services 1995:33), divorced and separated AFDC recipients accounted for only about one-third of all recipients while "parents not married" accounted for about 60 percent. Different definitions in the survey questions and table definitions apparently account for the disparity with the earlier Ellwood (1986) study, "Targeting Would-Be Long-Term Recipients of AFDC" that the Green Book relies upon. Then too the time difference of perhaps seven years may account for the change.

drawing upon the work of Danziger et al. (1982), Ellwood and Bane (1985), and Moffitt (1990).

Groeneveld, Hannan, and Tuma (1983) analyzed data from the sophisticated Seattle and Denver NIT experiments, discussed in the previous chapter, to predict the effects of a negative income tax on marital stability. In their frequently cited introductory review of the literature, they discuss whether the welfare system encourages marital dissolution by providing "more generous benefits to single-parent families than two-parent families" (Groeneveld, Hannan, and Tuma 1983:264). Generally, studies that utilized census data did not support contentions that welfare payments affected marital stability. However, interpretations from the census data were severely limited by incomplete information, limited points of measurement, and the problem of separating cause from effect in contemporaneously collected information, the "lag" problem (Groeneveld, Hannan, and Tuma 1983:265).

Similar technical problems also reduced the credibility of studies based upon longitudinal data from the PSID and the National Longitudinal Survey (NLS). After pointing to conflicting findings even among the more credible research and to their many methodological imperfections, Groeneveld, Hannan, and Tuma (1983) concluded that

> These studies of the effects of AFDC benefit levels on marital dissolution using data from the PSID and the NLS cannot be summarized easily. Given the mixed results it seems unlikely that the effect of AFDC on marital dissolution is strong. (266)

Yet, they never reconciled the differences in their findings, particularly between Sawhill (1975) that showed no effect and Hoffman and Holmes (1976) that did, making a conclusion of indeterminacy more plausible.

The experimental findings from the SIME/DIME provided ambiguous information about the effects of income security (or at least welfare guarantees) on marital dissolution among low-income families. Overall, the rates of family dissolution among experimental groups was approximately 40 percent greater than among controls. However, against expectations, marital dissolution was greatest among the experimental groups that received the *lowest* guarantee, producing what the authors describe as "the paradox of the guarantee level effects" (Groeneveld, Hannan, and Tuma 1983:297). Moreover, black and white experimental groups, but not Chicanos, were affected by the experimental conditions.

Since the control group was eligible for AFDC and Food Stamps and the lowest experimental guarantee provided only a slightly greater financial benefit than that to which the control group had access, it appears odd that the experimental condition created a much greater incentive for marital dissolution. At the same time, it might be reasonable to expect that the added financial security would have encouraged marital stability. Yet, a number of the black and white experimental groups that received the $3,800 guarantee experienced marital dissolution at *twice* the rates of the control groups, while some of the $5,600 experimental subgroups produced dissolution rates that were *below* those of the controls.

The authors refuse to accept their findings as spurious, even in light of very large attrition rates. They prefer to conclude that financial security does produce greater family dissolution. They offer three explanations for the paradoxical dissolution rates: experimental groups were more knowledgeable about their benefits than controls; they incurred fewer nuisance costs; and they suffered less stigma. However, these explanations appear weak on the surface (especially in consideration of the amount of stigma that Moffitt [1983] reports) and even weaker in explaining the declining rates of marital dissolution over time. If these three explanations hold, then dissolution rates should increase over time and decrease as the guarantee (an offset for stigma) increases. In the event, neither actually occurred.[5]

Moreover, the large attrition rates, frequently greater than 25 percent, may have produced noncomparable research groups. The authors' own sensitivity analysis, based upon the assumption that "marital dissolutions are undercounted for controls relative to experimentals," produced adjustments that reduced the disparity in dissolution rates between controls and experimentals (Groeneveld, Hannan, and Tuma 1983:308n). However, in a footnote, the authors concede that, after a search of court records, "attriting couples eligible for the high guarantee level programs, who had the most to gain from remaining in the experiment, had more divorces recorded than controls" (307n).

As in the case of work participation, SIME/DIME produced anomalous findings that were not scientifically credible. While expending an immense effort in torturing the interpretations of unreliable data, the experiments failed to produce information that would allow a judicious interpretation of their findings, such as they were. The findings could not refute the theory of family dissolution derived from economic rationality (Becker 1991). At a minimum, family dissolution becomes an uncomfortably noneconomic consideration, with the SIME/DIME experiment demonstrating a seemingly perverse decision to dissolve marriages at low levels of security and remain together at higher levels. The authors were decidedly loath to take on prevailing theory.

5. See, in particular, Groeneveld, Hannan, and Tuma (1983:Table 5.5, p. 294).

The experiments also ignored the issue of whether the dissolutions were socially desirable—whether the amount of family dissolution served the long-term interests of socialization, particularly of the children involved. SIME/DIME's assumption that simple dissolution rates are sufficient to determine public policy seems too cramped and parochial. A social policy that exacerbates bad marriages by forcing the cohabitation of incompatible parents may impede the successful socialization of children. In the end, Groeneveld, Hannan, and Tuma (1983) failed to produce a credible statement of the effect of welfare on family from either their review of the nonexperimental literature or from their analysis of the elaborate NIT experiments.

The subsequent work, commented on by Moffitt (1992), corroborates Groeneveld, Hannan, and Tuma's (1983) cautious review of the non-experimental literature, while it reports stronger effects, although still weak, of welfare on family dissolution. Yet, even this more recent research fails to provide any decisive proof of a relationship, underscoring the possibility of alternative explanations for family dissolution and poverty.

Danziger et al. (1982) demonstrated an extremely small effect of an income composite on family structure, estimating that AFDC raises female headship by only about 1 percentage point for nonwhites and about 2.5 percentage points for whites. Their model largely comprising economic variables seems very weak, however, and greatly underpredicts the actual increase in headship from 1968 to 1975. "Thus, while women are responsive to changes in their economic well-being in each headship status, the model does not predict such large increases in headship from the actual economic changes" (533).

Other problems with the Danziger study affect its credibility. It did not correct for selection bias; it relied upon income estimates from the CPS, which grossly underreports actual income; and more fundamentally it used cross-sectional data, failing to isolate causal variables. Its very small findings suggest that noneconomic factors, such as subcultural differences and perhaps the economic conditions of men, are probably important in explaining female headship. A more judicious conclusion would be that the determinants of female headship are still unidentified.

Moffitt (1990) displays trend data indicating that the sum of welfare benefits (Food Stamps, AFDC, and Medicaid) have been falling since 1975, while female headship has been rising. He cites these trends as "incontrovertible" evidence that welfare does not influence female headship or marriage. Nevertheless, his cross-sectional analyses, also based upon CPS data, suggest that welfare does provide incentives for female headship. Based upon the 1985 CPS cohort, Moffitt (1990) concludes that "a $100 increase in the benefit sum would lower marital probabilities by about 3.5 percentage points at the mean" (100–111). His analyses of 1969 and 1977 data suggest that this effect has been getting stronger over time. He interprets the difference between the trend data and the cross-sectional data to suggest that the reported changes in female headship over time "are simply the result of some other opposing force (e.g., the increase in the female wage)" (110). This conclusion seems to be supported by the fact that the size of the disincentive effect and its statistical significance virtually disappear when regional variations are taken into account. Those noneconomic regional variations may account for differing attitudes toward family and marriage and explain *both* variations in welfare and variations in marriage.

While supporting the notion from the repeated cross-sections that welfare's disincentives for marriage seem to be increasing, Moffitt's (1990) analysis also supports his surmises from the trend data that welfare fails to provide disincentives. Although it may be true that AFDC provides at least a theoretical disincentive for marriage, other factors may better explain family dissolution. After all, family dissolution has been increasing over this period with little reference to welfare.

Yet, without true experimental data, it is impossible to attribute the causes of female headship to any factor, such as nonwage and welfare income. Moffitt (1990) and others may have misconstrued the line of causation as running from local economic conditions to marital changes. Recalling the problems with Ellwood and Bane's (1985) analyses, marital changes by region may have produced local responses in welfare: regions that experience higher divorce may experience a growing tolerance for female headship, and larger political constituencies of the divorced and displaced (by their prevalence if not by their organized voice) may protect welfare benefits. Thus, the predominant direction of causation may proceed from cultural factors themselves, especially in reference to the behavior of society's poor, with only incidental concern for marginal economic incentives. The economic components of Becker's (1991) family model may be the least important in defining family formation and dissolution.

Welfare's only substantial effect seems to be on the number of subfamilies. Although finding much smaller effects than Ellwood and Bane (1985), Hutchens, Jakubson, and Schwartz (1989) report that subfamilies are encouraged to become independent families in states that provide higher AFDC payments to the latter. Still, increasing the differential between AFDC support for subfamilies and independent families only increases the probability of living independently by one percentage point. Moreover, the overall benefit level of AFDC appears to have no effect on the formation of independent families.

As with Ellwood and Bane (1985), this finding is also greatly impaired by methodological pitfalls. Hutchens, Jakubson, and Schwartz (1989) acknowledge the "imprecise parameter estimates" of their CPS data. Moreover, this nonexperimental study did not adjust or control for selection bias or state effects. People who remain in subfamilies may simply prefer them apart from any financial consideration. Moreover, the study also neglected the effects of the full welfare package, particularly in failing to include housing subsidies.

In any event, the actual problem of subfamilies is small; as Moffitt (1992) points out, the number of subfamilies converted into independent households accounts for only a small portion of the increase in female-headed households. Yet, as theater, the problem is large; Murray (1984) and the conservatives promulgate a scenario in which welfare payments encourage disobedient and ungrateful teenagers to have illegitimate children in an immoral attempt to escape parental control. This notion, despite the literature, has popularized the current welfare mood, realized in the welfare reform legislation of 1996 that cuts AFDC benefits for unmarried teenage mothers, presumably to maintain the penalty of remaining with their own parents as a disincentive for out-of-wedlock births. Yet, it seems likely that the adolescent decision to become a parent often reflects a pernicious home environment, and therefore the decision to perpetuate that situation through a neglectful social policy seems perversely counterproductive.

REMARRIAGE

Remarriage appears to be a major reason for departures from welfare (Committee on Ways and Means 1994:451). Welfare conceivably discourages remarriage by providing a more attractive alternative to a low-income marriage. But the small amount of evidence is mixed, and none of it is particularly credible or germane to social policy.

Analyzing 1970–1972 data from the PSID, Hutchens (1979) found that a 10 percent increase in the AFDC guarantee (not the same as a 10 percent increase in actual AFDC payments) would depress remarriage rates of AFDC recipients by between 0 and 8 percent over a two-year period. He notes that his findings contradict those by Duncan (1976) and Sawhill et al. (1975), who also utilized data from the PSID but over longer periods; they found no effect on remarriage rates. Hutchens

(1979) posits that attrition problems in the PSID during the period prior to his research may account for the differences. However, it is an open question whether the considerable differences in specifying variables between these studies, as well as their different time periods, may account for the differences. It is also noteworthy that none of these three studies was able to account for state or neighborhood effects.

It is also uncertain that any of Hutchens's findings would be useful even if accurate. An uncertainty interval between 0 and 8 percent is considerable, especially when paired with the observation that increased marital search may well be worth the extra welfare expenditure if it produces a more stable and satisfying marriage.

A more recent study (Hoffman and Duncan 1988) also contradicts Hutchens's (1979) findings that welfare affects remarriage rates. Its data are also drawn from the PSID and cover the fourteen-year period ending in 1983. Hoffman and Duncan (1988) analyze the data in two different models. Arguing that their nested logit model is more appropriate, they find that "increases in AFDC . . . do not act as a disincentive to remarriage" (Hoffman and Duncan 1988). Their other model produces a small relationship: cutting AFDC by 25 percent would increase the percentage of white women who marry by only 1.5 percentage points and of blacks by about 6 percentage points. As opposed to much of the literature (in particular Becker 1991), they find that neither AFDC nor wages have any effect on remarriage. Yet, the credibility of Hoffman and Duncan (1988) hinges precariously on the reliability of the PSID and the logic of their separate specifications and analyses.

The experimental data, collected principally from SIME/DIME, also have not settled the controversy over remarriage rates and welfare. The NIT appeared to lengthen the remarriage rates of only one group, Chicanos (Groeneveld, Hannan, and Tuma 1983:344). Whites and blacks were unaffected. Yet the SIME/DIME was a very imperfect experiment; a rise in payments in a more permanent welfare program might have a more notable effect on remarriage. It is also noteworthy that none of the research on remarriage, indeed none of the welfare research, is able to anticipate the effects of welfare per se. After all, there is no possibility of establishing a control group that is ineligible for existing programs. In the end, there is little evidence that welfare affects remarriage rates.

INTERGENERATIONAL EFFECTS OF WELFARE

The most disturbing possibility of welfare is that its putative harms to work participation and the family are carried over to subsequent generations, perhaps through the creation of "a pathology ridden and hostile underclass" that is dependent upon welfare (Gans 1995:157). The spectacle of American social and economic mobility—the bedrock myth of the American creed of advancement—thwarted by its own social policy sets the cornerstone of the conservative complaint with the welfare state. Welfare's effects on intergenerational poverty have been one of the most hotly contested issues. The search for the presence of an American underclass has occupied a large portion of social welfare history.[6] In addition to the issue of whether a true underclass subculture exists, the debate remains intense over the sustaining causes and, therefore the possible remedies for, intergenerational welfare dependency.

The fundamental tenet of the conservative's subcultural interpretation of success and failure is that the virtue of the American character is evidenced in social mobility. The ambitious, intelligent, and disciplined rise; the slothful and promiscuous fail. Strong families build strong character; welfare undermines strong families. The poor marginalize themselves. In this way, intergenerational dependency denotes a subculture of flawed families, whose deviant social values eat away at the nation's civic virtue.

In contrast, the liberal's structural interpretations of the intergenerational effect invoke the impermeability of American society, its tendency to isolate dysfunctional and poor groups, and its failure to provide equitable and corrective human capital investments (particularly family supports, education, and employment). Social conditions, notably opportunity and social investment, produce the personal characteristics that predict success. Imperfections in the society, such as racism and civic disregard, marginalize the poor creating the conditions for deviant subcultures.

If welfare receipt itself causes oppositional attitudes and destroys self-sufficiency, perhaps by relieving people of the obligation to work and by creating perverse threats to family solidarity that are passed on from generation to generation, then obviously its elimination would both reduce poverty and increase social equality. On the other hand, if other factors, such as social and economic isolation as well as racism, produce similarly dysfunctional experiences for different generations, then welfare itself has only a marginal impact on social failure.

There does appear to be evidence that AFDC receipt is correlated across generations. However, the evidence has failed either to settle the more important policy issue of whether welfare receipt per se causes the

6. See, as examples, Gans (1995), Garrity (1978), Himmelfarb (1983), Katz (1989), and Patterson (1981).

association or to identify the mechanisms of intergenerational transmission. Moffitt (1992) has summed up the evidence as showing consistent and "strong correlations between parental welfare receipt and later behavior of daughters" (36).[7] Based upon PSID data, Duncan, Hill, and Hoffman (1988) report that 64 percent of the daughters who grew up in homes that were heavily dependent upon welfare did not rely upon welfare. Still 36 percent dependence might be interpreted as considerable, especially since Duncan, Hill, and Hoffman (1988) employed only a three-year window, measuring welfare use when the daughters were between the ages of twenty-one and twenty-three.

The impression of considerable intergenerational welfare use is based particularly upon Solon et al. (1988), Gottschalk (1990), and McLanahan (1988). McLanahan (1988), also relying upon the PSID, found that "family welfare history is a significant predictor of daughters' future dependence," while the duration of a family's reliance upon welfare increases the likelihood that their daughters will also depend upon welfare (13–4). Solon et al. (1988) found a powerful effect among sisters, supporting notions of subcultural phenomena in explaining the transmission of dependency and illegitimacy.

Gottschalk (1990, 1992) observed that many of these studies may overstate the intergenerational correlation because they include families and daughters who are ineligible for welfare, while they may understate the true intergenerational effect by measuring welfare dependency during a limited time. In order to correct these earlier flaws in the research, Gottschalk (1990, 1992) employs a nineteen-year window, a considerable period of time, to compare the experience of daughters from eligible families who received welfare with those that did not. Gottschalk (1990, 1992) finds a large difference in the probabilities of welfare receipt: 55.3 percent for daughters with at least one child from families that received welfare, compared with 37.4 percent for those from eligible families that refused welfare. Moreover, the probability of welfare receipt for those whose families were ineligible was only 17.6 percent. These findings—especially Gottschalk's (1992) adjustments suggesting a small subcultural effect—could be taken as support for Murray's (1984) moral-hazards perspective that welfare policy itself affects intergenerational welfare receipt. However, Gottschalk (1990) points out that structural factors—

---

7. Five out of nine studies that Moffitt (1992) reviews relative to intergenerational welfare effects are working papers and speeches delivered at conferences, suggesting an even weaker literature than the following critique suggests. While the reliance upon ephemeral research is common in other econometric reviews of the welfare literature, it is notable here.

the similarity of social and economic conditions affecting both mother and daughter—offer alternative explanations for the same data.

The literature fails to resolve this interpretive ambiguity and thus the policy dispute over intergenerational dependency. The data sets themselves probably provide unreliable estimates of crucial variables. Gottschalk's (1992) imputed participation rates are considerably different than those in a comparable study (Ruggles and Michel 1987). He attributes these differences to the problems of the National Longitudinal Survey of Youth (NLSY), that "like almost all surveys, underreport the number of units receiving AFDC [while] . . . this underreporting of AFDC plagues all studies of intergenerational welfare participation" (263). McLanahan (1988) comments on the limited information from the PSID and its potential attrition problems (5). The direction and types of these problems with the PSID and NLSY, especially the narrow time periods during which the dependency of the daughters is measured, would seem to understate the amount of intergenerational welfare use.

In addition to flawed data, the more serious shortcomings of the research—in part resulting from its failure to approximate the nonexperimental designs in other areas of welfare policy and family structure—relate to its inability to establish credible conclusions or even reasonable surmises about the causes of intergenerational poverty and welfare dependency. The findings on intergenerational welfare receipt tend to support the presence of an intergenerational underclass, but they do not explain it. None of the studies employed an experimental design; this is impossible after all. Thus, the literature fails to establish conditions for testing cause by controlling for environmental influences. Moreover, it fails to satisfy any of the conditions for natural experiments that would allow nonexperimental data to define causal conditions (these conditions were established in Moffitt 1991). Rather, the studies suffer from serious selection bias problems: the conditions that may have predisposed recipients to opt for welfare may also have predisposed their children for welfare receipt. As Moffitt (1992) points out, none of the research controlled for omitted variables, notably "the human capital characteristics of the family" and the family culture itself (37). Thus, the central question—whether parental welfare receipt causes welfare receipt among their children—remains unanswered. Indeed, it seems unlikely that the minimal provisions of welfare could cause any subcultural response. Rather, the larger forces that create American stratification seem far more likely candidates.

It now appears to be generally acknowledged, even within the liberal camp, that America contains dysfunctional, undesirable subcultures and that these subcultures may transmit oppositional values that work themselves out through socially damaging and self-destructive behaviors, such as drug abuse, out-of-wedlock births, violence, emotional impairment, and so forth.[8] Even with this consensus, the main bone of contention has become the role of volition in these oppositional subcultures and how welfare may or may not sustain it. If dysfunctional subcultures are adaptations to the demographic and economic calamities of society, as well as to the injustices, deprivations, and cruelties of the dominant culture, then changes in basic social arrangements should produce a better socialized and more cohesive culture. Indeed, this is the central theme of the liberal literature worked out both ethnographically (see Bourgois 1995; Kozol 1995; Sheehan 1993) and quantitatively (see Massey and Denton 1993; Wilson 1987). Yet, tests of these propositions, Wilson (1987) in particular, based upon evaluations of programs that implemented their logic, marshal no consistent support (Mincy in Danziger, Sandefur, and Weinberg 1994). Moreover, the issue of personal responsibility, even in the face of social causation, remains philosophically ambiguous.

On the other hand, if gangs, broken families, and high-crime, low-work neighborhoods are simply collecting bins of the morally and cognitively impaired, then society is under little obligation to scrutinize its own behaviors, remaining justified in its inflated sense of its own charitability, justice, and virtue.[9] This position has faced acidic refutations (see Fraser 1995; Jacoby and Glauberman 1995).

The literature on intergenerational welfare fails either to clarify or to settle this conflict between liberal and conservative dogma. A true test of subcultural theory—its volitional content—would seem to rest with whether dysfunctional subcultures persist after the removal of the conditions that purportedly have nurtured them. This test is probably impossible to conduct, however. Still, there is little evidence that welfare de-

8. See, as examples, from both the subcultural and structural perspectives ethnographies such as Anderson (1990), Auletta (1982), Bourgois (1995), Divers-Stammes (1995), Harrington (1962), Kozol (1995), Lewis (1967), Liebow (1962), and Sheehan (1993). The more quantitative material suggests the same; see Massey and Denton (1993); Wilson (1987); Wilson and Neckerman (1986). This notion is still resisted stubbornly by some, notably Gans (1995) and Rank (1994). None of this literature has been able to distinguish the problem of social causation from personal responsibility. In reviewing Bourgois' book, Coughlin comments that "Mr. Bourgois tries hard to tread the fine line between not blaming the victims and relieving them of all responsibility" (Coughlin 1995:A16). However, this work and others finesse the issue. Their "fine line" is drawn more through literary appeal to an audience's sensibilities than through the systematic separation of cause and effect. The exculpatory notion of blaming the victim may be a logical canard.

9. Blankenthorn (1994) and Herrnstein and Murray (1994) are formidable statements of this position.

pendency itself traps people in an underclass; at the same time, the diminishment of a safety net has not been shown to hinder mobility.

The literature seems to have sidestepped the principal issues, preferring to focus on dependency instead of poverty or social marginality. Gottschalk, McLanahan, and Sandefur (in Danziger, Sandefur, and Weinberg 1994) have documented a stunning immobility among the poor: "between any two years, roughly 80 percent of persons in the lowest quartile remained in the bottom of the distribution" (92). Those who escape welfare do not move very far and frequently fall back again on public provisions. Similar analyses of welfare participation as well as studies of American income stratification suggest a small amount of mobility (Behrman and Taubman 1990; Hauser and Featherman 1977; Haveman 1987a,b; Solon 1992). Contrary to the conservatives' claim, American society does not seem to have routinely opened broad avenues to success for working people and the poor. The conservative contention that the openness of American society (but for racism and a counterproductive welfare policy) has provided adequate sorting opportunities has not been convincingly tested. Nor, for that matter, has the liberal line of argument stretching between social conditions and subcultural responses been credibly established. Rather, the issue of American stratification remains mired in fundamentally ideological preferences with liberals grasping for structural barriers and conservatives sensing their advantage in pointing to attitudinal impediments and oppositional subcultures. The debate for all its quantitative elegance has not gotten beyond the field's very porous ethnographies.

These same problems impede the interpretation of evidence that large differences exist among blacks, whites, and Hispanics on any number of variables related to welfare, work, and family structure. Again, the differences are variously attributed by liberals to structural factors, such as racism, social isolation, and unequal human capital investment, and by conservatives to inherent factors, such as cognitive incapacity and subcultural preferences abetted by a misguided social policy. If there is a true American underclass that systematically embeds its socially dysfunctional attitudes in its children, then its causes and cures remain undeciphered; they may be undecipherable. The role of welfare itself in cosseting this underclass is patently undefined.

CONCLUSIONS

If welfare does have an impact on family structure, it is not apparent to the unaided eye, or perhaps it is too subtle for the best of the existing literature to document. Intergenerational welfare dependency and intergenerational poverty are sizable problems, but there is little evidence that either are influenced by welfare itself. Still, for all of its evaluative wizardry, the major welfare policy research relies upon data of questionable reliability, notably related to the Edin problem; its methods are porous; and its conclusions are more ideological than scientific, emerging more from the political sympathies of the researcher and her love of hypothesis than from objective, experimental evidence.

The literature's blind allegiance to a raw economic rationality hints at a wide intellectual deficit in approaching social problems. Indeed, at the same time that American society shies away from the depth of its structural differences, it stubbornly refuses to address important subcultural differences. The social debate, instead, rages over relatively small effects, if any, of superficial social interventions.

A large portion of the literature justifies its narrow formulations in terms of Becker's (1991) laureate theory of the family. But the failure to produce credible findings is not due to Becker; his theory is certainly sensitive to social and psychological motives (Becker 1974). Nevertheless, to test Becker's (1991) theory would require an enormous complement of sociological, political, and psychological data and a heroic commitment to long-term randomized experimentation. Neither the requisite data nor the methodologies exist to do so, and the commitment to scientific objectivity, and not just a tone of neutrality, in social policy research remains elusive.

The crude reduction of "utility maximization and rational choices" to a series of easily measured financial incentives—usually defined as some form of welfare benefits—inadequately captures the reasons for family formation (Becker 1991:5). The thoroughgoing failure in the literature to document large effects of welfare on family structure hints at the limitations of financial incentives in understanding family decisions. Consequently, it should not be surprising to find that the minimal intrusions of welfare have not produced discernible impacts on families. The marginal changes in state interventions being discussed will probably have proportionately little impact on divorce, separation, and illegitimacy. Unfortunately, none of the broader sociological, psychological, or economic causes for family decline outlined in Haveman and Wolfe (1994), Hayes (1987), or even Hernandez (1993) has enjoyed any greater explanatory power.

Presumably, reducing the rates of family dissolution and out-of-wedlock births would greatly decrease reliance upon public welfare. However, the contention that a meaner welfare policy might achieve these ends is not demonstrated in the literature, even if such a policy would be an easier policy to implement—programmatically as well as politically.[10]

If large changes in behavior are desirable, then large changes in the underlying social conditions that give rise to them are implied. If middle-class outcomes are desirable, then middle-class circumstances need to be replicated. Moreover, middle-class outcomes are only rarely the product of entrepreneurial success itself; more often the middle class purchases its social opportunities through generations of favored access to better communities, schools, and educated parents.

Powerful experiments in social and economic equality have never been undertaken. The weak effects of welfare might best be explained by the weakness of its interventions, which, given Edin's findings, provide an even smaller portion of total income than the literature considers. However, the provision of greater social equality in basic social institutions—families, schools, communities, the job market—are not on the public agenda. For that matter, the popular mood seems closed to the more fundamental issue of social and economic stratification.

A position of greater social equality is difficult to maintain without rational support that the inequalities are the causes of social problems and not the results of inherent social differences and personal moral failures. Unfortunately, the research fails to adjudicate between different causes. Indeed, the literature provides little rigorous sense of what benefits society in the long run: whether bad intact families are preferable to functioning single-parent ones; whether welfare improves socialization and social cohesion; whether greater investments in social and economic equality will minimize social problems. Murray's (1993) call for two-parent families at any price may be no more satisfying than a reluctant tolerance for high divorce rates and the poverty and malaise they produce.

The central policy choices remain polemical, fueled by policy research that is little more than partisan ammunition. This dispute reached levels of ferocity around the issue of cognitive capacity and genetic determination, as witnessed in the recent *Bell Curve* debate (Fraser 1995; Jacoby and Glauberman 1995). The failure to settle these issues of cause—either the nature-nurture argument or the more pragmatic one of neglect versus generosity—and the subsequent problem of authoritative information for social policy shred any pretense that American social welfare policy-

10. In particular, Murray's (1996) claim that the family cap in New Jersey reduced additional nonmarital births among welfare recipients cannot be sustained on the basis of O'Neill's research (unpublished and undated but presumably 1994). See Epstein's (1996) commentary. The evidence from the other state-waiver experiments is slowly trickling in.

making is rational. There may even be a growing consensus that these issues are profoundly intractable both theoretically as well as practically (Manski 1992; Mead 1994; Moffitt 1991; Murray 1993).

In the absence of conclusive evidence that welfare has much of an effect on work or the family, conservatives are beginning to rehearse the argument that the social science literature itself is flawed beyond a capacity to test and therefore disprove their assumptions. Thus, the elements of a neglectful social policy become institutionalized as inherent ignorance serves a prioristic assumptions about the nature of man in society. In an appeal to common sense (probably as Kant's definition, "defiance without insight"), the conservative argument falls back on homiletics; Murray (1984) feels justified in employing the hypothetical case of Harold and Phyllis (while ignoring contradictory empirical evidence) to prove that welfare provides disincentives to work and to keep families together.

However, the same line of skepticism pursued more thoroughly undercuts the conservative position, especially if arguments are settled by the weight of evidence. On their part, however, liberals cannot take much comfort in their imperfect findings. The absence of rational discourse that has impaired much of the conservatives' rhetoric exists perhaps because liberals have not been able to realize its virtues.

Nevertheless, the policy community maintains the fiction of its scientific authority. It is notable that Ellwood and Bane (1985) on the liberal side at Harvard University and Bernstam and Swan (1986) for the conservatives at Stanford University's Hoover Institute explored similar data through similar state-level designs and reached the very similar conclusion that prevailing wages play an important role in welfare dependency. Yet, liberals assert that the research proves the desirability of greater human service investment, or at least relatively neutral effects of welfare on family structure, while the conservatives claim that the research supports cutting minimum wages and reducing the level of available welfare. This is less science than ironic testimony to the sociological truism that one stands where one sits.

With all of the limitations of the family structure literature, it is worthwhile to speculate that the increasing report and consequent belief in the influence of welfare on family structure indicated by Moffitt (1992) may be more a product of the analyst's enterprise than of social reality. There is little to distinguish the quality of the earlier and later research, and both were highly susceptible to a great variety of choices in specification and estimation. Perhaps the general social appetite for proof of the popular belief that welfare induces family dissolution subtly induced a conforming, although slight, social science response. Perhaps future research might profitably attempt through this literature to estimate the degree to which reported outcomes can be attributed to subtle social influences carried through as researcher bias (Rosenthal and Rubin 1978).

If, in the end, family breakdown and nonmarital childbearing reflect broader social conditions, then those conditions should be corrected or accommodated. The modern nuclear family may not be a uniformly viable institution to socialize America's children. Public supports for socialization may need to be provided through a variety of mechanisms that underwrite the civic culture. But attempts to augment basic social institutions have failed as profoundly as the cash welfare programs, and perhaps for the same reasons. Job training programs for the poor and for unemployed welfare recipients as well as specific social service arrangements—invariably underfunded and weak—stand as testimony to Rossi's observation: "If there is any empirical law that is emerging from the past decade of widespread evaluation research activities, it is that the expected value for any measured effect of a social program is zero" (quoted in Moynihan 1996).

5 Reforming Welfare with Work: Training Programs for Welfare Recipients

Work has long been a favored solution for welfare dependency. National responsibility for job training and work preparation programs for the disadvantaged began during the 1930s, intensified during the War on Poverty, and continues in one form or another today. Some are mandatory; others are voluntary. Some have been national, others experimental and confined to a few sites. At various times they have targeted minority and disadvantaged youth, welfare recipients, low-income populations, ex-addicts, ex-offenders, and other groups.

While structural approaches attempt either to anticipate the imperfections of the business cycle through macroeconomic fiscal policy or to compensate for its failures through public works programs and perhaps job retraining, training programs aim to overcome the impediments to employment that presumably reside in the individual. This individual approach to manpower includes counseling for the immature, troubled, unmotivated, timid, and mentally impaired; life skills for the socially impaired; basic education for the illiterate and semi-illiterate; job skill training for the unskilled; job search services and surveillance for the unknowing and unmotivated; public service employment and on-the-job training as bridges to unsupervised work for the inexperienced; and even, occasionally, in acknowledging some role for structural displacement, job retraining for technologically displaced workers.[1] The more super-

---

1. Job retraining can be either a structural approach where it is offered as an institutional characteristic of the labor market or a residual approach where it is a small and discretionary program targeted on a few favored workers. Individual approaches here carry the sense of residual, discretionary, and categorical as opposed to institutional and universal. Stigmatization, labeling, and social isolation are inherent concerns.

ficial work preparation efforts offer little more than job search support; the more intensive involve actual training and counseling.

Individual and subcultural approaches to increasing the work effort of welfare participants and other deprived and dependent populations are inherently more attractive than structural solutions. They have been far more popular in the United States than public works programs, promising to address the deep problems of social and economic deprivation inexpensively, customarily costing only a few thousand dollars per recipient.

All of the prominent national training approaches have been designed in tribute both to social efficiency and the old saw that it is better to teach a man to fish than to give him fish. They assume that a relatively limited investment in human capital is sufficient to achieve economic self-sufficiency through employment. The success of this essentially subcultural and personal approach to economic deprivation also relies upon a variety of other assumptions. First, individuals who are harmed by imperfect families, communities, schools, and labor markets can be made whole, or at least economically self-sufficient, without major investments in remediation and rehabilitation and within current institutional arrangements. Second, an adequate number of jobs are available to employ the trainees. Third, lacking an adequate number of jobs, the training approach assumes the presence of a sufficiently fluid market place that shares employment fairly among qualified applicants so that deprivation is not concentrated among particular individuals and groups. Job training is futile if a paucity of jobs or rigidities in the job market for workers at the lower end undercut the value of putting people to work.

Over the past three decades, public job training programs have touched tens of millions of the nation's least well-off citizens. They have been a constant companion of America's welfare strategies, providing the principal public bridge between dependency and work. Since the 1960s, a variety of direct employment strategies have been legislated by the federal government to reduce the welfare rolls and minimize unemployment among poor and other troubled populations. The Work Incentive Program was passed in 1967 and designed to provide "occupational rehabilitation" to welfare recipients. Building upon earlier legislated programs (Manpower Development and Training Act, Community Experience and Training Program, Title V of the Economic Opportunity Act of 1965), WIN provided "services and opportunities to assist recipients of AFDC in obtaining jobs and economic independence" (Ketron, Inc. 1980). At its most elaborate, WIN services included vocational training, on-the-job training, public service employment, work experience, and job placement assistance. The specific components of these services also included

basic and remedial educational preparation as well as a variety of counseling services. Approximately three-quarters of the WIN recipients were
women on welfare. Ketron, Inc. (1980) reported that WIN produced important benefits for participants.

The Louisville WIN Laboratories, operating prior to the 1982 OBRA
(Omnibus Budget Reconciliation Act) revisions that greatly reduced the
incentive for welfare recipients to work, conducted WIN experiments in
individual and group job search strategies. These WIN programs were
explicitly designed as low-cost techniques to reduce dependency. While
noting that these job search strategies were limited in their ability to reduce welfare expenditures or increase employment rates, the Manpower
Demonstration Research Corporation reported they had large impacts,
particularly on the employment of the less job-ready (Goldman 1981;
Wolfhagen and Goldman 1983).

The Supported Work (SW) program represented an effort in the early
1970s to provide support for "groups of individuals facing the most
severe problems in finding and maintaining employment" (Hollister,
Kemper, and Maynard 1984:3). These groups included women with
long histories of dependency on AFDC, disadvantaged and troubled
youths, ex-addicts, and ex-offenders. SW emphasized job placement, motivation, basic work skills, and basic work habits over job-specific training. MDRC reported that SW produced important gains, particularly for
long-term welfare recipients.

The Concentrated Employment and Training Act (CETA) passed in
1973 went well beyond AFDC recipients themselves to provide employment and training for youth and the economically disadvantaged. CETA
consolidated prior legislation, notably programs for youth, such as the
Neighborhood Youth Corps and the Job Corps, and provided local coor-
dination for the variety of manpower training programs in existence.
In 1983, the Reagan Administration replaced CETA with the Job Training Partnership Act (JTPA), which severely limited many of CETA's programs and its scope. CETA's range of services was similar to WIN's,
while its target populations and the depth of its services have varied with
different legislative changes. Notably, in 1978, CETA's eligibility was restricted to the very poor, and its public service employment component,
expanded during the recession of the mid-1970s, was eliminated in JTPA,
which also greatly restricted the use of stipends. Bassi et al.'s (1984) comprehensive evaluation of CETA reported similar outcomes to those of
WIN—small but important wage impacts for particular groups of recipients, notably women.

The Reagan Administration's Omnibus Budget Reconciliation Act of
1982 inspired a range of subsequent state experiments targeted at wel-

fare recipients. These experimental services customarily provided more intensive services than WIN, many of which were mandatory. The welfare/work initiatives undertaken in eight states along with California's Greater Avenues for Independence (GAIN) program were evaluated by MDRC using more credible research methodologies—randomized designs—than previous evaluation efforts.

The modest but consistent success of these OBRA work training experiences, reported in a series of MDRC publications, endorsed the welfare reforms of the Family Support Act of 1988. In particular, "GAIN is the nation's largest welfare-to-work program, and its passage in 1985 helped point to the pathbreaking federal legislation under which it operates, the Job Opportunities and Basic Skills Training (JOBS) Program" (Riccio, Friedlander, and Friedman 1994). The JOBS work preparation strategy continued the welfare/work program strategies and was also evaluated by MDRC at three sites. MDRC again found continuing benefits for these training programs.

The most recent experiences in the work training and preparation of welfare recipients occurred through a number of state experiments that were allowed by waivers of welfare regulations. These state waiver programs also embody a number of administrative constraints, notably the "family cap" in New Jersey and a variety of sanctioning (and other) changes in the Wisconsin Works program. These additional constraints are designed to reduce reliance upon welfare as well as provide disincentives for other behaviors, notably illegitimacy.

In reviewing the long-term experience of training and employment programs for the poor and disadvantaged, the social science literature (notably Gueron 1990; Manski and Garfinkel 1992; Moffitt 1992) comes to a cautiously optimistic conclusion on the basis of the best of the evaluative studies: there is a consistent but small net increase in earnings attributable to training programs for welfare recipients. While these programs fail to make major inroads against poverty, they provide a general cost/benefit dividend that is socially valuable.

Yet in spite of a widespread sense of modest success and occasional reports of considerable progress, the outcomes of these programs are routinely indeterminate even after enormous evaluative efforts. More seriously, even the best of the research can be reinterpreted as partisan statements that deflect political attention away from underlying social problems—the inability of society's basic institutions to successfully fulfill their functions. Schools, communities, families, and the market place routinely fail to prepare citizens for work and to assure that jobs are available.

Rather than cautious optimism, employment and training programs for the welfare population and other low-income groups are routinely in-effective against basic employment goals, let alone against grander hopes of alleviating poverty through adequate wages. This is hardly surprising since the customary training programs, even the higher-cost ones, pro-vide only minimal, short-term compensation for longstanding economic and social deprivations. From the perspective of the unemployed and the poor, the frequent tendency of the evaluations to contrive a redeeming cost/benefit virtue for these minimal social programs serves unfortunate political motives at the expense of broader egalitarian ideals.

The evaluation of job training programs for low-income and welfare recipients has reached perhaps the most sophisticated level of any social service program. Yet there remains considerable conflict between the two principal methodologies for evaluating program outcomes. Reduced-form evaluations, the principal methodology of demonstrations and ex-periments, make the simplifying assumption that the program be treated as a "black box," and thus only its outcomes need to be measured. After all, it is impractical to conduct the number of controlled experiments necessary to isolate the causal elements in a program to account for its outcomes. In contrast, structural evaluations are based upon nonexperi-mental observational data of program participants, their interactions with the program's elements, and environmental influences on their be-haviors.[2] Longitudinal panel data fail, however, to provide controls for self-selection, that is, the unique characteristics and situations that may motivate clients to participate in any program. Without appropriate ran-domized controls, research cannot distinguish between these unique characteristics and the intervention itself when explaining program out-comes. Indeed, once nonrandomized panel data are accepted as rea-sonable substitutes for experimental designs, this concession to rigor is likely to create a variety of biases. Moreover, persistent concerns threaten the value of the data from national longitudinal panels (such as CPS, PSID, SIPP, and so forth) and further circumscribe the utility of struc-tural approaches.

While Manski and Garfinkel (1992) argue that both approaches have their uses, the actual experience of evaluating social welfare programs suggests that both approaches have fallen far short of their goals. Never-theless, because of their ability to randomize participants, reduced-form experiments continue as the evaluative orthodoxy in spite of many recent demurrers. This dispute between experimental and nonexperimental ap-proaches to program evaluation has been reinvigorated as data from

2. Structural in this sense is not to be confused with situational theories of poverty. Un-fortunately, the same word is commonly used but with very different referents.

social experiments fall into greater disrepute (Manski and Garfinkel 1992). Unfortunately, the statistical manipulations of the structural approaches have not proven any more accurate or reliable.

The evaluation of a training program's success cannot be made in terms of employment rates, earnings, and welfare savings alone. Other costs must also enter the equation: the impact on wages and employment of increasing the supply of low-skilled manpower, the distributive impact on taxes (that is, the question of who is paying for the welfare savings), the impact on children for time lost with their parents, and the broader impacts on social cohesion and socialization.

WIN

The unequivocal goal of the WIN program was the reduction of the welfare rolls by improving the employment prospects of recipients. The components of the WIN program, carried in some form into almost all other manpower development programs for poor people, provided a variety of education, counseling, and skills training to overcome specific impediments to employment among low-income and poor people.

Ketron, Inc. (1980) conducted perhaps the most comprehensive and sophisticated evaluation of WIN 2, a "major longitudinal evaluation" of the program. Correcting a number of flaws in their earlier evaluation, Ketron, Inc. followed a large cohort of 1974–1975 WIN graduates for three years. Their evaluation involved over 3,700 WIN participants and another 5,000 AFDC recipients in a comparison group of WIN-eligible welfare recipients. Data were collected from record reviews and from four "waves" of interviews with research subjects that described their WIN service experience and their welfare histories, as well as

> supportive services provided by the WIN and welfare agencies,
> specific information on the client's welfare history, and most
> important, detailed information on earnings and periods of
> employment and unemployment. Program participants were also
> asked to describe their recent experiences in WIN components.
> (Ketron, Inc. 1980:11)

The early WIN 1 program, authorized in 1967, provided a comprehensive range of employment services: intake and assessment, orientation, basic and remedial education, institutional skill training, public service employment (PSE), on-the-job training (OJT), special works projects, work experience, and others. Social services, medical care, and child care were also provided in order to facilitate successful participation in the program. These services were supplied by a professional team of specialists: social workers and counselors, manpower trainers, and job developers. Moreover, many of the training programs paid stipends to the participants as well as subsidies to employers. The two major functions of these separate components were job training and placement.

The 1971 changes to the program that created WIN 2 reflected the growing political impatience with the failure of WIN 1 to achieve its goals as well as a sense that employable recipients were malingering on the welfare rolls. Still, participation in WIN 2 was effectively voluntary. WIN 2 emphasized job placement at the expense of training and implemented the mandatory registration of AFDC applicants while requiring that at least one-third of WIN funds be used for OJT and PSE. Moreover, the new PSE program prefigured later workfare experiments by replacing the special work projects of WIN 1 with a program that concentrated on clients who were currently employable but were waiting for jobs. In contrast, WIN 1's special work projects focused on a much more difficult group of welfare recipients with a low probability of job placement. A further overhaul of WIN in 1975 placed even less emphasis on training, focusing largely on job search and job placement activities.

WIN 2's key programmatic components were work experience, vocational training, OJT, PSE, and job placement assistance. The first four of these components are frequently considered intensive and high-cost manpower assistance, at least for welfare recipients and the poor. WIN 2's vocational training, the component of last resort after OJT, typically consisted of four to five months for both men and women; slightly more than 50 percent of participants completed their vocational training programs. OJT provided a subsidy to the employer and lasted less than one year. PSE was a very small component of WIN 2, providing only half the number of slots as OJT. The typical PSE placement lasted about six months. Vocational training, OJT, and PSE typically trained and placed women as typists, nurse's aides, and clerks; men as welders and auto mechanics.

Work experience, mirroring the earlier goals of the special work projects, focused on developing appropriate work habits for participants with little work history. It consisted of unpaid work and was limited to thirteen weeks. Finally, job placement assistance was the major emphasis of WIN 2; it largely consisted of job search and placement activities often unaccompanied by any specific training, counseling, or subsidy. Fully 40 percent of female and 55 percent of male WIN participants received only job search support with the largest number of them being defined as "unassigned participants."

It is notable in Ketron, Inc.'s (1980) large sample that only tiny percentages of WIN recipients received the intensive manpower services: 10.3 percent received vocational training, 6.4 percent basic education,

5.6 percent work experience, 6.7 percent OJT, and 3.0 percent PSE. At the same time, 62 percent of the sample went through orientation only or terminated their WIN involvement on their own (Ketron, Inc. 1980: Tables 2–5, p. 33). Only OJT and PSE resulted in sizable percentages of job placements (about 40 percent). Moreover, only 23 percent of those who terminated WIN prior to placement did so because they had found a job, presumably on their own. These percentages, calculated using WIN *participants* as the denominator, shrink even further when recomputed using the much larger number of *welfare recipients*—the population of true concern. Moreover, the rate of job placement in contrast to weeks worked or earnings may be the least valuable indicator of program success, in that it fails to convey information about the quality of employment or the long-term benefits of training programs (Gay and Borus 1980).

Nevertheless, the Ketron, Inc. (1980) evaluation concluded that WIN was largely a successful program, despite the fact that WIN produced only small increases in lifetime earnings for men and women and even smaller welfare savings, on the order of $5 to $10 a month in the basic AFDC grant. While the overall findings appear quite modest, due to the inclusion of participants who received only minimal services, the differential impacts of the separate services seem substantial. Work experience, for example, produced a $23,500 lifetime benefit for women relative to the comparison group, while vocational training produced a $15,000 benefit for women. OJT was "quite effective in raising annual earnings of both men and women"—about $7,700 for men and $5,100 for women. Remarkably, the greatest OJT gains were concentrated among those with no prior occupation. PSE apparently "contributes strongly" to earnings gains; in their first year out of the program, men earned $2,100 and women $1,200 more than the comparison group. Ketron, Inc. (1980) reluctantly reports that their cost/benefit analysis, which they take great pains to *undercut* on methodological grounds, shows *no* net benefit for the training programs; net benefits do not exceed program costs.

However, serious imperfections in the research invalidate all of their conclusions, raising questions about the use of government funds to evaluate its own performance and the complicity of contractors and social scientists in partisan research. In the first place, the gains themselves are extraordinarily modest and concentrated on a very small group of program registrants and even a smaller proportion of the AFDC caseload. Ketron's procedures for projecting lifetime earnings were suspect, relying upon a relatively short follow-up period in which "decay" rates were uniformly high. Indeed, the unprojected hourly wage differentials measured right after training are quite modest—frequently less than

55¢ per hour. Even more troubling, the gains of even the most successful program (work experience) work out to less than $1,000 a year over a thirty-year lifetime of work.

Their small findings are further vitiated by a number of serious methodological problems. Their comparison group was not chosen randomly. As Burtless (1989) argues,

> It seems likely that the choice not to participate in WIN made this comparison group quite different from the group that chose to participate, not only in measurable ways—such as age and education—but also in unmeasurable ways—such as intelligence and ambition. The two groups therefore differed from one another not just because only one of them has received WIN services, but additionally because one group may have greater average levels of intelligence and ambition than the other. (Burtless 1989:110)

In addition, some attrition from the wave-four comparison groups was accounted for by many who became WIN participants, presumably the more motivated and work-ready. This transfer into WIN and out of the comparison group by itself may account for the findings.

Moreover, assignment to specific elements of the WIN program also was not random. The true comparison groups should have been composed of AFDC recipients judged appropriate for each service and willing to enroll but who did not. These more capable recipients (perhaps those with higher education) might well have achieved similar job placement rates on their own. It is also suggestive that WIN 2 benefitted the better educated more than the less educated.

Attrition in both the WIN sample and the comparison group was enormous. Between the first wave of interviews conducted before the program began and the last wave three years after graduation, 46 percent of the WIN sample and fully 55 percent of the comparison group had been lost to the analysis. Ketron's (1980) insistence that attrition was not a problem because both the WIN and the comparison groups experienced similar losses is not convincing, especially in light of the creaming problem and the fact that the remaining cohort is used as the base for estimating outcomes. If their initial sample size is employed as the appropriate comparison, then their success rates, small as they were, are reduced by about 50 percent.

Even more problematic, the follow-up data on post-WIN employment and earnings may not have been reliable. Much of the critical data were drawn from retrospective interviews, recalling the Edin problem that besets all of the large longitudinal panel data sets. Ketron, Inc. (1980) issued no report on data reliability. Income, hours worked, and weeks worked may well have been reported differentially by those who had gone through training and those who had not. In any event, the problem of underreporting persists. Many welfare records themselves, especially concerning non-AFDC income and work, are probably inaccurate.

Finally, much of the superior performance of WIN graduates could be accounted for solely by the employer tax credit. Employers who took on WIN participants were allowed a tax credit of 20 percent of employee wages. The enormously steep decay rates in post-WIN wages and weeks worked, especially for men, strongly suggest a unique incentive to cut back on workers who had exhausted their subsidies.

In the end, the large pool of economically and socially deprived welfare recipients received few employment services through WIN. The typical experience was superficial. Trainees usually graduated into low-paying jobs. Even WIN's "intensive" services comprised little more than a few months of training, apparently inadequate to attain a livable income. It is not surprising that little if anything was gained.

Results from optimal program settings produced the same small, uncertain findings. The Louisville studies (Goldman 1981; Grossman, Maynard, and Roberts 1985; Wolfhagen and Goldman 1983), while correcting some of the methodological problems of Ketron, Inc. (1980), also failed to provide credible evidence of WIN's success. They continue a social science ritual of timid evaluations.

Mead (1986; 1988a,b; 1992) has made much of the WIN experience to argue that mandatory work requirements (one of the obligations of welfare entitlement) would go far to increase the employment of AFDC recipients and decrease the welfare rolls. Relying on state-level data, Mead (1988a,b) shows that administrative decisions that raised participation in welfare-to-work programs, usually through mandatory participation, achieved higher work levels. Aside from the problem of causality (whether the state regulations reflect or create local opportunities for employment), Mead's (1988a) data explain only a very small amount of job placement. Indeed, his study can be taken as an estimate of WIN creaming, even while it ignores the broader implications of increasing the labor pool at the bottom. Decreasing the AFDC rolls may be a desirable goal in theory, especially if it is produced by greater social and economic equality, but forcing more people into an unprotected pool of low-skilled, low-paid workers can have lamentable consequences if it depresses wages and employment.

It is difficult to avoid the conclusion that WIN 2 and the Louisville WIN Laboratory programs were parodies of sincerity, made even more farcical by biased "scientific" evaluations that lent legitimacy to an activity that earned none on its own merits. Ketron, Inc. (1980) and the more sophisticated MDRC evaluations devised myths of social efficiency in deference to national preferences for minimal welfare interventions. These politicized melodramas denied both the probity of economic reform and the value of adequate provisions for all low-income citizens.

SUPPORTED WORK

The SW experiments were targeted on some of the most persistently difficult groups in American society: long-term welfare recipients, ex-addicts, ex-convicts, and troubled youth. "In the sixties such people were referred to as the hard-core or structurally unemployed; today they are sometimes referred to as the underclass" (Auletta 1982). Initially modeled on a program developed by the Vera Institute of Justice for Bowery alcoholics in New York, SW assumed that its participants needed emotional support and guided work experience more than specific job skills in order to become self-sufficient:

> [SW] is based upon the premise that its participants can be
> successfully employed if they work in the company of their peers
> under close supervision by technically qualified people who
> understand the work histories and personal backgrounds of the
> crew members. The supervisors gradually increase standards of
> attendance, productivity, and performance until they resemble those
> of unsubsidized jobs. After 12 or 18 months, depending on the site,
> participants are required to leave their Supported Work jobs whether
> or not they have found other employment. Although participants
> are expected to learn some occupation-specific skills during the
> program, the emphasis is on the development of work habits, basic
> work skills, and motivation that will enhance employability. (Masters
> 1981:603)

The evaluation of SW took place largely between 1974 and 1979 at ten of the fifteen SW demonstration sites, providing MDRC its founding research task. With a blue-ribbon board containing some of the nation's most prominent social scientists, MDRC was established to conduct credible evaluations of manpower programs. Continuing the popularity of the NIT's earlier randomized designs, MDRC set a standard for subsequent research. Greenberg and Wiseman (in Manski and Garfinkel 1992) consider MDRC's evaluation of SW to be seminal, producing "an academic consensus that random assignment was a methodologically superior approach to program evaluation and evidence that such studies could in fact be carried out" (27). MDRC oversaw the project, contracting out the actual service provision to local auspices and much of the data collection and analysis to prestigious research organizations (Mathematica Policy Research and the Institute for Research on Poverty).

By establishing rigorous eligibility criteria, the project did appear to enroll their intended target groups, described at great length (Goldman 1981; Hollister, Kemper, and Maynard 1984; Masters 1981; and with a compelling drama by Auletta 1982). All participants were unemployed at the time of their enrollment in SW, having spent no more than three months in a job during the previous six months. The AFDC group had been receiving welfare for thirty of the previous thirty-nine months. Ex-addicts were eighteen or older and enrolled in a drug program; ex-offenders also eighteen or older had been incarcerated within the previous six months. Enrolled youth were between seventeen and twenty years of age and lacked a high school or equivalency degree, and at least 50 percent had a delinquency record. Also notable for the experiment's broader application, participation in SW was voluntary in 85 percent of the cases; prior to randomization, program managers screened out applicants who they felt would be too disruptive to their programs. Moreover, many of SW's participants had been referred by community agencies, presumably having been formally screened for suitability.

The detailed comparisons in Hollister, Kemper, and Maynard (1984) suggest that the final SW groups of participants were broadly similar to national samples of the four target populations. Although SW participants seemed to be long-term dependents, serious drug users and offenders, and troubled youth, they were not randomly *selected* from among target populations, though the project randomly *assigned* them to SW or control groups. Thus, the final SW sample, because of prescreening and convenience sampling, as well as the largely voluntary nature of participation in the program, may not be representative of the most difficult populations. The impact of the SW creaming—prescreening in the agency as well as at the project sites, plus self-selection—is not estimated; however, it becomes an important consideration in light of the modest outcomes of the SW experiment.

Within MDRC's broad guidelines, each of the fifteen SW program sites developed their own work experience projects as well as job assistance and other ancillary supports, such as counseling. Service projects—including clerical work, building maintenance, food services, and aide positions—constituted the largest category of training placements, accounting for more than half of all project days. Construction projects accounted for about one-quarter of project days. The remaining projects were spread among agriculture, forestry, and fishing, manufacturing, transportation and communication, and wholesale and retail trade.

SW sites were permitted to pay participants up to 25 percent of their work time for receiving ancillary services such as counseling, job search assistance, and other practical tasks such as training to obtain a driver's license. Many of these services, such as therapeutic counseling, were provided on referral to community agencies, some of which provided the initial referrals to the program itself. Moreover, all but two sites employed professional "job developers to line up job openings for participants" (Hollister, Kemper, and Maynard 1984:71). There was considerable variation among sites in the intensity and quality of the work experience and ancillary services.

Data for the evaluations were obtained from the participants usually in face-to-face interviews but occasionally by phone. The interviews took place at the beginning of placement, then periodically up to three years after graduating from SW.

According to the evaluations, SW was quite successful. One of the more restrained reports stated,

> From the viewpoint of society as a whole, Supported Work can be judged to have been successful for the AFDC and ex-addict target groups in terms of increasing opportunities and reducing dependency and social costs. For the youth group, Supported Work did not significantly alter opportunities or behaviors from what they would have been in the absence of Supported Work experience. For the ex-offender group, no firm conclusion can be drawn; some aspects suggest positive net effects, others negative net effects. (Hollister in Hollister, Kemper, and Maynard 1984:43)

Most others connected to the MDRC project were not so restrained, claiming that SW produced "large earnings impacts"—significant and important differentials between the SW groups and their controls that recommended broader adoption of the program (Friedlander and Gueron in Manski and Garfinkel 1992:187). Some were even effusive:

> Supported Work, in essence, demonstrated that society need not acquiesce to the existence of a permanently disadvantaged group of citizens. There are ways that some of these individuals can be reached; they can be assisted in a way that will enable them to earn a livelihood so that they and some of their children can escape from what is often otherwise a dead-end track. (Ginzberg, Nathan, and Solow in Hollister, Kemper, and Maynard 1984:311)

The impact of SW varied by target group as well as by site. AFDC recipients were the most successful of the target groups. The long-term (three-year) average impact of the program on AFDC recipients amounted to $50 a month in earnings or about $600 a year (presumably in 1979 dollars), approximately 25 percent more than the control group. The control group monthly mean was about $210. Thus, the AFDC sub-group of SW participants earned about $260 a month (after small adjustments for inflation and SW subsidies), a wage below both the poverty line and welfare benefits in most states at that time (all data from Masters 1981). Welfare savings were negligible. It is also notable that only two out of seven sites evaluated by Masters (1981) produced statistically significant earnings gains for the AFDC group.

Masters's (1981) findings were largely corroborated by Grossman, Maynard, and Roberts (1985), who relied upon Social Security data for earnings reports and extended the follow-up to five years. At that time (the fourteenth quarter), Grossman, Maynard, and Roberts (1985) estimated that SW almost doubled the control group's monthly mean earnings of $180. Because of "cohort effects," however, the eleventh-quarter gain of $50, over the control group's mean of $229, is a better estimate. This increase of about 22 percent was highly significant statistically but insubstantial for purposes of escaping welfare or poverty.

Still, much is made (Grossman, Maynard, and Roberts 1985) of the fact that those who were the most welfare-dependent seemed to gain the most, suggesting opportunities for program targeting. However, these differentials were neither consistent across measures of the welfare-dependent nor usually statistically significant, and the differentials themselves were small.

Statistically significant benefits for ex-addicts did not emerge until more than one year after their graduation from SW. Measured at the last follow-up, thirty-four to thirty-six months after the beginning of their participation in SW or about eighteen to twenty-four months after graduating from the program, ex-addicts showed marked improvements over their controls: 17 percent more were employed, working twenty hours and earning $100 more a month. Still, the mean figures for the controls were low: only 32 percent worked an average of fifty hours a month, earning about $220 (Skidmore in Hollister, Kemper, and Maynard 1984). It was puzzling that these long-term differentials were not reflected earlier; during the year after graduation from SW, there was hardly any difference between the participants and their controls. Moreover, the interviews confirmed that SW did not have any impact on drug use. Still, Skidmore happily concludes that SW while "far from a panacea" provides "some support" that SW "facilitates [ex-addicts'] return to a drug free and independent lifestyle" (in Hollister, Kemper, and Maynard 1984:168).

Compared with the AFDC group and ex-addicts, ex-offenders and youth fared poorly. SW ex-offenders made no statistically significant gains over their controls at any point after graduation from SW. The differential in monthly hours worked between ex-offenders and their controls was only 8.2 at the two-year follow-up. The mean for the control group at this time was only 66.8 hours of work a month. Moreover, the thirty-six-month cohort showed greater deterioration than their controls in terms of arrests (not statistically significant) and drug use (statistically significant). Finally, there were no statistically significant benefits for SW youth after graduation.

On balance, SW produced very modest benefits, so small that few of its participants could escape poverty and even fewer could obtain employment at a livable wage. Moreover, these modest benefits were accrued by a thrice-creamed group of participants (by self, by their referral agency, and by SW itself), whose representativeness of the underlying population is questionable. In the end, SW was as ineffective in improving the employment prospects for troubled people as other personal social service approaches have been in handling a variety of related impediments (discussed in the next chapter).

Hollister argues that external labor conditions, in particular the economic recession of the mid-1970s, may have affected the SW outcomes. "The recession not only made it more difficult than expected to create jobs in which the participants could work while in the program, but it also made postprogram placement quite problematical" (Hollister, Kemper, and Maynard 1984:37–8). Still, it also seems likely that the recession could have produced a group of participants who were especially motivated to find jobs. The recession may have provided a wake-up call for a more receptive group of people to enroll in SW, one for whom the subsidized work and job placement activities were most crucial. Thus, SW's highly screened participant pool was probably further distorted by prevailing economic conditions. Instead of an understatement of SW's potential, the findings may exaggerate its ability to rehabilitate and affect employment.

Furthermore, the design of the experiment prevents the attribution of findings to any particular program element. The findings are so small and the pool of participants so highly screened that it seems plausible that the low-cost job search activities—matching skills and attitudes that the participants brought to the project with available jobs—may have accounted for its small amount of success. Work experience and the ancillary activities may have provided no more than temporary work relief.

Other factors also may have minimized the credibility of the differentials. The experiments were clearly time-limited demonstrations, so that agencies and staff may well have exerted atypical efforts, especially in job placement, to achieve success. If the program were routinized, those efforts would probably fall off, together with any demonstration dividend.

The data were collected from interviews and from groups whose veracity is highly questionable. The experiment may have created biases that predisposed SW participants to report their work behaviors differently than the controls. Perhaps out of loyalty, gratitude, or affection, SW participants may have reported their employment more accurately (or exaggerated it) relative to the controls, who might have hid their employment in illegal jobs. Recalling the Edin problem, SW participants and their controls may have differed only in the degree to which they were employed in the underground economy. The project made little effort to verify the accuracy of its data, conveniently accepting at face value self-reports of income, drug use, and crime.

The large variation among evaluated sites and the persistent report of negative findings argue against an ability to replicate SW at other locations. The highest-quality programs, as judged by MDRC staff, did not produce the best results. A few sites tended to account for much of the positive outcomes, perhaps reflecting idiographic situations. This fact alone should raise questions about whether the program or the peculiar characteristics of certain subjects and other external factors are responsible for the outcomes.

Furthermore, Piliavin and Gartner (in Hollister, Kemper, and Maynard 1984) note that in both the ex-offender sample and the ex-addict sample the settling down of older participants (over thirty-five years of age) seems to explain a large portion of success rates:

> One of the trends noted in the crime and drug results was that, among older ex-offenders (especially those over 35 years of age), experimentals were consistently more likely than controls to remain arrest free and to abstain from drug use throughout the three years during which follow-up observations were carried out.

> Furthermore, among controls, those who were older were more likely to report being arrest free and abstainers from drug use. Our interpretation of these findings is that they suggest that Supported Work provides a particularly important opportunity for a conventional lifestyle to a key group of ex-offenders, namely, those who, with the passage of time, are withdrawing from a long-term pattern of crime. (Piliavin and Gartner in Hollister, Kemper, and Maynard 1984:198)

This also seemed true of older ex-addicts both in SW and generally. In this event, it again seems likely that the aggressive job placement activities of SW provided a greater benefit than any of its minimal work programs or ancillary counseling services.

SW was one of the most expensive training programs in the literature, but it produced minimal and questionably credible results. SW's claims to have found an effective work program for large portions of the underclass are threatened by its small and sporadic findings, creaming, the unreliability of its data, deviations from the eligibility criteria, demonstration effects, maturation effects, and external economic conditions. Even acknowledging some program benefits, it is not clear whether they were due to SW's core elements or to its job development activities. In the end, SW demonstrated little more than the ability of sophisticated researchers to conduct self-serving research.

The limitations of the project suggest the depth of need, the extent of the human impediments that must be overcome, if marginal groups are to earn adequate incomes in the job market. One-and-one-half years of job experience together with ancillary supports seem inadequate to produce economic independence, let alone an adequate income for deprived and troubled people. By insisting on SW's success, MDRC failed to provide a true advocacy for those in need. Moreover, it failed to provide a voice for a much larger group of economically insecure Americans: SW's creamed participants, particularly its AFDC group, may have been more broadly representative of the tens of millions of economically precarious American families than just those at the very bottom.

Further, the basic premise of SW may have been off the mark. Supported Work may not be as essential for economic independence as the availability of jobs; job training may not be as powerful a tool in combatting poverty as a livable wage. But the project did not address the desirability of increasing the number of jobs through public action and did not address the problem of job displacement. After all, a public jobs program, especially if it pays adequate wages, is much more expensive than SW. Indeed, only infrequent concern is raised that training programs capriciously favor participants over other low-income applicants when employment decisions are made and that programs that increase the low-wage pool of workers force the least well off to subsidize each other. SW seemed designed as a concession to popular desires for a reduction of the welfare rolls, geared to increase income but not necessarily to the level of either a livable wage or one that could enable the participant to escape welfare.

This desire was a palpable goal of MDRC's funding auspices. Anticipating its role "as an agent of the states," which had employed it to work on the OBRA demonstrations (Greenberg and Wiseman in Manski and Garfinkel 1992:65), MDRC was acting in SW as an agent of those funders' social philosophy. The funding auspices of SW—six federal agencies, the Ford Foundation and other local philanthropies, and state and local governments—are institutions committed to notions of social efficiency. SW tested the ability of a rational expression of social policy to achieve important goals through the design and implementation of a relatively inexpensive and socially compatible intervention. While neglect may be at the core of the conservative vision, SW's rational helping hand was emblematic of liberal social welfare policy, and its failure testifies to the implausibility of this strategy. Yet MDRC's ideological commitment to liberal social welfare interventions may well explain the distortion of its evaluative role, raising a more troubling concern about the conduct of social science: its apparent inability to transcend factional politics in favor of an objective policy role.

CETA

Bassi et al. (1984) is probably the most comprehensive and thorough evaluation of CETA. Its findings were remarkably similar to the Ketron, Inc. (1980) evaluation of WIN, probably for similar reasons: CETA's and WIN's services and recipients were similar; both evaluative methodologies were seriously and similarly flawed; and both sets of evaluators may have been organizationally compromised by accepting evaluative contracts from the administrative auspices of the programs.

Bassi et al. (1984) evaluated CETA's impact on low-income populations and youth while attempting to estimate its effects on welfare dependency. They relied upon fiscal year 1976 data from the Continuous Longitudinal Manpower Survey (CLMS) to describe CETA participants and drew their comparison groups from the CPS and the PSID. Social Security data provided estimates of earnings both prior to the CETA training year and for the two years afterwards. All of the files except the Social Security data relied upon self-reported earnings and welfare participation.

In spite of acknowledging "some very serious technical and methodological difficulties," Bassi et al. (1984) insist that their findings are credible estimates of true CETA outcomes, even pressing on to draw conclusions for public policy. Like Ketron's evaluation of WIN, Bassi et al. (1984) found that economically disadvantaged women and women who were welfare recipients benefitted more from the program than similar men, although their earnings gains were modest, usually less than $1,000 a year for each of the two years after training. These earnings did not show the rapid decay of the WIN data.

However, CETA had only a small impact, if any, on the probability of welfare receipt in future years. In all cases, benefits were defined in relation to comparison groups that were not randomly drawn from a single pool but were demographically matched from other data sets.

CETA's results were mixed for youth. PSE was shown to be the only CETA program effective for those under twenty-three years of age. Even then, PSE was effective only for females, and its gains in the first post-program year were very modest and decayed rapidly in the second for Hispanic and black females. The largest gains were made by Hispanic females, approximately $1,700 in the first postprogram year, which fell off to about $300 during the second year. Most of the other program activities for males and females—classroom training, on-the-job training, youth work experience, and multiple activities—reported lower gains than the comparison group. CETA males actually did more poorly than their comparison group, a disparity that *grew* during the two postprogram years. This generally negative finding is not that surprising since the CETA youth sample was much more debilitated than the comparison group, which was drawn from the CPS.

Indeed, the study's CPS comparison group of youths was inappropriate since the true reference group should have been a similar population of debilitated youth. Moreover, the contamination problem (the degree to which the comparison group contained CETA participants) probably produced underestimates of the true difference between the CETA sample and the CPS comparison group.[3] Lacking a randomized design, the research had no ability to compare its outcomes with an appropriate control group.

Bassi et al. (1984) report that the labor market activity of CETA youth increased after the program. Again, however, without appropriate controls, the research cannot attribute this increase to the CETA programs themselves or to natural maturation, the tendency for youths to work more as they age into their twenties.

On the basis of their findings, Bassi et al. (1984) draw a number of important conclusions for public policy:

Our findings indicate that CETA programs were effective for economically disadvantaged adult women and for young women (most of whom are economically disadvantaged). Programs that

---

3. The contamination problem is quite large. The authors estimate that as much as one-third to one-half of all comparison groups—of youth and adults—may contain CETA graduates. This also hints at the many tens of millions of poor and low-income Americans who have passed through public training programs.

integrated individuals into the labor market (OJT and PSE) were more effective than those that did not.

> The fact that OJT does work for women would suggest that efforts be made to expand their participation in this program. In the past, local prime sponsors tended to assign OJT slots disproportionately to white males. Consideration should be given to more balanced assignments. The move toward more training (and less work experience) and greater participation by the private sector under JTPA has the potential of increasing the effectiveness of the program. (Bassi et al. 1984:122)

Yet, the pitfalls of the study design undercut the credibility of all its findings, except the sporadic concessions to its methodological ambiguity. In the first place, the adult participants, like the young participants, were neither randomly selected from the deprived target populations nor were they randomly assigned to the comparison groups. Self-selection remains an unanswerable point of skepticism in attributing the outcomes, modest as they were, to the training programs and not to some unmeasured motivational factor. Matching to create comparison groups fails to pick up these factors. Adult CETA participants were disproportionately better educated, younger, unmarried, and with slightly larger families than their matched comparison groups. They were also self-selected. Thus, any conclusion drawn from the experience of the samples is not broadly relevant for public policy. The corrections that the authors attempt to make for differences between comparison groups and CETA participants are suspect in the same way as the Heckman corrections for self-selection were in previous studies; the corrections assume an unproven similarity between the self-selected and demographically similar members of comparison groups (in particular see Grossman, Maynard, and Roberts 1985).

Second, recalling the Edin problem, the basic data may not be reliable. Ignoring the probability that illegal income is underreported, Bassi et al. (1984) only picked up income that was contained in the Social Security files. To the extent to which CETA graduates differentially ended up in legitimate employment as a result of the program, little more than haphazard sorting may have taken place. But even here, the research fails to measure the extent to which CETA simply provided a job placement advantage to participants over similarly qualified people who had not participated in CETA.

Third, attrition was an enormous problem. The authors sidestep the issue, except to point out that the rates of attrition were similar across the different groups. On this basis, they assume that there is no attrition bias, a heroic assumption with attrition rates of approximately 35%. Attrition at this level, however, even without the creaming that results from self-selection, creates insurmountable challenges to representativeness.

In the end, Bassi et al. (1984) fail to justify the value of CETA either on grounds of increasing labor force participation or income. Their small reported benefits were highly suspect estimates of the program's impact. The differential findings among CETA's component programs were probably more a result of program creaming than any training benefit. The consistent report on CETA and WIN that PSE provides the greatest benefit could easily be reinterpreted to suggest that there was a ready labor pool for any job that paid a steady income instead of the research's preferred conclusion that income gains through PSE were tributes to the training. It is also notable that CETA as well as WIN trained its participants for a series of low-wage, dead-end jobs.

CETA provided only superficial interventions targeted on labor force participation and the reduction of welfare dependency to the exclusion of adequacy of employment or longer-term personal and social outcomes. The Bassi et al. (1984) evaluation relies upon compliant and sophisticated social scientists to transform customary job-seeking behaviors, program creaming, and convenient sampling procedures into an illusion of programmatic success and a ceremony of social compassion. This misleading factional study camouflages feckless training as a noble social mission and obedient research as grand science. Its insidious effect is to deprive the least well off in society of a true advocate, a voice in behalf of their needs. Rather than an important investment toward economic self-sufficiency, CETA may well be a melodrama of labor force discipline that fails in its few weeks of educational and vocational pantomimes to compensate for inadequate basic education or skill preparation.[4]

THE STATE WELFARE/WORK EXPERIMENTS

The Omnibus Budget Reconciliation Act of 1982 created federal mechanisms to allow states to experiment with a variety of initiatives designed to reduce welfare dependency by increasing the employment of recipients:

> . . . the consolidation of authority for AFDC-related employment operations within state welfare agencies; community work

4. Evaluations of JTPA largely followed the same path as CETA. The results of the JTPA study also mirrored CETA's small findings and uncertain evaluative methods (Bloom et al. 1994). For criticisms, see in particular Hotz (in Manski and Garfinkel 1992) and Lafer (1994). Hotz concludes, "Clearly, despite significant efforts on the part of the designers of the Study, a design which guaranteed external validity was not achieved" (110).

experience; a work supplementation program that permitted use of welfare grants to subsidize client employment in public, private nonprofit and (after 1984) private for-profit organizations and businesses; and expanded authority for requiring participation in job search programs by both AFDC applicants and recipients. (Greenberg and Wiseman in Manski and Garfinkel 1992:26–7)

Many states took advantage of the OBRA provisions to mount welfare/work experiments. MDRC in collaboration with the states and a variety of other sources of funding evaluated programs in eight states.[5] These evaluations, employing randomized designs, objective measures, and follow-ups, are perhaps the most credible of the twenty-four available outcome studies of the OBRA state initiatives. The claims have been widespread that MDRC's evaluations, constituting a large portion of "a remarkable collection of new information on the consequences of employment related welfare innovations," strongly influenced the enactment of the Family Support Act (Greenberg and Wiseman in Manski and Garfinkel 1992:28; also see Baum 1991; Haskins 1991; Szanton 1991). The act, touted by its sponsors as a radical overhaul of the welfare system, was actually a modest reform of AFDC emphasizing skills development and employment. It enjoyed almost universal congressional support.

The eight MDRC sites enrolled three different groups: AFDC recipients, AFDC applicants, and AFDC-UP recipients. MDRC produced findings suggesting that a variety of skills development strategies were successful both in raising the earnings of AFDC and AFDC-UP recipients and in lowering welfare costs and dependency. The programs were far less successful with AFDC applicants, a less welfare-dependent group and one that includes many with greater skills and presumably greater motivation to find work on their own. While the gains and the savings were modest, they were sufficient to recommend broad adoption of these training and job search programs, a recommendation implemented by the Family Support Act and carried into the 1996 welfare reform.

The annual earnings effect per participant—the difference in earnings between those enrolled in the experimental groups and those in the control groups—varied from about $1,000 in Maine to as little as $10 in

5. These eight constitute the two demonstrations in San Diego as well as the programs in Arkansas, Cook County, West Virginia, Virginia, Baltimore, New Jersey, and Maine. The Louisville WIN Laboratory and AFDC Homemaker-Home Health Aid Demonstrations are not evaluated here. SW was considered above.

Cook County.[6] While small, the effects represented as much as a 33 percent increase over the earnings of controls, which were typically less than $500 a quarter and less than $2,000 a year. The earnings gains from the programs were clearly inadequate to escape poverty or welfare.[7] Moreover, many of the annual differences and most of the quarterly differences failed to reach statistical significance, and a scattering of negative, but not statistically significant, effects further muddied the water (Greenberg and Wiseman in Manski and Garfinkel 1992).

The net welfare effects (average per capita differences between experimentals and controls) ranged from small increases in Maine to annual savings of over $500 in San Diego. The net program costs for each experimental participant ranged from about $2,000 for the "higher cost" intervention in Maine to less than $200 for "lower cost" programs in Arkansas and Cook County.

Still, while actual gains in employment, earnings, and welfare savings were weak, MDRC's methodological shortcomings were serious enough to undercut the credibility of the studies. Any conclusion except the indeterminacy of the findings themselves or the failure of the programs seems unwarranted. Even MDRC's recent and most cautious conclusion seems to exaggerate:[8]

> In sum, while prior expectations and some evidence suggest that higher-cost services can have a greater impact on income, by affecting job quality and stability, collectively the studies suggest that welfare-to-work programs for AFDC single parents may have to be complemented by other policy tools (for example, an increase in the minimum wage or Earned Income Tax Credit and increased child support collections) to reach the goals of not only reducing welfare receipt but also reducing poverty. (Friedlander and Gueron in Manksi and Garfinkel 1992:188)

6. The various sources are not always clear about the years of the reported dollars. Presumably most are in or about 1985.

7. These summary data as well as those below, except where specifically indicated, are drawn from Gueron and Pauley (1991).

8. MDRC's interpretations of their own findings have become more cautious and restrained over time as criticisms of its research have increased. The tone and claims of the initial site studies (Friedlander et al. 1985a,b; Friedlander et al. 1986; Friedlander et al. 1987; Friedlander 1988; Goldman et al. 1985) is more buoyant than MDRC's early congressional testimony and studies that endorsed the FSA (Gueron 1986a,b; Gueron 1987). Recent work is even more balanced but still insists that the state programs convincingly demonstrated important gains for most of the interventions (Friedlander and Gueron in Manski and Garfinkel 1992; Gueron 1990; Gueron and Pauley 1991; Gueron 1995).

The actual site data only feed skepticism of any beneficial impact of the minimal training and job search strategies. Of MDRC's eight research sites, Maine's On-the-Job Training Program (TOPS) was the highest cost service, Arkansas's WORK program the lowest cost, and Virginia's traditional "workfare" approach (Community Work Experience Program) fell in between.

Maine's TOPS program, costing about $2,600 per recipient, recalled the "intensive" casework approach to welfare dependency. It was designed specifically to place long-term dependent welfare mothers in private sector jobs. The TOPS sequence was implemented in three phases: prevocational training that lasted two to five weeks; work experience that consisted of a maximum of twelve twenty-hour weeks; and finally for "participants who demonstrated their motivation and acquisition of basic work skills," on-the-job training in subsidized positions, primarily in the private sector, for up to six months. Moreover, the employer was subsidized up to $50 a week per trainee.

Among the MDRC welfare/work sites, TOPS produced the greatest work success. By the third year after the program, TOPS participants were earning almost $1,000 more—about $20 a week—than the $2,000 earned by the controls. However, "three quarters of the overall earnings impact in the post program period was due to increased wage rates or hours worked for those who were employed, *rather than to a higher proportion of experimentals who were ever employed*" (Auspos 1988, emphasis added). Equally high proportions of both the TOPS participants (81.8 percent) and their controls (80.2 percent) worked at some point during the follow-up period. Almost all participants in both groups relied upon AFDC at some point, although payments to TOPS participants were slightly higher. Moreover, based upon soft responses to interviews, the authors conclude that the Maine experience produced a net social gain.

However, a number of biases and flaws undermine even these modest findings. The TOPS program did not adjust or control for its demonstration effects—the possibility that highly motivated program staff would make an unusually great effort to train and place participants during an experimental phase, one that might well affect their careers. Moreover, here as in many other research situations, income may have been differentially reported by participants and controls. After all, the TOPS participants were under surveillance while the controls, similar to Edin's sample, were probably underreporting illegal income. The amount of income underreported in Edin's study—a few thousand dollars a year—would create a situation in which nonparticipants were in the end better off than TOPS participants.

Yet the most serious problem with the Maine experiment, and perhaps with all of the MDRC sites, emerges from the process of selecting participants. The 444 who volunteered for the program were decidedly unrepresentative of the pool of AFDC recipients either in Maine or in the nation. Voluntary participation in TOPS presumably resulted in a highly motivated group of participants. Moreover, the TOPS staff "exercised considerable discretion in deciding whether a particular client was 'appropriate'," which meant that the recipient had arranged for child care on her own, was in good health, and was literate (Auspos 1988). Thus, voluntary participation, the screening process, and Maine's recessionary labor market created a group of prime candidates for employment, not a set of hard-to-employ welfare recipients, those who justified the experiment in the first place.

Indeed, Maine may mark the upper limits of employability in the AFDC pool since TOPS did not fill its full complement of slots. It is noteworthy that only sixty-nine of the 444 TOPS enrollees reached the job training phase, sixty-three of whom continued their employment after training. However, fully 70 percent of these positions entailed service or clerical jobs, most paying less than $4 an hour. Moreover, TOPS delivered a highly motivated work force to employers, as well as offering them subsidized wages and lower search costs for new hires. Often having appropriate skills and attitudes to begin with, these "displaced homemakers" represented only a tiny fraction of Maine's 3,000 women on welfare with children over six years of age and an even smaller percentage of the total number—16,500—of women on welfare in the state. In short, the Maine experiment failed to realize adequate wages for a highly creamed group of recipients. Even so, the TOPS experience cannot be generalized, and therefore offers no policy wisdom for handling the underlying populations of concern that gave rise to the experiment in the first place (Epstein 1993a).

The Arkansas WORK program cost only $118 per recipient.[9] It provided traditional WIN-type services in which participants "received virtually no services beyond assessment (Friedlander et al. 1985a:148). WORK offered two weeks of group job search followed by sixty days of individual job search and finally mandatory unpaid work of twenty to thirty hours a week for those who did not find jobs. Still, it produced an annual gain over the controls of $337 (less than $7 a week) and welfare savings of about $3 a week by the third year. The controls averaged only $650 earnings per year by the third year (Epstein 1993a).

---

9. Portions of this section on Arkansas appeared in Epstein (1993:123–25).

WORK staff were instructed to spend more time with highly employable participants. This also seems to be the pattern in the other experiments: low participation and a tendency to favor the more employable. The reasons for nonparticipation, attrition in many cases, were not measured, although here as in other sites it seemed to stem from a combination of factors: leaving welfare for a job or marriage, a reluctance by staff to penalize nonparticipation (creating a largely voluntary program), and true attrition.

The possibility of large attrition may raise the specter more eloquently than any poorly conceived and possibly reactive survey of client attitudes that workfare has been unpleasant, abusive, and stigmatizing. The enrollees' nonparticipation—a tacit strike—supports the speculation that the programs have caused harm. In any event, the research did not check into this possibility.

In spite of these problems, the Arkansas study concluded that "against the backdrop of low pre-program employment, the WORK Program was effective in helping its enrollees achieve modest improvements" (Friedlander et al. 1985a:xvii). "Clear reductions in welfare receipt were found for WORK Program enrollees" (Friedlander et al. 1985a:xviii). This "clear" reduction—only 6.9 percent and only in the third quarter of the follow-up period—was associated with a third-quarter welfare savings of $43, or about $3 per week.

The plausibility of the these tiny, marginally significant findings is sabotaged by the study's many design problems. For one, the findings may result from a few motivated recipients in the experimental group being given a chance for unsubsidized work. This sort of creaming does not testify to the slight but palpable value of the intervention but to a more reasonable conclusion that a weak intervention produced inadequate results, if any at all. Particularly at this site and probably at the others, the researchers exaggerate the success of the experimental intervention. "Over the nine month follow-up period welfare savings per recipient were nearly six times higher than the savings per applicant" (Friedlander et al. 1985a:xxii). But the actual savings were only $176 for experimentals versus $29 for controls, which is only $4.60 per week versus $0.75 per week.

The authors also tend to ignore their fifth-quarter follow-up on applicants that showed the controls doing better than the experimentals. For the follow-up year, controls averaged $813 in total earnings, while experimentals earned only $633. Again the average weekly difference is tiny as are all of the others. None of the differences was statistically significant. Yet statistical significance did not bar the authors from reporting trends in the other, shorter-term data that tended to support their views of WORK's effectiveness. Finally, the gains in employment and earnings were not sufficient to offset losses to recipients in Medicaid and AFDC. In other words, by removing people from assistance, the program benefitted taxpayers more than participants; it is noteworthy that this occurred amid the wretched poverty and low wages of high-unemployment Arkansas.

The true conclusion is that no conclusion should be drawn about the effectiveness of the experimental intervention except that they did not appear to be beneficial. The experience, particularly in Arkansas, might also raise the question of whether the program's goals were reasonable or even laudable. In whose interest was it to force unremunerative jobs, ones that left workers below subsistence, on impoverished people? In exercising their interpretive discretion, whom did the researchers represent, and in crafting their myths of program efficacy, whose position were they advocating?

Clearly in Arkansas, the researchers used weak, contradictory, and implausible findings to construct the decisive metaphors of the myth of work. Apparently, too, the consultants to the project and the MDRC board, who allowed it to be published, were satisfied with the study. Moreover, the WORK program, being no program at all, might stand as a placebo control, a way to measure the demonstration effect of the MDRC experiments at other sites. It may even represent the degree to which the researchers' expectancy bias—a love of their own hypothesis—produced confirmation of that hypothesis.

In Virginia, two experimental conditions—a low service intervention and a moderate service intervention—were compared with a control group that was offered no services. WIN-eligible recipients and applicants were enrolled. In one experimental condition, participants went through job search (individual or group) followed by unpaid work in government or a not-for-profit agency. In the other experimental condition, the participants went through the same regimen but were also referred to an approved educational or training program, including adult basic education, preparation for the GED, vocational education, and other publicly funded activities (through the JTPA).

The experiments were conducted in only eleven of Virginia's 124 public welfare agencies because the state (its Department of Social Services) "considered them generally representative of Virginia's welfare agencies," their data systems were appropriate, and "they had all expressed a strong interest in taking part in the study." The reported costs were similar to Chicago, $388 per experimental participant. In Virginia, however, "overall the study found that (both experimental conditions) lead to modest employment gains and welfare savings" (Friedlander et al. 1986).

As in other sites the differences were minuscule and possibly artifacts of multiple comparisons. For the three quarters of follow-up, controls drew only $84 more in AFDC payments than experimentals (less than $3 a week); only 3.3 percent more experimentals than controls were employed. After segregating applicants from recipients only one statistically significant finding remains—recipients in the control group drew more welfare than experimental participants, but again by a small amount. Although these differences are statistically significant they are unimportant, especially given the nonrandom process for selecting sites. The burden for demonstrating representativeness lies with the researchers and should entail more than bland assurances from the state.

The Virginia study suffers the same flaws as the other MDRC sites, impeding any interpretation of the findings. The possibly biased selection of welfare agencies—signalled by their "strong" desire to participate in the study, demonstration effects, and the positive attitude of the authors to noncoercive Virginia—again suggests that the source of variation between sites lies more in the head and heart of the researchers than in the intervention itself.

Similar methodological and interpretive problems marred all the site evaluations. The problem of unreported income was particularly acute, with MDRC acknowledging that in West Virginia at least the state's employment records did not include many sources of income (such as that from domestic work). The authors were quick to point to convenient "trends" in the data, that is, findings that were not statistically significant but that supported the programs' effectiveness, and they just as frequently failed to address negative and perverse results that were not statistically significant, such as the fifth-quarter follow-up report in San Diego that showed controls earning *more* than the experimental group. In spite of a frequently creamed experimental sample of relatively employable people, the income gains in all the sites were inadequate to allow them to escape welfare or achieve a livable wage. Aside from cost, there were few other legitimate distinctions between lower-cost and higher-cost interventions: both provided only a pittance of help despite MDRC's forceful protestations to the contrary (Friedlander and Gueron in Manski and Garfinkel 1992).

The cost/benefit analyses that MDRC conducted suggest that even though the gains were small the investments in the projects paid off in the long run; recent analyses are more equivocal (Friedlander and Burtless 1995). However, all of these analyses ignored many of the possible extended effects of the programs: displacement of potential workers who were not program participants, downward pressure on wages by increasing the low-wage pool, and capricious distributive effects whereby poor people are subsidizing each other. This perverse subsidy occurs when a welfare recipient is placed in a job at the expense of a low-wage worker. This reduces the costs of welfare to the taxpayer, but the savings are paid for by other relatively poor people who must compete in an increasing labor pool for a relatively fixed number of low-paying jobs. The cost/benefit analyses also ignored the implications of these problems for social cohesion.

If anything, the MDRC welfare/work research reaffirmed an old truth: you get what you pay for. Their very low-cost and superficial interventions produced very little. In truth, they probably did nothing at all to reduce long-term welfare dependency and may even have reduced total income. These experiments teach that dominant political preferences for low-cost training, a central pillar of contemporary liberal thought that inspired both the FSA and the 1996 welfare reform, reject a programmatic assault on poverty, inadequacy, and social inequality.

GAIN

Spanning both the pre- and post-FSA periods, California's Greater Avenues for Independence program was a mandatory OBRA experiment and perhaps MDRC's most credible study. It was the largest of the welfare/work programs. MDRC made its most unambiguous claims for manpower training programs on the basis of GAIN, which is frequently cited in support of the FSA's basic reform—the JOBS program:

> GAIN can change the basic character of welfare to make it much more work-focused, and in doing so get people jobs, reduce welfare costs, and save taxpayers money.

> GAIN had some notable successes in all six study counties, but results varied considerably. While, overall, GAIN increased single parents' three-year earnings by 22 percent and cut welfare payments by 6 percent, impacts were particularly large in one county, where earning went up 49 percent and welfare costs fell 15 percent.

> This most successful county (Riverside) set a new standard of achievement returning taxpayers $2.84 for each $1 invested. While many factors probably contributed to this success and to the county's relatively low average costs, key were a strong and pervasive employment-focused message (including the active use of job developers), a balanced use of basic education and job search, and adequate resources and commitment to extend a serious participation mandate to all GAIN-eligible people on welfare.

GAIN demonstrated the potential to succeed with a wide range of groups in the welfare population, including very long-term welfare recipients and people in a major inner city (Oakland). (Riccio, Friedlander, and Freedman 1994:v–vi)

In addition to any merit that they have as an objective assessment of the actual outcomes of GAIN, MDRC's conclusions constitute a powerful political statement, a play to the contemporary furor to limit AFDC, emphasizing the obligation to work above a commitment to address poverty. They are made to further a particular perspective as well as the organizational health of MDRC. Indeed, MDRC has lobbied extensively on the basis of its findings (Oliker 1994; Szanton 1991). To the extent it can resolve the conundrum of welfare and work, by producing both effective programs and accurate evaluations, MDRC's policy expertise and its contractual profile would rise. Unfortunately, MDRC's claims are neither scientifically credible nor complete.

The credibility of the research lies in its large sample sizes, multisite implementation, long follow-up period (three years), multiple measures of outcome, and randomization procedures. The research involved more than 13,000 participants from both AFDC and AFDC-UP, who were randomly assigned to the different GAIN programs or to control groups in six counties.[10] Randomization began in 1988 and about 55 percent of the research sample had been assigned by July 1989 when GAIN officially became covered by JOBS (when FSA took effect). Information describing welfare utilization as well as employment and earnings were obtained from county and state administrative records, which also supplied background data on research participants. Periodic surveys of study participants produced information about their participation and satisfaction. GAIN staff were surveyed for their opinions about the administration of the program.

The intensive programmatic strategies of the six California counties that participated in GAIN featured case management and professional job search. Case management assigns each participant to a trained worker who identifies the particular factors that impede employment, develops a specific course of action (the necessary training, education, and support services), arranges for those services, and monitors progress (Doolittle and Riccio in Manski and Garfinkel 1992):

> After registration, eligibility workers refer new [and appropriate AFDC] registrants to the GAIN office for orientation and appraisal.

---

10. Except where explicitly indicated, all GAIN data are drawn from Riccio, Friedlander, and Freedman (1994).

At orientation, the opportunities and obligations of the program are explained, and the registrant takes a basic reading and mathematics test. As part of the appraisal interview, the assigned case manager reviews the registrant's background characteristics, including circumstances that might prevent her or (much less commonly) him from participation in GAIN. The registrant is then either referred to a GAIN activity or deferred (i.e., temporarily excused from participating). GAIN's support services, such as child care and transportation, are arranged at this time if the registrant needs them to take advantage of the program's activities. Participation in GAIN is expected to continue until the individual finds employment, leaves welfare, or is no longer required to participate for other reasons. Failure to comply with program rules can result in a "sanction" (i. e., reduction or termination of the monthly welfare grant). (Riccio, Friedlander, and Freedman 1994:3–5)

It is notable that GAIN was targeted on AFDC applicants as well as recipients. Presumably, applicants are a more motivated and skilled pool of potential workers than recipients.

In addition to orientation, the GAIN activities included basic education, job training, job search, and a great variety of support services, such as counseling for personal and family problems that impede employment. With a large amount of variation among sites, the total amount of participation in all GAIN activities averaged 7.5 months, 3.7 months more than controls; the most time was spent in vocational education and basic education. The GAIN strategy was implemented differently in the six counties, with some emphasizing quick job entry and others emphasizing basic education:

Supporting the quick job entry approach is a view that almost any job is a positive first step, and that advancement will come through acquiring a work history and learning skills on the job. Support for the second approach comes from the view that low paying jobs will not get many recipients off welfare or keep them from returning to the rolls. (Riccio, Friedlander, and Freedman 1994:51)

Generally, job search components were contracted out, as were other components of GAIN, including case management. The average gross cost per GAIN registrant ranged from a low of about $3,500 in Riverside County, which stressed the quick job approach, to a high of $7,000 in Alameda County, which stressed personalized services and basic education. These costs, incurred through the early 1990s, are commensurate with those of more intensive welfare/work experiments, although considerably below those of SW. In contrast, controls absorbed a maximum of $2,000. Thus, GAIN provided a net increment of service that ranged from as much as $6,000 per participant in Alameda County to as little as $1,600 per participant in Riverside County. Alameda spent an average of $2,900 on all basic education, other education, training and work assignments, while Riverside only spent $23 per participant on these activities.

Yet in spite of these efforts, the employment and earnings benefits, as well as the savings to welfare, were very modest and quite inadequate to achieve any important social goal, including work participation. Notably, the least expensive program—that of Riverside County—produced the largest employment and welfare results. Three years after leaving the program, the average total earnings for GAIN participants were higher than controls in all of the sites; the statistically significant differences (in four of the six counties) ranged from 40 percent in Riverside County where controls earned $2,600 to 20 percent in Tulare County where controls also earned $2,600. The percent ever-employed during the third follow-up year was also higher for GAIN participants in all of the sites; the statistically significant differences ranged from 2.4 percent in Los Angeles County where 16 percent of controls were employed to 6.6 percent in Riverside County where 25 percent of controls were employed. Statistically significant welfare savings (four of six sites) in the third follow-up year ranged from $600 in Riverside County where welfare payments averaged $3,500 for controls to $275 in Los Angeles County where they averaged $5,000. This incremental benefit for GAIN participants works out to little more than $10 a week. Indeed, the total wage increment for GAIN participants in Riverside County amounted to only about $20 a week more than controls. Nevertheless, in most sites earnings and employment gains increased between the first and third follow-up years.

Many methodological problems eat away at GAIN's very small successes, however. As in most other sites, small differences may really be tribute to unusually dedicated staff and receptive employers anxious to take advantage of an emerging fashion in charitability. These demonstration effects could well disappear in a routinized program that competed with the large pool of unemployed job seekers not on welfare. It is notable, too, that on-the-job training was subsidized. Furthermore, the income and employment data may have been distorted, with controls more likely to work illegally and underreport their income.

The design of the evaluation cannot separate the impacts of the job search activities, frequently conducted by outside professionals, from the effects of training and basic education. Indeed, Riverside County's emphasis upon quick job entry is very suggestive that placement and not training made the largest impact on employment, wages, and welfare savings. Moreover, MDRC refused to discount their apparent successes by the degree to which potential workers not on AFDC were denied employment, or to which wages were held down by an increased pool of low-skilled labor, or to which poor and low-income families perversely ended up paying for the welfare savings.

Among those formally assigned to GAIN, only between 40 percent and 60 percent participated in any of its activities. Moreover, even measured over a five-year period, participation in GAIN's central activities, including training and basic education, was typically short—a matter of months. It is not at all surprising that such superficial interventions are associated with such modest outcomes. Indeed, the superficiality of the interventions underscores the likelihood that the job development activity of GAIN's staff was the chief reason for its modest success.

The great variation among the six counties suggests idiosyncratic local conditions, the possibility that regional job markets and not the nature of the interventions themselves explain the outcomes. MDRC devotes considerable attention to an analysis of the six sites precisely for this reason. But as the authors point out "this type of comparative analysis cannot be of the same level of rigor as the analysis of program impacts *within* each country," and indeed it was not (Riccio, Friedlander, and Freedman 1994:21). Yet this caution does not inhibit MDRC from reinforcing their strong conclusions:

> These limitations notwithstanding, the three-year findings [of the site analyses] do bolster two important conclusions offered in previous reports. First, the fact that all six counties produced modest-to-large earnings gains or welfare savings, or both, indicates that GAIN's effectiveness is not just a one-county story: GAIN can lead to increased earnings and reduced welfare payments even when operated under a variety of local conditions, when targeted toward different types of welfare recipients, and when implemented using different approaches. At the same time the data support a second preliminary conclusion of the earlier reports: that the particular combination of implementation conditions and approaches identified in Riverside may have the largest and most consistent impacts for [welfare] registrants, and the most consistent payoff from a benefit-cost standpoint. (Riccio, Friedlander, and Freedman 1994:270)

Moreover, because of the enormous amount of demographic variation between the counties (urbanization and unemployment rates, employment gains, ethnic variations) as well as large differences in administering and implementing the program (staff differences, philosophies, program emphases), the site analyses are best interpreted as six separate case studies. This enormously deflates the degree to which GAIN's findings can be generalized.

The largest benefits were so concentrated in a few locations—notably Riverside County—as to raise the issue of whether randomization was subtly breached, whether extraordinary staff efforts were made to place GAIN participants in available jobs, or whether local transitional and unmeasured characteristics of the labor force produced an unusually large number of work-ready GAIN participants. Unemployment rates were nearly 10 percent in Riverside County during the period in which GAIN enrolled many of AFDC's work-ready registrants as well as its long-term recipients. Quite possibly, many GAIN registrants had been displaced from steady employment by the local recessionary labor market.

In spite of its high unemployment rate, Riverside County's gains in employment were the highest among the six sites, suggesting that GAIN registrants, already motivated and sufficiently skilled, were favored for local jobs as they opened. Riverside County's GAIN program simply might have exploited temporal employment fluctuations, giving preference to GAIN participants through its job search activities. In the absence of job search, the same amount of new employment might have been spread more equitably among GAIN participants and the control groups.[11]

Job preference for AFDC recipients may have serious social implications. The real Riverside story might well be much less virtuous than MDRC's tale of scientific benevolence in which a wise county adopted a humane and useful job search strategy to prevent the unemployed from becoming long-term welfare recipients. Rather, because the GAIN program favored AFDC registrants over other low-income job seekers, the latter nonwelfare population spent down their already meager resources to become eligible for welfare. Thus, GAIN came to serve the conservative desires of the local community: an expanded pool of low-wage workers, downward pressure on wages, low welfare dependency, and a diminished tax burden.

---

11. Riccio, Friedlander, and Freedman (1994) argue that Riverside's growth rate fails to explain the success of GAIN participants. They show that the growth rates did not occur evenly over the years while benefits were accruing over the years. Moreover, the benefits occurred in different offices within the county. Yet there is no reason to believe that the office of registration necessarily represented the site of employment. The growth rates were huge during follow-up years one and two and slightly negative during year three. The authors also fail to address the possibility that the GAIN referrals for employment may have been favored by local businesses and that the high unemployment rates may have produced an unusually motivated pool of job applicants.

Instead of an inspired direction for welfare policy, GAIN's "investments" more accurately provide low-level, inadequate, and intermittent work for society's poor and deprived. GAIN fails to fulfill any sort of noble vision of work, social participation, or civic success. Many of GAIN's reported successes, if they existed at all, were likely to have resulted from the native talents and skills of its participants combined with the opportunity for work provided by GAIN. Yet MDRC's evaluative enterprise is packaged to deny the desirability of a broad-based jobs program that offers livable wages.

It is notable that GAIN achieved so little and ominous that this overrated activity would so profoundly influence national policy. Yet GAIN's utility may lie less in its production function as a manpower program and more in its ceremonial role of justifying a socially efficient national policy toward underemployment, unemployment, and poverty. In the same way, MDRC, and by extension the social sciences, may serve more to create comforting myths than to estimate the objective reality of program effects. A public that had been growing increasingly inattentive to the claims of the poor was receptive to GAIN's reported effectiveness. Yet MDRC's evaluation of GAIN was not modest, and, buttressed by the appearance of scientifically credible research, it served to deflect policy attention away from the problems of American inequality.

MDRC transformed programmatic failure into a myth of success. It draped its evaluation of GAIN in the robes of science, transmitting the decisive metaphor of work as the comforting illusion that an intensive effort had been made to remedy personal dysfunction. MDRC wrote a morality play, an allegory for our times, in which a Good and Generous Nation Wisely undertakes a Benevolent yet Sensible Mission to offer Yet Another Chance for the Improvident, Inattentive, and Lazy to Reform Themselves through Work. Repentance came cheaply but with little impact on sin.

CONCLUSIONS

By 1992, following criticism of their hopeful findings, even MDRC made an important concession to the skeptics about manpower training programs for the poor, at least in the context of JOBS:

> In sum, while prior expectations and some evidence suggest
> that higher-cost services can have a greater impact on income,
> by affecting job quality and stability, collectively the studies suggest
> that welfare-to-work programs for AFDC single parents may have
> to be complemented by other policy tools (for example, an increase

in the minimum wage or Earned Income Tax Credit and increased child support collections) to reach the goal of not only reducing welfare receipt but also reducing poverty. (Friedlander and Gueron in Manski and Garfinkel 1992:187–9)[12]

Still, there are apparent needs for manpower programs: an enormous number of Americans lack adequate skills to achieve economic independence. Their vocational deficits may result from personal failures or from the failures of basic social institutions to prepare them for employment. However, the national training strategies to deal with their deficiencies—WIN, SW, CETA and the JTPA, the OBRA experiments, JOBS, as well as the state-waiver experiments—have routinely failed, perhaps because of their superficiality.

The homogeneity of the American culture may justify conflating the past thirty years of manpower training programs for poor and dependent populations into a single experience. American society may provide largely similar conditions under which the different training programs were instituted. Yet the results are very similar; evaluations of recent programs mirror those of earlier studies.[13]

12. Throughout their chapter concerned with the precursors to the JOBS program, Friedlander and Gueron (in Manski and Garfinkel 1992) refer to "high-cost" services as frequently as "higher-cost" services. In truth, even when compared with the costs of a year of public schooling, all of the manpower services, and notably those that purport to provide basic skills, are really low cost. One of the major difficulties in attempting to assess the depth of deprivation is that true high-cost services representing deep investments in deprived populations have not been tried. Yet the seeming high cost of the earlier SW, whose direct project costs came to about $6,000 per participant in 1976 dollars, does not represent a large expenditure when measured against continuous medical treatment for addicts, incarceration for offenders, or institutional services for youth (Hollister, Kemper, and Maynard 1984:244). However, even SW failed to produce any notable benefits for participants.

13. Evaluations of both the JOBS programs that was created under the FSA and the more recent state welfare initiatives are still fragmentary (Wiseman 1993, 1995). Similar to its other evaluations, MDRC's preliminary evaluations of the JOBS programs, perhaps in an attempt to fulfill its support, report modest, statistically significant findings that, like those in its earlier studies, are ambiguous and open to a variety of methodological criticisms (Freedman and Friedlander 1995; Pavetti and Duke 1995).

Not surprisingly, the waiver experiments are focused on self-sufficiency either through some sort of work program, teenage pregnancy prevention strategy, or change in the administrative rules of welfare (Wiseman 1993, 1995). There have been more than thirty waiver experiments to date. The evaluations of these programs seem to be among the most factional of the studies. O'Neill's evaluation of the family cap in New Jersey is seriously flawed and incomplete (Epstein 1996). The Hudson Institute, on contract to the Republican governor of Wisconsin to evaluate Wisconsin Works, has heralded its success in news-

Typically, the evaluative studies report only small gains, and these are uniformly compromised by a variety of methodological pitfalls: inaccurate and biased data, demonstration effects, selectivity biases, attrition, incomplete and shortsighted measures, inappropriate controls, and so forth. The studies uniformly assume that preferentially hiring the participants in the training programs—expressed as job development and search efforts—is beneficial for society. The studies neglect to measure any broader social effects beyond earnings, employment, and welfare savings. Yet, displacement, effects on wages, perverse subsidies, and other impacts on social cohesion may eclipse any narrow benefit of limited training for the recipients themselves.

The body of outcome research has been formed in a highly contentious policy atmosphere tilting increasingly toward the preferences incorporated into the 1996 welfare reform: state devolution of national authority, welfare reduction over poverty reduction, and mandatory and punitive administrative changes in social welfare programs. Excusing state variation in manpower programs as experimental "laboratories of democracy" seems disingenuous when these experiments occur almost entirely to shortchange and deny social equality. While some variation did occur in the states' programs, in large part both the higher-cost and the lower-cost services were superficial and inadequate to provide marketable skills and compensate for deep social deprivations. They were little more than rituals of social concern, in which job search support may have accounted for the large portion of very small reported benefits. The recent state initiatives, far from magnanimously addressing social problems if from a variety of points of view, actually undercut the egalitarian impetus of the original Social Security act to provide national standards, intrastate equality, and cost-sharing between wealthy and poor regions.

The manpower training programs elevate the goal of welfare reduction high above any concern with poverty or economic adequacy. Work for subsistence wages and the discipline of toil blot out the need for livable wages and a sense of citizenship, civic unity, and social cohesion. In consideration of the target populations for these programs—notably, welfare recipients, unwed mothers, and delinquent teens—the na-

letters and press clippings but is unresponsive to requests for their data, program design, and analysis (see Hudson Institute 1995). In contrast, the social science community has been routinely forthcoming in opening its analyses to scrutiny both through timely and relatively complete publication as well as through responses to informal requests.

tion's thirst for "deservingness" seems to constrain allocation of sufficient funds.

O'Neill's preferences for mandatory jobs programs and greater sanctioning are supported by her evaluation of then-Governor Dukakis's Employment and Training Choices (ET) in Massachusetts (O'Neill 1990). The failure of ET, cited along with the MDRC studies, has encouraged O'Neill to support other conservatives, notably Mead (1988a,b), in calling for more restrictive welfare-to-work programs that provide low-paying jobs and low-cost services for the inexperienced alone. Yet the same findings might argue for a more generous approach, such as a national jobs program (Lafer 1994). If anything, the failure of the manpower training experience argues forcefully for a more direct strategy of job creation. While more costly, a jobs program that provided work at livable wages may in the long run prove more congenial to the hopes of American social cohesion. Its other impacts are hard to know, except for the near certainty of its great expense and political unpopularity.

MDRC's experiments, recalling the experience of other social experiments, were grievously flawed. It is no wonder that with such imperfectly applied experimental designs, a preference for longitudinal panel data with their ability to get inside the interventions, is reemerging. However, neither approach has been able to provide credible and reasonable approximations of the true program experience, except perhaps to reaffirm Rossi's skepticism that social welfare interventions typically fail. The conflict between reduced-form and structural evaluations comes down to a question of the quality of both the data and the research design. These remain the sticking points in producing scientifically credible estimates of outcomes.

The changing fashions in evaluative design are failing to resolve the basic problems of scientifically credible research. Without adequate resources for evaluative research, no approach seems tenable while the researcher is safe to excuse accommodations to political orthodoxy on grounds of insufficient funding. As Greenberg and Wiseman (in Manski and Garfinkel 1992) and Oliker (1994) begin to argue, MDRC makes a political statement through their research. They acted as agents of the states and as program advocates far more than as neutral social scientists committed to the truth of their evaluations. "Their deployment of resources through interorganizational networks of policy experts, media, and policy makers" overshadowed their role as credible social scientists (Oliker 1994:41). Yet this role was not simply political and rare but ideological and common. MDRC is not an isolated case of accommodation but emblematic of the manner in which modern society makes social policy. In leading a consensus toward the desirability of the 1988 FSA, they were following popular tastes for conservative welfare reform more than the dictates of their experiments.

> The format of [MDRC's] interpretation and publicity was simplified and oriented to vernacular persuasion. And the researchers adroitly publicized it before their analytical operations could be inspected and criticized by peers. Evaluation researchers deployed their knowledge resources among a broad array of actors and organizations in the welfare arena, in a way that established an authoritative and effective appeal for their claim that "something works." The conviction that a widely-shared idea (welfare mothers should work) could be made into a program that would have some impact at little cost eased the bipartisan consensus on the FSA. (Oliker 1994:208)

Evaluative research, depending as it does for support on the very institutions (both organizational and ideological) that it seeks to assess, characteristically ends up as advocate and spokesperson, an agent for the reigning orthodoxy. The different experimental training and job search interventions were expressions of social efficiency, endorsing the fundamental notions that well-planned and focused programs that entail marginal expenses and fit into the existing context of society are adequate to remedy deep social problems. After all, this is the consensus of government as well as its attendant private philanthropies, notably the Ford Foundation. Indeed, MDRC's constituency contains the pinnacle of contemporary American benevolence and the centers of liberal politics. The actual results of MDRC's experiments, however, challenge these comforting beliefs.

The evaluative studies were unable to establish that the manpower training programs were socially efficient and effective. None of them proved capable of providing marketable skills, long-term benefits for participants, or social benefits, and no evaluation established the causal relationship between the program and the defined outcomes. While the evaluators may have been formally free to select outcome measure, they picked only a narrow range of criteria, perhaps because of political considerations. There was little if any concern with socialization, adequacy, social cohesion, or other long-term impacts on the family, the community, or society. Yet by boosting contrived, positive outcomes, the evaluations created myths of governance—in this case, that relatively inexpensive interventions were capable of producing important social effects.

While this sort of conclusion provides little solace for the poor or working class, it does reinforce the utility of the social sciences for contemporary political orthodoxies. This may not be a very noble role but it does provide some social prestige and it does pay the bills. Still, such a role is problematic for the social sciences. Instead of creating acultural truths for democratic discourse, its evaluations and studies have simply endorsed the symbols of rule.

In point of fact, the manpower training programs probably failed, largely because they lacked sufficient resources to compensate for prior deprivations. They provided neither jobs nor the expensive interventions needed to educate, train, and counsel individuals, or to create appropriate alternative environments. The failure of the training programs marks the degree of failure in more basic preparatory institutions, notably the family and public schooling. Rather than social efficiency, an expensive strategy to achieve a greater parity in the institutional experiences that precede a successful work life may be necessary both to prevent and to remedy social problems.

Why have the primary program evaluations so consistently overstated the value of manpower training programs? Much of the answer lies in the fact that these evaluations are most frequently purchased by the program auspices themselves and he who pays the piper. . . . A number of pointed criticisms of these evaluations appeared in the social science literature but apparently came too late to affect policy. More to the point, public policy has been steadfast in spite of the criticism. These social science "bickers" (as Greenberg and Wiseman call them) have little effect; intellectual debunking only seems valued after the public has made up its mind.

The manpower training programs may be little more than tests of deservingness—a puritan's valuation of election and worth. In this sense, if program participants fail at training and refuse to get a job, they certify their own worthlessness and excuse social neglect. Still, the training programs provided little opportunity to overcome personal, subcultural, or structural obstacles to employment. Their meager provisions were seemingly intended more as a sop to participants and a symbol of charitability in the social dialectics of welfare than as a serious attempt to transmit skills. It takes more than a few months of cursory training to prepare a productive worker. Moreover, the training itself seems cruel and futile unless it leads to employment that can provide a livable wage.

In the end, the impediments to scientifically credible program evaluations may be insurmountable, seriously limiting the possibility of rational policymaking. Yet even while inconclusive, the evaluations of manpower training programs played an important role in social policy. Indeed, the social sciences are seemingly more distinguished for their ceremonial functions in creating and reinforcing social myth than for their rationality.

In addition to manpower training programs, many other personal social services address impediments to work as well as the personal dysfunctions that precipitate welfare dependence and broader social problems. Unfortunately, they have been as ineffective and superficial as manpower training programs. Evaluations of personal social services have been even more accommodating of ideological orthodoxies, more frankly embracing the ceremonial political functions of the social sciences.

6 Personal Social Services and Welfare

Manpower training, as well as the welfare rules designed to promote work and family solidarity, are frequently joined with personal social services, usually some form of counseling. Personal social services that focus on poverty and dependency typically address individual barriers to employment: motivation, criminal and delinquent behaviors, mental and emotional health, family dysfunction, educational deprivations, out-of-wedlock pregnancy, particularly among teenagers, drug and alcohol addiction, school performance, and others. All of these behaviors interrupt successful employment. The mentally ill cannot work; the unmotivated will not work; criminal behaviors are directly antithetical to appropriate work behaviors. Broken, single-parent families, by creating two households where there was one, have been a major source of the increase in poverty over the past few decades. Teenage mothers, lacking appropriate education and training do not have the skills to escape poverty. Substance abuse dramatically curtails work. Poor school performance interrupts education and leads to low wages and unemployment.[1]

The personal social services devoted to these problems have largely followed strategies that either provide substitutes for failed social institutions (such as the family, the school, and the community) or attempt through some form of counseling and psychotherapy to directly induce conforming behaviors, or both. Foster care for children is the classic surrogate service, providing substitute homes and home-like environments for children without adequately supportive natural families. Psychotherapy is the quintessential example of a socially efficient strategy to

---

1. Some personal social services do not directly relate to work—such as care for the chronically ill, many educational and health programs, recreational programs, and so forth. This chapter focuses only on those social services that have been sanctioned largely to remove barriers to employment, that is, personal social services that are at least partially evaluated by the degree to which they affect the employment or employability of their recipients. Nevertheless, the analysis and conclusions of this chapter are equally applicable to most other social services as well.

achieve conforming behavior inexpensively, usually through some process of rational induction. The two strategies are often combined, as in residential care (a home-like surrogate) for disturbed adolescents that provides psychotherapeutic treatment.

Whether social services are provided as entitlements or as discretionary care, they customarily focus on personal adaptation, not on the reform of systemic imperfections. Clearly, both types of personal social services—surrogate care or psychotherapy—justify themselves by serving at least one of three functions—prevention, treatment, and rehabilitation.[2] In pursuing socially efficient solutions for social problems, both types of personal social services narrowly identify the trigger points that precipitate impediments to normal social participation, such as work.

In this way, drug programs either prevent abuse or treat and rehabilitate addicts. While drug rehabilitation programs are humane in themselves, especially if they interrupt addiction, they are more broadly justified in the political discourse as improving social harmony (if not safety) by restoring the addict to a life in the mainstream, notably involving work and economic self-sufficiency. In a similar fashion, child care is a type of surrogate program that is intended to alleviate the responsibility for daily child supervision from able-bodied single parents, and free them up for work. Other personal social services, while providing care that may be satisfying to recipient populations, similarly are justified as efficient methods to achieve more acceptable and conforming social behaviors.

There is an immense range of personal social services focused on employment and dependency. They have constituted the heart of traditional private philanthropy: child and family service agencies; mental health programs; programs to treat addicts, criminals, and juvenile delinquents; programs aimed at the motivations of the poor; educational programs for welfare clients and potential welfare recipients; intensive casework services, child welfare services; family preservation; psychotherapy; and so forth. A variety of federal initiatives, mirrored in state legislation, have provided public support for these efforts and in a large number of cases—notably in child welfare—have overtaken the private sector's efforts. Still, the traditional philanthropic sector has not been eclipsed. Rather, the

---

2. Nevertheless, they could be justified on other grounds, namely equality, without attention to whether they prevent, rehabilitate, or cure. In this sense, the only outcome concern is that recipients be afforded an environment that achieves cultural parity with some predetermined target experience or group. There is a lot to recommend dropping the concern with treatment outcomes and focusing on equality. However, this would also imply dropping an overarching will to provide socially efficient solutions for social problems, an unlikely event.

public sector has frequently provided financial support and subsequently some regulation of their activities.

Social service agencies play out the conflicts between the dominant culture and the needs of the intended recipients. These conflicts arise over the goals of the programs as well as the actual levels and intensity of the interventions themselves, including the conditions under which conforming behaviors are to be achieved. The critical literature of the social services has elaborated the divergent interests between social service agencies and their recipients. The former have frequently been indicted for administering an illegitimate social control (see Epstein 1993a; Piven and Cloward 1993; Polsky 1991), for failing to fulfill the conditions of citizenship for recipients (Smith and Lipsky 1993), and for stigmatizing or asserting the nondeservingness of recipient populations (Gans 1995; Katz 1989). In these ways, the frequent failures of social services are interpreted as political choices that deny sufficient resources to recipients, that neglect underlying social conditions, and that refuse the claims of recipients for social support.

Social services are political compromises in the negotiations among competitive groups over social ascendancy and scarce resources. They fulfill two roles in this political process: first as providing specific measurable outcomes—social service production functions—and second as ceremonies of social values—mythic functions. The mythic function is impelled by the notion of deservingness and relates to social priorities. Deserving groups achieve a sanction for social support; the undeserving receive justifiable neglect or punishment. On the other hand, the production function relates to the quality and success of the services. Without serving a true production function in modifying dysfunctional personal behaviors, the social services are left with only a ceremonial role in the drama of American deservingness.

The American social welfare system has made a number of defining choices in providing services to the poor and nonworking populations. Personal social services are preferred over cash welfare. Rehabilitative programs have undercut structural reform, so that short-term treatment is preferred to prevention. The conservative preference for private sector solutions is resurgent over institutionalized rights to public assistance. The voluntary, charitable impulse is again overtaking professionalized public services. These preferences for socially efficient services are endorsed to the extent to which the services are effective, providing a true production function. Their ceremonial function emerges more clearly in the absence of a demonstrated ability to resolve social and personal problems.

This chapter reviews the experience of the more prominent personal social services in achieving their production functions—particularly relative to the impediments to work participation—and interprets their shortcomings in terms of their ceremonial functions. It evaluates their core interventive strategies as well as a number of the basic implementing programs: psychotherapy and counseling, drug treatment and prevention programs, programs for juvenile delinquents, the constellation of social work interventions (in particular, family preservation services associated with foster care), Head Start, and programs to prevent out-of-wedlock births.[3]

With a few notable exceptions, the literature has confronted neither the general ineffectiveness of social services nor the weakness of the empirical research testing program outcomes. Nevertheless, the detailed empirical research that attempts to define the instrumental role of services in handling social problems provides the fundamental justifications for the provision of social services. While the research appears to focus on the production functions of services, it also forms social attitudes toward both the services and their recipients. Thus, as the rational capacity of the social sciences is undermined by poorly conducted, porous research, their ceremonial function becomes ever more apparent.

PSYCHOTHERAPY

The language of modern discourse relies heavily upon psychological explanations of human behavior, encouraging society to deny expensive structural solutions for its problems. The recourse to psychological explanation runs deeply in the American consciousness, powerfully reinforcing the traditional individualism of the American ethos. Herman points to the field's practitioners as

> ... clinicians who heralded the healthy personality as the basis for
> democracy, insisted that mental health could be mass-produced
> and purchased, and welcomed psychotherapy as a strategy for
> the manufacture of normality. All claimed loyalty to a psychology
> capable of revealing universal laws about human experience,
> personality, social life, and subjectivity. All melded the understanding
> of individual and collective behavior, and in doing so, contributed
> significantly to the characteristic features of the postwar United

---

3. A full treatment of all the personal social services is beyond the capacity of a single chapter. However, the experience of these programs and interventive techniques is largely mirrored throughout the social services.

States. . . . [P]sychological experts have been a critical force in the recent convergence between private and public domains, cultural and political concerns. Joining the comprehension and change of self to the comprehension and change of society was their most enduring legacy. (Herman 1995:12)

This legacy has expressed itself in the contemporary design of the personal social services with their emphasis on psychotherapeutic techniques promising cure, prevention, or rehabilitation. A trained practitioner identifies the specific causes of the aberrant behavior in the experiences of the patient or patient group (typically a family or problem cohort) and then through a variety of relatively inexpensive and socially compatible techniques embarks upon a treatment for the dysfunctional behavior. The psychotherapeutic approach to deviancy exemplifies the engineering logic of the social sciences by promising to resolve deviant behavior in a relatively short period of time, with minimal cost, and without disrupting the customary patterns of social life.

Psychotherapeutic techniques lie at the heart of most personal social services that are justified as efficient solutions for social problems. Psychotherapy, and its use in a variety of counseling approaches, has been employed for social and mental problems as well as serious personal problems, all of which interrupt customary work behavior: drug and alcohol addictions, depression, poor school performance, illegitimacy, delinquency, spousal abuse, child abuse, phobias and other behavioral disorders such as anorexia, bulimia, post-traumatic stress disorder, panic disorders, motivational deficits, and so forth.

The standing of psychotherapy as a modern profession derives from its clinical effectiveness rather than its theoretical elegance. Without proof of its clinical effectiveness, however, the social standing of the field shifts to its mythic role and away from its ability to provide a true production function in treating social and personal problems. In the absence of clinical validation, psychotherapy is reduced to an ethical metaphysics, a series of prescriptions for behavior that reflect social and political preferences and embody the penalties and judgments of modern society. Lacking a true production function, the coherence of scientific psychotherapy and behavioral change becomes supplanted by an elegant, scientistic social sanction: the practitioner becomes priest and judge in a secular religion; therapy becomes blame; diagnosis becomes labeling and stereotypy. Through these ceremonies the programs that provide psychotherapy emerge as brokers between recipient populations and controlling social interests.

The running debate over the effectiveness of psychotherapy was considerably quieted by Smith, Glass, and Miller's (1980) citation classic, *The Benefits of Psychotherapy* (SGM).[4] Earlier reviews of the outcome literature had reached their conclusions either through intuitive summary procedures or through box-score comparisons.[5] Both procedures were seriously marred: the first lacked explicit evaluative criteria and frequently reached idiosyncratic conclusions; the second permitted only a crude tabulation of outcomes. SGM utilized a meta-analytic technique that permitted detailed and adjusted comparisons across studies through an objective, standardized measure—the effect size.

SGM reviewed the entire extant body of the clinical literature to identify the most scientifically credible outcome studies of psychotherapeutic practice. Four hundred and seventy-five passed their methodological screen, conforming with "the acknowledged canons of experimental science," which included control groups, quantitative measures, and quantitative analyses (8):

> All controlled studies of the effectiveness of any form of
> psychotherapy formed the population of interest for this project. . . .
> No form of psychotherapy was excluded if the therapy (1) involved
> clients identified by themselves or others; (2) if the clients sought
> or were referred for treatment; (3) if the treatment or intervention
> was psychological or behavioral; and (4) if the person delivering the
> treatment was identified as a psychotherapist by virtue of training
> or professional interest. (Smith, Glass, and Miller 1980:55–56)

SGM found that psychotherapy was impressively effective. "[T]he average person who would score at the 50th percentile of the untreated control population, could expect to rise to the 80th [in actuality, the 82nd] percentile with respect to that population after receiving psychotherapy" (88). Since the control groups represented the 50th percentile, the average 32 percentage point improvement covered almost two-thirds of the possible range of improvement. Moreover, some of the different psychotherapies appeared to be enormously effective. Patients treated with cognitive therapies were better off than 99 percent of control subjects.

---

4. Prior to SGM, a small critical literature raised questions about the effectiveness of psychotherapy: Eysenck (1952, 1961, 1965), Rachman (1971), Stuart (1970), the early Bergin in Bergin and Garfield (1971), and very few others. Even after SGM, the critical literature in psychotherapy remains very sparse (see, as recent examples, Dawes 1994; Dryden and Feltham 1992; Epstein 1995; Grunbaum 1984; Kline 1988; and Polsky 1991. But even this later body of criticism often exaggerates the effectiveness of psychotherapy perhaps in service to its preferred commentary on the field's inappropriate social role.

5. See Bergin and Garfield (1971 as well as later editions) as an example of the former, and Luborsky, Singer, and Luborsky (1975) as an example of the latter.

188 Personal Social Services and Welfare

Following SGM's seminal study, many meta-analyses appeared that endorsed its findings in specialized areas on the basis of subsequent primary research and reanalyses of SGM's base of research.[6] Yet the logic of SGM's analysis and the subsequent research it generated were deeply flawed, invalidating many of the conclusions. In the end, there has still not been even one evaluation of the outcomes of psychotherapy that is scientifically credible. At best, the outcomes are indeterminate. More probably, psychotherapy is ineffective, while the persistent report of patient deterioration across many studies raises unsettling questions about its harms.

SGM compared the effects of psychotherapy to a variety of nontreatment controls, notably subjects on waiting lists and other similar comparison groups, as well as to placebo controls. Their large finding of about 30 percent improvement emerges from the comparison with nontreatment controls. However, the comparison with placebo controls reduces patient benefits to only about 10 percent since the placebo controls improved about 20 percent on their own. Bergin's conversion to the effectiveness of psychotherapy took place on the insistence that the placebo effect is a true benefit of psychotherapy (Bergin in Bergin and Garfield 1978).

Still, the more reasonable position—especially in light of the field's social ambitions for professional standing—rests on the ability of psychotherapy to add value above structured time activities and the ministrations of the untrained. Indeed, society need not turn to highly trained professionals simply to create supportive settings and a belief in self-healing and cure. Moreover, most of the SGM controls were *not* composed through randomization, and thus the possibility of bias through self-selection, especially among the unmatched comparison groups, and the problem of comparability among the others, remains a serious threat to the credibility of their outcomes.[7]

In spite of their claims to include only rigorous studies, SGM also included analogue studies, those that were not controlled (quasi-experiments that took pre- and post-measures only on an experimental group),

6. See, as examples, Andrews and Harvey (1981); Giblin, Sprenkle, and Sheehan (1985); Landman and Dawes (1982); Shapiro (1985); and Shapiro and Shapiro (1982a,b).

7. Studies frequently advertise for patients. Those who respond are not necessarily typical of the underlying population of concern, having distinguished themselves perhaps by their unusual motivation in seeking treatment. Self-selection is a serious threat to representativeness in these studies. Additionally, many studies recruit their subjects in emergency rooms; without appropriate controls, these studies are rigged for success since the most severely acute patient groups will naturally return to a lower level of distress with the passage of time.

and results that did not reach statistical significance. Strangely, they even criticized more rigorous reviews for imposing

> . . . textbook standards; these methodological rules, learned as dicta in graduate school and regarded as the touchstone of publishable articles in prestigious journals, were applied arbitrarily; for example, note again Rachman's high-handed dismissal on methodological grounds of study after study of psychotherapy outcome. (Smith, Glass, and Miller 1980:38)

SGM's rejection of rigor is particularly puzzling since they themselves (see their chapter 2 in particular) and the field have widely accepted the standard scientific position that the burden of proof for effectiveness rests on the therapist and not on the skeptic. Rachman's (1971) dismissals were occasioned by the routine absence of appropriate controls, particularly randomized controls, that are needed to account for spontaneous remission, seasonality, and maturation. Some conditions may spontaneously cease, while a number of patients may grow out of their problems. In addition, researcher bias itself has been a prominent explanation for many outcomes (Rosenthal and Rubin 1978). Therefore, in order to establish the fact of a therapeutic outcome as well as its enduring value, research requires a methodological rigor that includes randomized placebo controls and other methodological protections, notably blinding, reliable assessment procedures, and follow-up measurement. Even this minimal level of rigor is routinely absent from the primary research and the summary reviews.

Still, a multitude of additional problems cripple the research. Wait-list controls, even if randomized, are not credible since patients may inaccurately report their conditions to maintain eligibility for service. Self-report is also a serious problem. Few independent or behavioral measures are available to assess objectively the outcomes of psychotherapy, while the self-reports of subjects are amenable to a large variety of biases. Moreover, sample sizes are routinely small; researchers evaluate their own patients; interrater reliabilities are low (that is, discrepancies among the judges abound); measurement validity is often impaired; and attrition rates are frequently unacceptably high.

Therefore, the small 10 percent benefit of psychotherapy that SGM substantiate on the basis of placebo comparisons needs to be further discounted by a number of possible biases. Moreover, in a more credible reanalysis of SGM's own data, Prioleau, Murdock, and Brody (1983) shrank SGM's 10 percent benefit to only 6 percent. Modest additional adjustments for bias would push the true means into the area of deterioration. Even more troubling, Rosenthal and Rubin (1978) reported that in the area most closely related to psychotherapy, researcher biases were huge, accounting for a distortion of more than one standard deviation or, in SGM's terms, well over 30 percent.

Furthermore, SGM presented the means of the effect sizes for the different therapies as if they were populations of patients instead of populations of means. In this way, their reported standard deviations are actually standard errors with the effect of exploding tightly organized normal curves into a Wild West of patient outcomes.[8] Thus, not only does the possibility of patient deterioration recur, but the amount of deterioration might well be substantial. In this regard, it is also noteworthy that the literature is created in optimal settings by presumably the best therapists—university-based research that employs accountable professionals, frequently professors in the field. The live conditions of practice might offer a bleaker assessment of psychotherapy. Outside the research setting, patient deterioration may even be a more common occurrence than improvement, resulting from the technical incapacities of psychotherapy as well as malpractice among largely unsupervised, solo practitioners.

The recent base of primary research appears to have improved upon the rigor of SGM's earlier 475 studies.[9] With a greater prevalence of multisite, randomized controls, multiple outcome measures, larger samples, more sophisticated statistical procedures, and the use of multiple judges, the research after SGM seems to have achieved a greater scientific credibility. Meta-analyses based upon this research continue to report large benefits for psychotherapy. However, the many pitfalls of the research continue to vitiate its findings, endorsing deep skepticism of psychotherapeutic interventions.

Such failures, even in the best of the current research, reinforce the conclusion that the effects of psychotherapy are still indeterminate. Possibly the most elaborate and certainly one of the most extensive studies of psychotherapy outcomes provides little grounds for optimism that the field is capable of providing scientifically credible outcome statements.

Elkin et al. (1989), Imber et al. (1990), and Sotsky et al. (1991) report the findings of a large-scale experiment conducted on behalf of the federal government: the National Institute of Mental Health (NIMH) Treatment of Depression Collaborative Research Program (CRP).[10] "Two hundred thirty-nine outpatients with major depressive disorder according to the Research Diagnostic Criteria entered a 16-week multi-center

---

8. See Epstein (1984) for a more detailed discussion of this problem.

9. See Epstein (1995) for a detailed analysis of the psychotherapeutic literature.

10. The description of the CRP is reprinted from Epstein (1995).

clinical trial and were randomly assigned to interpersonal psychotherapy, cognitive-behavior therapy, imipramine with clinical management, or [drug] placebo with clinical management." Interpersonal psychotherapy "focuses on the 'here and now' and relates the patient's depressive condition to a number of areas of interpersonal difficulties: unresolved grief, role transitions, role disputes, and interpersonal deficits" (American Psychiatric Association 1989:1732).

Reporting on the CRP, Imber et al. (1990) conclude that their "predictions about differential treatment effects were not supported in general" (355) by their large-scale comparison of alternative therapies:

> [N]one of the therapies produced clear and consistent effects at the termination of acute treatment on measures related to its theoretical origins. . . . [Nevertheless] most patients seen in this program had a successful course of treatment, regardless of modality. . . . Perhaps the most parsimonious interpretation of our findings is that there are core processes that operate across treatments, overriding differences among techniques, that is, the common factors noted earlier. (Imber et al. 1990:356–7)

Unfortunately their measures were largely based upon self-report; attrition of their samples averaged about 38 percent; interrater reliabilities were variable; and success in treatment was not consistent across many measures. Most notably, no true nontreatment control existed for psychotherapy, and only a drug placebo for imipramine. Moreover, there was a "general lack of significant differences between the psychotherapies" and the drug placebo group (Elkin et al. 1989:978).

The study began with 250 patients. Eleven dropped out before treatment; of the remaining 239 patients, only 155 completed treatment and had complete records. Completion of treatment was defined as attending 75 percent of the sixteen sessions. The researchers created another problem in failing to consider alternative "core processes" that could have produced their findings, namely, the expectancies of the therapists and researchers and the subtle manner in which their positive hopes for treatment success may have encouraged patients to report nonexistent improvements. It is particularly relevant that those patients who received "supportive clinical management," supposedly the least intense of the treatments, fared *better* than the other groups along a variety of scores— most noteworthy, the combined "endogenous" score that measured personal changes—as well as sleep disturbances, appetite changes, psychomotor changes, and so forth. At the end of therapy, 71 percent of the supportive clinical management group did better than the median as compared with only 49 percent of the next most successful group.

If anything, the CRP study suggests that a range of superficial interventions are incapable of producing powerful effects in severely debilitated patients. Sixteen weeks of intermittent discussions, even supplemented by drugs that can directly affect mood, are inadequate to sustain improvements in depressed patients. But the authors did not say this, choosing instead to reaffirm the creed of therapy in spite of their own data and porous research methods.

The CRP also reported that

> . . . the results of this collaborative clinical treatment trial comparing the efficacy of two specific forms of psychotherapy with active and placebo pharmacotherapy demonstrate the relevance of patient characteristics for the prediction of outcome from an episode of major depressive disorder. (Sotsky et al. 1991:1004)

However, the design problems of the study, especially attrition, will not sustain this conclusion. The huge amount of attrition raises the likelihood that subjects self-screened themselves for the therapy most consistent with their own styles. Rather than predicting cure, patient characteristics may have predicted the most favored type of ceremony for their own natural remission.

An occasional note of skepticism creeps into the Elkin et al. (1989) report:

> Further work will be directed toward understanding the therapeutic properties of the PLA-CM condition in the study. The present findings do raise the possibility that some type of minimal supportive therapy in the hands of an experienced practitioner may be sufficient to bring about a significant reduction of depressive symptoms (at least in the short run) for the less severely depressed patients. The findings, if replicated, also raise questions regarding the need of antidepressant medication or for highly specified forms of psychotherapy for the resolution of the depressive episode in these patients. (Elkin et al. 1989:979)

Perhaps, too, all the conditions of treatment and their "core processes," superficial as they were, constituted placebo care. Instead of pursuing the obvious inability of short-term therapy to provide gains over a nontreatment control, Elkin et al. (1989) pressed to reinterpret the nontreatment control as true treatment in an attempt to present the findings as universally effective. It is also noteworthy that McLean and Taylor (1992) pointedly fail to corroborate the Elkin et al. (1989) reanalysis.

In spite of a few tortured acknowledgments to skepticism, the CRP reports adopted a pervasive tone of buoyant optimism, while their analyses and reanalyses strained to provide evidence of effectiveness. Their hopeful science was not a private venture, however. It was funded and apparently sanctioned by the NIMH, expressing not simply a sectarian bias for positive findings but a deeper social demand, delivered through the federal government, for socially efficient myths, in this case that relatively inexpensive care provides substantial gains against serious depression. The demand for results favoring the profession and the expectations of government for politically viable findings are subtly transmitted through funding decisions. Even the peer review process, whether blind or conscious of authorship, that determines which research proposals are funded is open to a variety of institutional, methodological, and reputational biases. It is difficult to avoid the conclusion that this large experiment in treating severe depression became a project in producing compatible findings, not one that provided scientific scrutiny of psychotherapy's clinical effectiveness.

The remainder of the literature testing depression outcomes made similar positive claims for psychotherapy, testifying to the effectiveness of a variety of treatments in curing depression and related mood disorders, and suffered from similar errors. In spite of the fact that the length of therapy seems to have declined over the past few decades—with short-term intervention the treatment of choice and the preference of managed-care insurers—outcomes are as rosy now as they were before SGM. Nevertheless, the short-term interventions appear to be so superficial and their controls so inadequate that natural remission—depression resolving naturally over time—seems as likely a cure as Thompson, Gallagher, and Breckenridge's (1987) twenty sessions of bibliotherapy, Nezu and Perri's (1989) ten sessions of problem-solving therapy, McLean and Hakstian's (1990) ten-week course of nondirective psychotherapy and relaxation therapy, or Lewinsohn et al.'s (1990) fourteen-session Coping with Depression course.

The other outcome research is routinely less credible: smaller samples, more biased measurement, less representative subjects, and so forth. Butler et al. (1991) and Marchione et al. (1987) fail to prove that psychotherapy is effective against agoraphobia and anxiety; Brom, Kleber, and Defares (1989) cannot sustain the ability of three different therapies to treat post-traumatic stress disorder; Kazdin et al. (1989) fail to provide evidence that psychotherapy is effective with children; neither Woody, McLellan, and Luborsky (1987) nor Miller (1980) proves that psychotherapy is effective with substance abusers; Hall and Crisp (1987) fail with anorexia nervosa, Mitchell et al. (1990) with bulimia, and Alexander et al. (1989) with sexual abuse. Culturally sensitive practice is patronizing and ineffective (Malgady, Rogler, and Costantino 1990; Szapocznik et al. 1989). The family therapy research is even weaker than mainstream psychotherapy research, still apparently glued to qualitative case studies for testimonials to its effectiveness. Neither psychological functioning, nor psychosocial adaptation, let alone work behavior, appears to improve as a result of psychotherapy.[11]

The ineffectiveness of psychotherapy is not particularly surprising. It fails to compensate for the deprivations of the basic culture, particularly the absence of adequate socialization. Rational induction and philosophic reflection seem to be poor substitutes for nurturing environments and policy attention to those in need. Indeed, by opening emotional wounds and questioning cherished albeit dysfunctional behaviors, psychotherapy may exacerbate personal problems. If anything, the history of psychotherapy indicts superficial interventions, recalling the need for attention to underlying structural conditions. Yet the field endures even without any demonstrable effectiveness in handling the pathology of socialization.

Psychotherapy's powerful mythic role may explain its persistence. The myth is best understood as a drama of social sanction that underscores individual responsibility and the desirability of a laissez-faire social policy. Psychotherapy provides symbolic comfort that socially efficient solutions are plausible. Perhaps for the same reason—the triumph of ceremony over substance—psychotherapy remains the preferable tech-

---

11. The most recent defense of psychotherapy, the Seligman (1995) study, is rebarbative, falling back on weak methods to nourish happy conclusions. In spite of its technical report in the *American Psychologist* and its popular presentation in *Consumers Reports* (1995), it speaks more to the need for unquestioning belief in psychotherapy than any objective ability of the field to treat emotional and mental problems. Seligman attaches questions about the use of psychotherapy to the *Consumer Reports'* annual car survey, which is sent to 180,000 subscribers to that magazine. Twenty-two thousand responded of whom 7,000 responded to the mental health questions. Of these 7,000, about 2,900 saw a mental health professional. In other words, the survey's response rate was only about 12 percent, small enough to disregard any finding. Looked at another way, if 10 percent of the American public sees some sort of mental health professional each year, then the survey only received responses from about 16 percent of the target group (2,900 divided by 18,000). Moreover, respondents were decidedly not like the customary psychotherapy patient, being older, wealthier, and far more stable. Yet none of these serious problems bridle Seligman's enthusiasm: "The [*Consumer Reports*] study then is to be taken seriously—not only for its results and its credible source, but for its method. It is large scale; it samples treatment as it is actually delivered in the field; it samples without obvious bias those who seek out treatment . . ." (Seligman 1995:974).

nique in many social work services, resolving the paradox of professional longevity without the ability to fulfill basic service promises (Leiby 1978; Lubove 1965).

SOCIAL WORK

Social work services, defined more by the field's activities than by any elegance of theory, constitute the largest and most intense array of personal social services. Cutting across problems in education, health, mental health, and social adjustment, social work services focus on an enormous variety of different populations—children, adolescents, adults, and the aged. While psychotherapy has been the "nuclear" intervention of social work for decades, the field still embraces a large number of services constructed around surrogate provisions, particularly child foster care, adoption, and protective services as well as institutional care for a variety of different groups (Lubove 1965).

Largely reflecting the broad political insistence on social efficiency, the field has adhered to the position that minimal and personal (largely psychotherapeutic) interventions are adequate to resolve social problems. The social work community in step with the American public has increasingly rejected structural theories of social problems as well as services designed to provide more equal environments for deprived populations. The demise of redistributional impulses since the 1960s and the rise of conservative politics have reflected this refusal to attend to underlying inequities in American society. Paradoxically, the field of social work still strains to maintain that it performs an advocacy role on behalf of deprived populations.

In light of the inability of the field's research to demonstrate the effectiveness of its services, this advocacy emerges as a patronizing ritual of noblesse oblige—the insistence by dominant groups that they know best the interests of the deprived even while they reap the tax benefits of minimal public provisions.[12] Indeed, without clinical verification of its production function in social services, professional social work is left with deviance management—a role that institutionalizes prevailing social interests.

---

12. This sort of self-deception extends to calling service recipients "clients" as if they had engaged the allegiance of their social workers in the manner of a lawyer's relationship with her clients or of a doctor's relationship with her patients or of a divine's relationship with her flock. In distinction, a social worker's relationship with his "client" is intruded upon far more than the medical, pastoral, or legal relationship.

Claims for the field's effectiveness have been examined in a series of summary reviews. Infrequently these reviews employ meta-analyses and box scores; more frequently, they simply summarize the more credible primary research. Disputes over scientific credibility in social work have pressed the boundaries of the common understanding in the social sciences. A preference for a qualitative, "practical" epistemology, following the fashion of postmodernism, has reemerged in social work.[13] Heineman (1981) has even insisted that simple professional wisdom provides adequate grounds for certifying effectiveness. Nevertheless, "practical" epistemologies that are customarily partnered with claims for the efficacy of postmodern (or perhaps New Wave) psychotherapeutic interventions have been profoundly rejected by others.[14]

Yet Wootton's (1959) early skepticism toward the effectiveness of social work has not been dispelled in spite of the buoyant reviews of the field's more rigorous outcome studies. To the contrary, attention to that base of research forces the conclusion that even the best of the field's outcome evaluations employ porous methods that routinely transmit their biases. Moreover, studies frequently report ineffectiveness. If anything, the consistent failure of social work to document any success indicts the basic assumptions of social efficiency itself. Minimal, superficial, under-funded, and short-term personal services are patently unable to compensate for the underlying deprivations of American institutions, notably the family, or to remedy embedded social problems, whether directly or indirectly related to work. These failures of service and scholarship pull understanding of the field back toward its ceremonial functions. Indeed, without credible scientific methodologies, even the best of the field's research adds little more than ornamentation to the already baroque rhetoric of social dialectics.

In 1981, Fischer declared the scientific revolution in social work. On the basis of "procedures of demonstrated effectiveness" (meaning behavioral interventions) and "new processes of knowledge development" (referring to single subject designs) Fischer concluded that social work was achieving a true professional maturity, a giant Kuhnian step of progress:

> In essence the practice of social work appears to be moving away
> from the use of vaguely defined, invalidated and haphazardly or
> uncritically derived knowledge for practice. In its most salient
> characteristics, the paradigm shift appears to involve a movement

13. See, as examples, Bloom and Fischer (1982); Heineman Pieper (1989); and Proctor (1990), and for a discussion of them see Epstein (1993b).

14. See Epstein (1993b) and Wakefield's (1993a,b) articles on Heineman Pieper and Heineman (1990) and his response to critics.

toward more systematic, rational, empirically oriented development and use of knowledge for practice. For want of a better phrase, this could be termed as movement toward *scientifically based practice* in social work. . . . [S]ocial workers are increasingly explicating new approaches that are systematic, clear, and oriented to both the rigors of research evidence and the realities of practice. (Fischer 1981:200)

Curiously this sudden advance had taken place only eight years after Fischer (1973) reviewed all the credible outcome studies of casework's effectiveness—eleven studies—and concluded that "at present, lack of evidence of the effectiveness of professional casework is the rule rather than the exception" (19). He even found evidence of harm.

Fischer's 1973 conclusions reinforce a small, earlier number of unusually thorough and thoughtful reviews. Anticipating both Rossi's (as cited in Moynihan 1996) bleak assessment of social services and Martinson's (1974) conclusion that nothing works in corrections, Segal (1972) could find "no study of outcome with respect to social work therapeutic interventions with both an adequate control group design and positive results" (3).

On her part, Wootton (1959), a magistrate and Fabian socialist, wrote an elegant but devastating critique of socially efficient interventions arguing for minimal structural solutions to social problems. She reviewed the entire body of psychiatric, psychological, and social work literature in pressing toward the conclusion that solutions based upon reforming the individual instead of social institutions were doomed. Wootton (1959) indicted the body of contemporary knowledge as a transmittal of the social bias to treat "the infected individual rather than to eliminate the infection from the environment" (326).

Ironically, Wootton's conclusions undercut the Fabian's Pygmalion minimalism as well as social work's attention to personal deviance:

By tracing the springs of anti-social behavior to the individual rather than to his social environment, we are, after all, only following what has long proved itself to be the path of least resistance; for, difficult as it is to cope with the mishaps of individual men and women, the institutions in which they enchain themselves are even more obdurate still. Conditions which favor pathological developments, either in the medical or in the social sense, are notoriously awkward to deal with. . . . Always it is easier to put up a clinic than to pull down a slum, and always it is tempting to treat the unequal opportunities of the slum and of the privileged neighborhoods as part of the order of nature. If only for these reasons, theories which direct attention away from social conditions towards the deficiencies of individual personality are bound to enjoy a considerable practical advantage. They are comfortable. (Wootton 1959:329)

Wood (1978) continued the skeptical tradition with her review of twenty-two credible outcome studies refusing to accept their implications. Her review covered social work services for criminals and delinquents, the aged, the poor, and children as well as the conditions of the interventions themselves (that is, short term versus long term). Like earlier summaries, she found methodological flaws in the base of the research and numerous studies concluding that social work was not effective. However, instead of embracing the conclusions of Segal, Fischer, and Wootton that superficial interventions targeted on the individual's deviance were fundamentally flawed, Wood (1978) preferred the comforting alternative of "appropriate treatment." She claimed that "quality practice" achieved through a rigorous and rational problem-solving approach was effective. Thus, services for the poor would be successful if social workers "accurately define the problems in the case, what is causing them, and what can realistically be done about them within the limits of available time and services" (446). She ignored the issue of resources—that ineffectiveness was the product of poorly funded services and that no amount of improvement in efficiency at such meager levels of funding could compensate for structural inadequacies.

The studies included in the skeptical reviews by Segal, Fischer, Wootton, and Wood covered social work's role in counseling as well as public service. The typical intervention involved an interchange between a recipient and a trained social worker. That interchange was usually verbal and sporadic, customarily involving no more than a few hours of face-to-face contact each week. Even the interventions of so-called "intensive casework" rarely involved more attention and rarely included the provision of generous amounts of concrete care, such as child care, food, cash, housing, employment, and other material supports for daily living. Institutional care was rarely evaluated. In most cases, the interventions involved motivational types of interventions and were concerned with innovations in interventive techniques.

The contemporary social work literature has reviewed similar services. The field has found great relief in Fischer's (1981) scientific revolution, going on to produce primary studies and reviews of those studies that endorse a perception of its growing effectiveness. Reid and Hanrahan (1982) identified twenty-two studies between 1973 and 1979 that met their inclusion criteria: random assignment of subjects to a control and an experiment condition and interventions by social workers with the goal of improving the recipient's social functioning. In contrast with earlier reviews, these authors appeared to document social work's effectiveness:

> All but two or three of the twenty-two studies yielded findings that could on balance be regarded as positive. . . . [L]ess than a third of the (Wood) studies produced findings that could on the whole be regarded as positive. . . . Also in marked contrast to the earlier experiments, no recent study that involved a comparison between treated and untreated groups failed to yield at least some evidence of the positive effects of social work intervention. The findings of the recent experiments are grounds for optimism, but they are no cause for complacence. (Reid and Hanrahan 1982:331)

Shortly afterward, Rubin (1985) screened the entire social work literature between 1978 and 1983—probably more than 6,500 articles—and identified only thirteen studies that met his methodological inclusion criteria. He claimed that these thirteen studies further supported Reid and Hanrahan's (1982) growing optimism. Other recent reviews (see Sheldon 1986; Thomlison 1984; Videka-Sherman 1988) and the vast majority of the contemporary experimental literature (Epstein 1993a) further endorse the field's sense of its own efficacy.

Yet all of the studies after Fischer (1981) are as flawed as their predecessors, stepping into the same methodological puddles while boosting interventions that are as inadequately funded and superficial. Indeed, the earlier and later studies are so similar in their deficiencies that the differing conclusions of the reviews regarding social work's effectiveness might be more easily attributed to the mood of the times than to any objective evidence. In a period that questioned authority, institutional social work produced skeptical reviews, and, in a time of orthodoxy, the field is producing comfortable reassurances.

A close reading of the base of studies themselves endorse none of the optimism of the summary reviews. To the contrary, they undercut any claim to either methodological sophistication or to efficacy. Fischer's (1973) happy conclusions about behavior therapy and a few other areas of social work that preceded his 1981 epiphany were largely drawn from single-subject experiments. However, these uncontrolled experiments routinely failed to control for natural remission, maturation, seasonality, or research biases. His other conclusions rely on the same sorry base of research. Indeed, the sea change that Fischer claims for the role of science in social work was less the product of his literature review than his own intuition, inspired by "material presented at social work conferences, from the literature and from less concrete sources of evidence such as the new 'spirit' or 'world view' that seems to be emerging among many social workers" (Fischer 1981:199).

Reid and Hanrahan's (1982) base of twenty-two studies contained fifteen with very small samples—twenty-five subjects or fewer. Moreover, many of the studies reported findings that were far more ambiguous and far less optimistic than Reid and Hanrahan acknowledged. Many of the studies violated randomization, contained noncomparable groups, employed biased reporters and unreliable instruments, failed to take follow-up measures, and seriously violated blinding.

Only one of the seven studies that Rubin (1985) claimed to be methodologically sound was actually credible. And even this study, a gem by Stein and Test (1980), contained serious problems—questionably representative samples and a unique demonstration situation—that undercut its value.

The current literature in social work, perhaps best exemplified by the studies that test the outcomes of family preservation programs, is similarly flawed. It tends toward optimism and weak methodologies. However, the failure of the most credible of this research—Schuerman, Rzepnicki, and Littell (1994)—to adequately assess outcomes raises serious questions about the role of the social sciences in the policymaking process. Effectiveness and proof in social work as well as in the welfare debate are at best indeterminate.

Codified into federal law in 1980, family preservation services are the latest in a long tradition of interventions intended to prevent the problems that seem to attend family dissolution—poverty, dependency, child abuse, and neglect. The family preservation strategy was specifically developed in acknowledgement of the severe problems of the American foster care system. Child foster care has been routinely condemned for its inability to either place children in decent environments or to handle the results of their abuse and neglect (Barth et al. 1994; Costin, Karger, and Stoesz 1996; Lindsey 1994; Pelton 1989). Compared with other American children, foster children are routinely reported to engage in more criminal activity, to be poorer, to attain less formal education, to suffer greater problems with drugs and alcohol, to be sicker and more emotionally disturbed, and ultimately, through all of these problems, to work less and at lower-paying jobs (Cox and Cox 1984; Kavaler and Swire 1983; Rowe et al. 1984; Thrope 1980). By repairing families at imminent risk of dissolution, family preservation promises to short-circuit the horrors of the foster care system as well as poverty itself.

Family preservation, initially modeled on the Homebuilders Program, recalls many of the intensive casework interventions as well as short-term therapy. Although the programs vary considerably from state to state, family preservation is customarily provided for less than one year and optimally for less than six months; it utilizes case managers, usually social workers, to sort through the family's problems. The case managers, who tend to work intensively on relatively small caseloads, have access to a great variety of social services. Moreover, such services are family-centered as opposed to child-centered, crisis-oriented, home-based, and community-oriented.

Family preservation has stimulated a sizable pool of outcome studies.[15] While many reported that family preservation produces large, positive effects, their credibility is vitiated by a host of methodological problems involving sampling, bias, reporting errors, comparison groups, and others. In contrast, the most credible studies, employing randomized designs and large samples, reported small and usually insignificant effects. The Illinois experiment, Families First, reported by Schuerman, Rzepnicki, and Littell (1994) is the most carefully conducted and comprehensive of these studies. Indeed, this evaluation compares favorably with the most sophisticated experiments ever conducted in the social sciences (including the NIT experiments and the MDRC studies). Yet, like the others, Families First failed to provide credible policy information, perhaps transmitting the preferences of its skeptical authors in the same manner that the rosier family preservation research has transmitted the biases of their credulous program advocates.

Putting Families First (PFF), the evaluative enterprise and not the service providers themselves, set out to test whether family preservation services in Illinois produced better outcomes than the customary services provided through the Illinois Department of Child and Family Services (DCFS). In pursuit of a scientifically credible study, PFF incorporated a classical, prospective experimental design: large samples, random selection and random assignment, multiple sites, multiple measures, follow-up, neutral measurement, and so forth. Service recipients and applicants were randomized either to the experimental condition in which family preservation services were provided or to the DCFS control at a variety of different sites throughout Illinois.

PFF's services were similar to many other family preservation programs. They were targeted on families at imminent risk of dissolution (the children being placed in foster care), the theory of the services being that early and intensive intervention could lower the need for protective

15. For recent examples, see Feldman (1991); McDonald and Associates (1990); Meezan and McCroskey (1993); Pecora, Fraser, and Haapala (1991); and Schwartz, AuClaire, and Harris (1991).

and foster care services. This was a broadly popular idea across the political spectrum: conservatives would be satisfied with lower public costs and liberals with improved outcomes. PFF's experimental families received a median of 108 days of service, considerably more than the ninety days that were originally planned. "There is substantial evidence that the Family First program provided both a wider range and far more intensive service [to experimentals] than cases in the regular service group" (Schuerman, Rzepnicki, and Littell 1994:109). Workers reported that the average experimental recipient received 3.8 concrete services and 3.2 counseling services while controls received only 0.8 and 0.8, respectively. The cost per experimental case averaged close to $4,000.[16]

In tribute to Rossi's pessimism, PFF failed to report any significant difference in placement rates between experimental and control groups. There was even a curious, although not statistically significant, rise in placement rates among those who received family preservation services. The authors found

> . . . little evidence that the program affects the risk of placement, subsequent maltreatment, or case closing and some evidence that the program may be related to short-term progress on case objectives. However, these results must be viewed in the context of considerable variation among sites and variations in outcomes that are due to characteristics of cases and the services provided to them.
> (Schuerman, Rzepnicki, and Littell 1994:188)

In addition, PFF seemed to produce a "net widening effect" through which "more families become involved in the public system than would have without the program" (Schuerman, Rzepnicki, and Littell 1994: 23). Moreover, the attentive case managers accounted for a dramatic increase in services for their caseloads. But once again, these services did not appear to assure any improved outcomes. By further reinforcing two other large randomized studies that also failed to find positive outcomes (Meezan and McCroskey 1993; McDonald and Associates 1990), PFF seems to dampen enthusiasms for family preservation. Yet its many methodological imperfections, especially taken in context of the mistargeting of the family preservation services themselves, impede any conclusion.

---

16. The authors have not evaluated the cost material. This is an estimate based upon a phone discussion with Rzepnicki. The true cost differential is also difficult to estimate since no assessment was made of the costs of customary DCFS services during the experiment. Still, the amount spent on PFF experimentals recalls the amounts spent on other intensive casework programs.

In the first instance, the predictors of imminent risk are imprecise. As a result, PFF's services appear to have been mistargeted. In other words, family preservation was not fairly tested on its intended target group. Yet even while perceiving this problem early in the evaluative process, the researchers refused to abort the experiment.

Second, the experiment bypassed randomization for 24 percent of its subjects: 7 percent due to court orders and 16 percent at the discretion of caseworkers. While none of these cases (those that did receive the services) was included in the analyses, their exclusion compromises the representativeness of the samples. Indeed, the exclusions may account for the poorly targeted samples. Moreover, the fact that these exclusions did no better than any other group raises the troubling possibility that family preservation, acknowledged as "intrusive," may exacerbate family problems.

Third, the study is marred by many measurement problems. PFF's outcome instruments never demonstrated acceptable levels of reliability. The authors report that "evaluations of family preservation will continue to make use of measures of uncertain reliability, validity, and sensitivity" (Schuerman, Rzepnicki, and Littell 1994:212–3). Further, methods to gather data varied between the experimental and control groups. Moreover, the interviews with the experimental families were conducted by different groups of interviewers presumably with different interviewing skills; the early interviewers were relatively inexperienced and untrained while the later interviewers were professionals. In this way, the outcomes of the interventions may reflect the shifting attitudes and skills of the interviewers more than actual changes in target families.

Fourth, the treatment integrity of the family preservation intervention is suspect. PFF failed to independently check the actual receipt of services, relying on the reports of workers to measure the amounts and kinds of services. Fifth, neither interviewers nor subjects were blind to their assignment. Sixth, the fundamental outcome measure of the experiment, foster care placement rates, may have been an inappropriate measure of the true impact of the services; it may also have been an artifact of the experiment, an instance of Heckman's experimentation bias, where the intense surveillance of the experimental condition temporarily suppressed the actual family behaviors leading to placement, while the superficial surveillance of the control condition failed to pick up abuses. In any event, family dissolution is frequently desirable to protect the child; deferring placement may only serve the short-term interests of taxpayers. Still, this remains speculative in light of the poor targeting of intervention.

Finally, PFF faces a debilitating demonstration problem in that the experiment enjoyed unusual worker motivation, intense surveillance by researchers, and creamed clients. Its experience may be unrepresentative of live service conditions, actual clients, or prevailing worker behaviors.

In the end, PFF emerges as an unreliable study whose outcomes are at best indeterminate. Yet the authors pushed on to general recommendations about the American child welfare system that appear compatible with contemporary political tastes:

> The expansion of the purview of the child welfare system that has occurred in the last few decades should be stopped and reversed. This requires that lines be carefully drawn between our aspirations and what can be reasonably expected. . . . The state cannot accept responsibility for the optimal development of all children. Nor should it even endeavor to assure the "well-being" of all children given the impossibility of achieving that goal, even if well-being could be adequately defined and measured. . . . Emotional harms can, of course, have serious effects on the child, on the development of services to help parents better relate to their children. But these services should be voluntary, outside the abuse and neglect response system. (Schuerman, Rzepnicki, and Littell 1994:245)

However, the research never established "reasonable expectations" nor in any way measured the desirability of state action. The authors offer triage and targeting efficiency, which may be near impossibilities, by way of arguing for a limited state role, and remain silent on the broader concern for the seemingly entrenched problems of American poverty and institutional neglect. Nevertheless, the authority for this partisan statement is not drawn from the research.

In light of the very minimal interventions of family preservation—its intensity is apparent only in relation to the customary neglect of families—PFF established little more than the probability that prior institutional and social deprivation exceeds the corrective capacities of intensive casework. The personal service approach to social problems may be inadequate to compensate for the structural problems and growing institutional inequalities of American life. The failure of family preservation services suggests that case management, even under optimal conditions when a variety of superficial treatment services are available (not the common experience), may still be ineffective.

More than any other evaluation of personal social services, PFF approximated rigorous research, conforming with Rossi's (1991) call for randomized experimentation. The authors of PFF were unusually forthcoming in defining their methodological problems, but this clarity does not shift the burden of proof from their shoulders. As a result, the policy arena is deprived of credible information about the impacts of family preservation services, except for the general observation that, whoever the recipients and whatever their needs, intensive casework appears to be ineffective.

The deepest criticisms of social work seem to be supported by its clinical record. A self-righteousness suffuses the field, in which its interventions serve the normalizing interests of the society. Yet social work services do not appear to promote either emotional self-actualization or the desires of the nation to return the idle to work. Services are generally ineffective even by the weakest criteria. Family preservation does not preserve families.

If anything, social work's interventions provide a mild surveillance of deviant populations, which may retard their inclinations to harm. The state of research is, in the manner of Wootton's (1959) British restraint, "unfortunate." Horowitz's (1990) nightmare experience with social workers may be common. The field's professional absorption with psychotherapy has crowded out concern with the deeper problems of deprivation that affect many tens of millions of Americans, failing to provide either effective services or a voice on their behalf.

The skeptical tradition in social work and the social services, small as it is—Segal, the early Fischer, Cloward and Piven, Cloward and Epstein, Wootton, Epstein, Polsky, Smith and Lipsky, and a few others—draws considerable support from the near-uniform failure of the field's intellectual life to credibly identify the benefits of services or to acknowledge their weakness. After decades of insubstantial research, the failure of advocates to defend the value of their programs endorses the skeptic's prudent surmise that social work is ineffective. Nevertheless, social work paradoxically continues to be sustained. Its acceptance seems to be based more on its symbolic representation of social efficiency than on any production function of cure, prevention, or rehabilitation.

DRUG AND ALCOHOL TREATMENT

Drug and alcohol treatment programs, customarily involving some form of counseling or psychotherapy, epitomize the frequent preference for medical auspices to treat social problems. Viewed as a medical disease, addiction offers the hope that a socially compatible clinical cure can be applied conveniently and inexpensively. But as a reflection of social imperfections that impel people to escape from reality, addiction threatens America's complacent belief in its social success. As if to affirm civic faith in the exceptionalism of American society, the literature plangently reports hopeful leads from the battlefronts of the War on Drugs.

Unfortunately, the history of addiction treatment and prevention programs is uniformly bleak. Neither the outcomes of the interventions nor the quality of addiction research endorse the wisdom of a clinical medical approach to social problems. The closest approximations of cure—such as methadone treatment for heroine addiction—are routinely ineffective and entail ancillary social costs, notably neglect of the problem itself.

The principal evaluations of addiction programs have been funded through a variety of federal agencies: National Institute on Drug Abuse (NIDA), National Institute on Mental Health, Office of Substance Abuse Prevention, Office of National Drug Control Policy, and others. Yet all of these agencies, along with a number of private funding sources, have failed to uncover any credible clinical approach to addiction (which is not to suggest that any prevention program whether dealing with "supply" or "demand" has provided any benefit either). Indeed, they probably do no better than acupuncture, meditation, and exercise, reasonable candidates for treatment placebos. Nevertheless, all of the public agencies have produced volumes of claims that a variety of approaches are successful, raising not simply the issue of professional misfeasance but also the problem of government propaganda.

Two large data sets—Drug Abuse Reporting Program (DARP) and Treatment Outcome Prospective Study (TOPS)—both funded by the federal government purported to evaluate the outcomes of treatment. DARP collected reports on approximately 44,000 addicts who entered treatment from 1969 to 1973. Texas Christian University conducted this enormous data collection activity on contract with NIDA. Sells and Simpson (1979) concluded that

> the gross outcome results . . . showed substantial reductions of drug use and criminality during all treatments and smaller but statistically significant improvements on other criteria as (productive activities, employment, beer and wine consumption). Overall, methadone maintenance showed more effects than other types, particularly no opioid use and criminality. (Sells and Simpson 1979:318)

Yet the reports were filed with DARP by the drug treatment programs themselves, not by neutral evaluators. Moreover, an immense amount of data was lost. Due to patient noncompliance and a variety of other "substantive" factors, the original 44,000 reports resulted in only 28,000 research files. Also, very few patients completed treatment: 14 percent of youth, 15 percent of those in therapeutic communities, and less than 30 percent in all other programs. Of greater concern, the follow-up interviews did not routinely include any laboratory tests—neither urinalysis nor blood checks—and the reports relied upon the addicts themselves, a notoriously unreliable source of information. In addition, patients were not randomized to treatment and control groups, nor were they randomly selected from among the addict population, nor were participating programs randomly chosen from among the pool of all drug treatment programs. In spite of these large potential biases, treatment reportedly achieved "substantial reductions" in addictive behaviors. A far more accurate summary of the findings might conclude that no treatment gains were demonstrated in spite of biased selection and measurement procedures and enormous amounts of attrition, customarily denoting treatment failure.

TOPS, collecting data from 1979 to 1981, fell into many of the same pitfalls. Predictably it reported that drug-related problems decreased during treatment. However, it suffered enormous attrition; its follow-up evaluations did not include laboratory corroboration of patient self-reports; it failed to employ a randomized design; and it failed to assure that its study population was representative of the underlying addict population.

A variety of other government and government-funded agents published reports of programmatic success (Amatetti 1989; Beschner and Friedman 1979; Friedman and Beschner 1985; Gerstein and Harwood 1990). All put a cheerful face on failure. They relied on case studies, enthusiastic panel reports, optimistic research that was not screened through a peer review process, inaccurate data (frequently from DARP and TOPS), and poorly conducted research. Indeed, the reports are more budget justifications for federal agencies than serious program evaluations.

More recent studies fared as poorly; their analyses are uniformly suspect. Nirenberg and Maisto (1987) report that methadone maintenance is successful with heroine addicts. Methadone permits treated addicts to lead a relatively normal life and to work while addicted. However, more than 60 percent of those on methadone abuse other drugs; in addition, methadone and associated drugs (naltrexone and others) produce a number of physiological side-effects. The small number of successful methadone patients is customarily older, and age itself is a frequent predictor of success in all drug treatment programs. The host of methadone studies have routinely failed to separate out the factors that contribute to success. Indeed, it is not clear that methadone, an addictive substance itself, increases cure rates over natural remission.

Dolan et al. (1985), Hawkins (1988), Magura, Casriel, and Goldsmith (1987), McAuliffe (1990), and Szapocznik et al. (1983)—a sampling of the best of the contemporary research—also fail to provide any credible evidence that drug treatment programs are successful. Most programs utilize some form of counseling after inpatient detoxification. Most report success, although limited; some report failure. All rely upon laboratory verification. Yet, in the end, they distort measures, fail to provide reasonable follow-up data, suffer high attrition rates, and employ unreliable and frequently irrelevant measures. In contrast with Platt, Husband, and Taube's (1990–91) compliant endorsement of treatment, McLelland et al. (1994) cast great doubt on the success of treatment programs, suggesting that patient characteristics and their degree of substance abuse (not the treatment services they receive) are the greatest predictor of recovery.

The alcohol treatment literature is as flawed as the drug treatment literature. Not only is it weak, but Miller and Heather (1986) conclude that "the list of elements that are typically included in alcoholism treatment in the United States . . . evidenced a commonality: virtually all of them lacked adequate scientific evidence of effectiveness" (122). They apply a rigorous and skeptical eye to traditional American interventions—Alcoholics Anonymous, alcoholism education, confrontation, disulfiram, group therapy, and individual counseling—finding no credible evidence of their success. Littrell (1991) corroborates this conclusion in her exhaustive study of alcoholism: "studies in which alcoholics are observed over 20 years or life time intervals suggest that those in the treated group fail to display higher rates of sobriety than those in the untreated group" (169).

Miller and Heather (1986) identify a series of interventions based upon both psychotherapy and behavioral interventions that they claim are successful: aversion therapies, behavioral self-control training, community reinforcement, marital and family therapy, social skills training, and stress management. They even recommend a differential approach to treatment, matching appropriate patients with appropriate treatments. Yet the outcome literature of these interventions, covered in part in the previous discussion of psychotherapy, is as flawed as those that they disparage. Moreover, in contrast with the availability of objective clinical tests of drug use, alcohol treatment studies must rely more on subjective reports from patients and their collaterals.

Alcoholism remains a problem and treatment is a very uncertain enterprise. Cure when it occurs, or better said, remission when it occurs, may be more a result of maturity, social situation, the extent of prior alcohol abuse, genetics, and other factors than the alcohol treatment program itself. Yet, it is clear that the literature has failed to separate the factors and provide credible estimates of the power of the interventions.

Even more clearly than with the other personal social services, the substance abuse literature appears to be the victim of social hope. Especially in light of the enormous and popular desire for an answer to addiction, the public sector is pressed to demonstrate at least some progress. The federal government through its tendentiously funded research has produced ephemeral evidence of victories over drug abuse. Social science has met this political need with convenient research.

JUVENILE DELINQUENCY

In 1974, Martinson published the conclusion that "nothing works" in corrections. On the basis of an exhaustive review of the best research—231 minimally acceptable studies that appeared between 1945 and 1965 (Lipton, Martinson, and Wilks 1975), he argued that

> *With few and isolated exceptions, the rehabilitative efforts that have been reported so far have had no appreciable effect on recidivism.* Studies that have been done since our summary was completed (i. e., after 1967) do not present any major grounds for altering the original conclusion. (Martinson 1974:25; emphasis in the original)

Martinson also commented sourly on the quality of the research. Like Wootton (1959), he was disturbed by the absence of methodological protections against research bias—the expectancy effects of "optimists" that distort findings.

Martinson's conclusions still hold true. The research on juvenile delinquency has yet to produce any credible statement of the success of any program to treat or prevent it. Moreover, a critical review of the research confirms that correctional programs for youth may not be having any positive influence.

Martinson's comments were focused on the then-current fashion for intensive supervision and community treatment of juvenile offenders. The Community Treatment Program (CTP), which operated between 1961 and 1974, provided intensive case management by a parole officer to juvenile offenders. The parole officer, who was assigned a small caseload over a period of years, was able to make additional referrals to a variety of counseling and service agencies. Large numbers of youth were randomly assigned to CTP or to a control that received the customary care of the California Youth Authority. CTP reported great success both with the typical youthful offender and with the more difficult ones (Palmer 1974). Those who received the intensive services were much less likely to be rearrested than those who did not.

However, both Martinson (1974) and Lerman (1975) criticized the experiment for artificially creating its own success. The evaluations of the project's outcomes, notably parole revocations, depended upon the very staff—the parole officers—who had the greatest stake in the CTP's success. Obviously committed to community treatment, these parole officers were reluctant to revoke parole and in the later stages of the experiment they simply substituted a form of house arrest for actual revocation.

In addition, treatment integrity was not assured; many of the services received by CTP participants were also received by the controls, although not from the same sources, while much of the so-called intensive supervision was expended on administrative chores. Finally, Lerman's (1975) description of CTP suggested that it operated far more as a detention program than CTP acknowledged in its own mimeographed project materials. Martinson (1974) wryly concluded that "the 'benefits' of intensive supervision for youthful offenders may stem not so much from a 'treatment' effect as from a 'policy' effect," that is, from administrative policies that reduce the number of *reported* failures (46). Still, community treatment was less expensive than incarceration.

While Martinson (1974) took the soft "nothing works" position, arguing that some approaches *might* be promising, two subsequent reviews were more condemnatory of the literature and even more decisive in pointing out that nothing had worked while there were no promising leads. In one of their rare criticisms of the practice of social sciences, the National Academy of Sciences squared their shoulders:

> [T]he entire body of research appears to justify only the conclusion that we do not know of any program or method of rehabilitation that could be guaranteed to reduce the criminal activity of released offenders. Although a generous reviewer of the literature might discern some glimmers of hope, those glimmers are so few, so scattered, and so inconsistent that they do not serve as a basis for any recommendations other than continued research. Sechrest, White, and Brown 1979:3)

A later, even more thorough review came to equally dreary conclusions about treating juvenile delinquency. Rutter and Giller (1984) outlined the short-lived effects of behavioral approaches: counseling and psychotherapy "are of no value"; institutional rehabilitation approaches produce no consistent effects; and so forth. It is noteworthy that for all of the programs reviewed, in all of these extraordinarily thorough reviews, not one provided a generous environment that approximated a desirable home-like situation. Every program offered a relatively superficial intervention that was justified by its low cost compared with incarceration. Indeed, the budgets of correctional systems and the social logic of their operations seem defined by two pillars of social efficiency: reducing the costs of incarceration and minimizing expenditures for treatment.

Subsequent research on diversion programs for juvenile offenders continues to exaggerate the outcomes and to employ faulty, even bogus, research methods. Gottfredson (1987) reviewed a series of diversion and treatment programs that used a sometimes highly confrontational treatment technique—Guided Group Interaction (GGI). GGI assumes that juvenile offenders must learn to conform with conventional behaviors and, to this end, employs coercive group interactions and severe organizational sanctions. Gottfredson's (1987) review covered the Highfields Project, the Essexfields and Collegefields demonstrations, the Silverlake and Provo experiments, the Marshall Program, and a variety of school-based interventions. The most intensive of these interventions claimed to achieve substantial behavioral changes in only a few months. While pointing to the many self-serving distortions in the project evaluations, Gottfredson (1987) concludes that at least the Essexfield program seemed to produce positive results. Less favorable conclusions, in line with the CTP experience, would seem warranted, however, especially since GGI can easily be seen as both ineffective and frequently cruel.

Other more recent box scores and meta-analyses of outcomes in juvenile corrections similarly point to promising leads. Garrett (1985) reports that "yes, treatment of adjudicated delinquents in residential settings does work" (303–4). Andrews et al. (1990), carrying the torch for psychotherapy, find conclusive evidence for a strategy of "appropriate treatment." They celebrate the scientific maturity of corrections, contending that it offers a differential ability to appropriately match offender with treatment. Izzo and Ross (1990) conclude that corrections programs containing a cognitive treatment component were "more than twice as effective as programs that did not" (138).

Nevertheless, the base of primary research upon which these reviews rely contains not one single definitive test of any intervention. To the contrary, every study purporting to demonstrate even minimal effectiveness can be pushed aside as simply a partisan salvo that lacks the methodological rigor to support its claims. Occasionally, it can actually be reinterpreted, in the manner of CTP and GGI, as an instance of failure. Indeed, two reviews—a box score (Lab and Whitehead 1988) that was later confirmed by a more sophisticated meta-analysis (Whitehead and Lab 1989)—actually endorse skepticism toward the effectiveness of youth corrections, if not actually their harmfulness:

The results are far from encouraging for rehabilitation proponents. Disregarding tests of statistical significance, 45 of the comparisons showed no impact or negative impact for the various interventions with juvenile offenders while 40 interventions showed positive impact. Where authors reported tests of significance, only 15 comparisons were in favor of the experimental group, whereas 33 showed no impact or a negative impact. Based on these statistics, it is hard to reaffirm rehabilitation. (Lab and Whitehead 1988:154)

The youth corrections literature covers residential and nonresidential programs, psychotherapeutic and behavioral interventions, boot camps, shock treatment programs such as Scared Straight, work programs, counseling and education programs, and a host of others. Some are very expensive, especially incarceration and residential treatment. All seem to fail: recidivism remains high, emotional and psychiatric problems persist, social adjustment is not achieved, and the crime rate seems unaffected. Yet it is quixotic to expect, as these programs do, that a few months in a decent environment (in the rare instances in which it is provided) is sufficient to change behaviors that have become habitual over many years spent amidst inadequate and abusive families, deficient and uncaring communities, and unconcerned, underfunded schools. It is all the more fanciful to expect rehabilitated behaviors, in the few instances that they take place, to persist when the youths are returned to precisely the situations that nourished their deviance in the first place. If nothing else, the failure of youth corrections measures the depth of prior deprivations and the extent of resources, still untested, that will be needed to overcome them.

TEENAGE PREGNANCY AND PARENTING PROGRAMS

Because of the absence of experimental designs, the outcomes of programs to prevent premarital births are indeterminate. Still, it appears that sex education programs "affect knowledge, but rarely have they been found to strongly affect behavior" (Hofferth 1991:13). More generally, considerable controversy has surrounded programs for adolescents that are designed to prevent first pregnancies by either delaying intercourse or through birth control. Mirroring the targeting problems of family preservation services and the ambiguities that arise from recipient self-selection, many of the reported benefits of prevention programs might more appropriately be attributed to the motivations that participants bring with them to the program. As with family preservation services, the efforts may also have been targeted on low-risk populations.

This is not the problem with programs designed to prevent repeat births to unwed teenage mothers. By definition these programs focus on high-risk youth (defined minimally as already having had a child out-of-wedlock, but frequently too as living in poverty). Many of these programs take a "comprehensive" approach under the assumption that the young women have been deprived of the skills, the opportunities, or both to avoid teenage motherhood. Besides offering a variety of counseling services, the "life options approaches" (following Hofferth 1991) also provide employment skills training and sometimes job placement.

Commenting on these kinds of treatment programs, Hayes (1987) observes that they

> . . . tended to improve outcomes for those areas on which they were specifically focused, for example, reducing the number of pregnancies or keeping pregnant teenagers in school. Substantial long-term effects, however, especially on delay in subsequent fertility, have yet to be demonstrated. (224)

> [Yet] only a few programs have been rigorously evaluated; many have not even collected basic pretest and posttest data to indicate outcomes along specified dimensions. Among those for which outcome information is available, there is some evidence of positive short-term effects on targeted goals. (229)

This sort of summary puts the best face on research that simply does not have the methodological rigor to attribute any of the programs' reported outcomes to their interventions. While these "comprehensive" programs offer more than barren neglect, they do not offer sufficiently intense interventions to substantially affect behaviors.

One of the most comprehensive, Project Redirection claimed at the five-year follow-up that the program provided "the strongest supporting evidence yet that comprehensive programs designed to benefit young mothers can have positive long-term effects for the mothers and for their children" (Polit 1989). Yet this optimism is not sustained by either the program's outcomes or by its design. Indeed, the repeat pregnancy rate among program participants was 20 percent *higher* than the rate among the comparison group. Educational, employment, and welfare outcomes favoring the project's participants were small. Their importance, especially in terms of repregnancy, could not be established, while many measures of life improvement were soft responses to survey questions that may well have been coached by participation in the services themselves.

Furthermore, the small earnings gains by program participants ($23 a week above the comparison group's earnings of $45) might be explained by the fact that at the beginning of the experiment more comparison group members were enrolled in school than program participants (64 percent versus 46 percent) and were presumably less available for work. More troubling in terms of the general welfare of the two groups, the comparison group appeared to be slightly better off ($19 more in monthly household income than the experimental group) after five years.

In short, there is little evidence to sustain any optimism that Project Redirection offers an attractive model of services to handle illegitimacy among adolescents. Moreover, Project Redirection, perhaps the most expensive of the treatment approaches to adolescent pregnancy, spent only about $4,000 a year on each recipient, an amount that recalls family preservation services and intensive casework. It is notably an expenditure less than the customary cost of a year of high school and far, far less than residential care.

Maynard (1995) reports mixed outcomes from the best-evaluated and most ambitious programs targeted on teenage parents, including New Chance (Quint, Musick, and Ladner 1994), that mirrored the interventions and outcomes of Project Redirection. Project Redirection's higher repregnancy rates were found in a number of the other experiments, notably New Chance, and many of them failed to produce any employment or educational achievements. Indeed, a number of the studies reported declines in measures of social adjustment among program participants. Nonetheless, the gains in education and employment, when they did occur, were modest, while no efforts were made to assess their long-term impact.

Maynard (1995) also describes an experimental reform of the welfare system for teenage parents:

> Over the course of two and a half years, the demonstration programs enrolled nearly 6,000 teenagers who had their first child and were already receiving or started to receive welfare. Half were randomly selected to participate in a new welfare regime—the enhanced services programs—requiring them to engage in approved self-sufficiency-oriented activities or to risk a reduction in their welfare grants of about $160 a month. These young mothers also received a fairly rich bundle of support services to facilitate and promote their compliance with these requirements. The other half of the mothers received regular welfare services. (Maynard 1995:317)

Similar to the other employment efforts for the welfare population, the demonstration had only modest impacts on school enrollment, job training, and employment. It failed to increase support from noncustodial fathers. Most important, it failed to reduce repregnancy rates (increasing doubt concerning O'Neill's similar efforts, also in New Jersey). Strangely enough, out of this mash of conflicting findings and often weak research, Maynard (1995) still concludes, in support of Mead, that mandatory programs with clear goals can be successful.

Nevertheless, there is nothing in any of these programs to sustain hopes that minimal interventions offer promising short-cuts to social cohesion and family stability. To the contrary, their consistent failure to produce substantial effect draws attention back to their superficiality, even at $4,000 a year. It seems a reasonable response to the tenets of social efficiency that if there are to be fewer adolescent parents then there needs to be fewer poor and otherwise deprived adolescents. Programs that pursue fewer births among teenagers without assuring greater cultural parity, notably less poverty, may be destined to fail.

HEAD START

Head Start was established during the War on Poverty as a preschool strategy that provided comprehensive child development services to low-income families. It encompasses education, medical, and nutritional supports as well as parental involvement. Essentially, Head Start assumes that the key to addressing poverty for deprived children depends upon early intervention to combat the problems in families and neighborhoods.

The Westinghouse Study, published in 1969 (Westinghouse Learning Corporation 1969), concluded that Head Start was largely ineffective; its short-term effects wore off within a few years after entering school. However, the Westinghouse Study along with subsequent national studies have been largely rejected on methodological grounds:

> These studies have been criticized for: (a) the narrowness of their outcome measures, (b) possible selection biases in who attended Head Start itself, (c) the question of program continuity, (d) the failure to examine the effect of different program curricula, and (e) the failure to examine the role of family process variables. (Cole and Washington 1986:94)

Indeed, no evaluation of Head Start has utilized a rigorous randomized design. Consequently, the controversy over its impacts, first introduced by the Westinghouse Study, has continued to the present.

Despite its many methodological problems, the findings of the Westinghouse Study have been sustained by a variety of reviews (Cole and Washington 1986; Consortium for Longitudinal Studies 1978; McKey et al. 1985; Zigler and Muenchow 1992; Zigler and Valentine 1979). Yet, these reviews have failed to identify a pool of credible studies even while the large body of primary research, customarily produced by program advocates, seems to contain disturbing hints of actual deterioration among Head Start students compared with their controls.

The Consortium for Longitudinal Studies (1978) found that early educational interventions produced sizable benefits in later years: less assignment to special eduction, fewer children held back a grade, and less underachievement. Yet the twelve demonstrations that provided the base for these findings used very weak research methodologies, which were initially published in the field's ephemeral literature. Only a few of the twelve employed randomization and even these constituted only "approximately" experimental designs in the consortium's own terms. Attrition was an immense problem; only three of the demonstrations retained more than 85 percent of their enrollees while attrition occasionally exceeded 50 percent (Consortium on Developmental Continuity 1977: Table B-5). Moreover, it was not clear whether the recipients of the services were either representative of deprived children or typical Head Start students.

Zigler and Valentine (1979) reach a more equivocal conclusion:

> [I]f Head Start is appraised by its success in universally raising the IQs of poor children and maintaining these IQs over time, one is tempted to write it off as an abject failure. On the other hand, if one assesses Head Start by the improved health of the tens of thousands of poor children who have been screened, diagnosed, and treated, it is clearly a resounding success. (496)

On the basis of a meta-analysis of 210 outcome studies of Head Start, McKey et al. (1985) present similarly varied findings that actually highlight occasional deterioration. McKey et al. (1985) estimate that three years after graduation from Head Start the global cognitive measures and school readiness and achievement scores of enrollees and controls were equivalent, while the performance of enrollees on IQ tests were worse than the controls (3–11). The weaker outcome studies that relied on pre/post designs reported larger benefits than the controlled studies. The longitudinal studies showed the greatest amount of deterioration.

While McKey et al. (1985) report immediate gains in a variety of areas—socioemotional development and scholastic achievement, to name two—few of these gains are sustained over time. Again a number of measures—such as self-esteem and achievement motivation—indicated that enrollees did worse than their controls.

Unfortunately, none of the conclusions of the summary reviews is based in credible research. The simple fact of convergent findings would be more believable if the different studies were independent. Yet, in the very homogenous culture of the United States, the biases that affect one experiment quite possibly affect all. Indeed, much of the Head Start literature has been generated by a research community dependent on the program for its livelihood. In light of the very porous primary research, it is plausible that the common positive evaluation of Head Start is simply the product of the hope that a few hours a day of early schooling can overcome the enormous deficits of culturally deprived children.

The persistent finding that the Head Start advantage rapidly wears off seems a reasonable conclusion, especially considering that it is intended to compensate for deep failures in the family, the neighborhood, and the school system. Its putative benefits are even less credible when considered against the backdrop of Head Start's targeting problem. It is unclear that the children enrolled in Head Start are the most deprived or even representative of the underlying population of concern. Head Start children did after all have parents concerned enough about their welfare to enroll them in the program, and some of these children are not deprived, at least culturally, in spite of the possibility that their family incomes are low.

It is curious that Head Start should be so popular after the many ambiguous reports on its outcomes. Without a long-term production function in education, however, Head Start still seems to benefit many different constituencies: it is relatively inexpensive; it provides needed day care; it emphasizes education not jobs, opportunity instead of an equality of outcome; it fits comfortably into current social service arrangements.

In a less rosy interpretation, one might conclude that a shred of preschool education is patently insufficient to compensate for the inadequacies of families, schools, and neighborhoods. If children are to come out of high school with more mainstream emotional and educational development, then their families, schools, and communities also need to be more mainstream.

CONCLUSIONS

If there is any truth to the beneficence of American society in providing personal social services to the poor and disadvantaged, it has not materialized in evaluations of them. At a minimum, the effectiveness of personal social services is still indeterminate. Social interventions inspired by psychotherapy and social work, notably family preservation, as well as rehabilitation programs for addicts and juvenile delinquents, programs to prevent repeat out-of-wedlock pregnancies among adolescents, and Head Start, have all failed to produce evidence that they achieve their goals. There are considerable grounds on which to conclude that they are routinely ineffective.

The social sciences have abided weak and porous evaluations of the outcomes of such service programs, frequently retreating into the fancy of practical research that relies upon the subjectivity of the practitioner and the researcher. Yet the decades of biased and poorly conducted research authored by committed program advocates and funded by government agencies press for a conclusion that encompasses social motive as well as program operations. Society itself seems to be more concerned with creating comforting symbols of its charitability than with alleviating the economic, social, and psychological distress of its poor and dependent citizens. Ceremonial roles in social belief seem to dominate the production function of the personal social services.

The myth of social service effectiveness passes into proverbs through the formal social science literature and more ephemeral publications—a variety of programmatic initiatives, reports, evaluations, hearings, and proposals. Their partisan conclusions invoke the authority of science but offer only political symbols for social dialects. Ultimately focused on the legislative process and public policy, these factional manifestoes contend for social belief by accessing popular and emergent social values.

The Carnegie Report (Carnegie Council on Adolescent Development 1995) represents a pure form of the impulse to provide a relatively inexpensive response to social problems. It follows the typical logic of contemporary liberalism: the existence of a problem is displayed demographically through the extent and the importance of those who are affected; the pivotal role of the problem relative to important social concerns is defined in terms of specific causative agents; and a series of interventions, usually some combination of personal social services, is proposed to handle the causative agents. The justification for this logic is vested in scientific proof—the testimony of objective tests of effectiveness—that the interventions are credible solutions for the posed problem. The Carnegie Report is unusual only in proposing a relatively extensive series of interventions.

The report makes a number of structural assumptions about appropriate socialization focused on the critical importance of adolescence:

> Many adolescents manage to negotiate their way through this critical transition with relative success. With caring families, good schools, and supportive community institutions, they grow up reasonably well educated, committed to families and friends, and prepared for the workplace and for the responsibilities of citizenship. (Carnegie Council on Adolescent Development 1995:9)

Unfortunately, many other adolescents do not follow this path, presumably because "caring families, good schools," and the other customary social institutions are not in place. As a consequence, the Carnegie Report proposes compensatory programs as surrogates for these institutional failures. Sidestepping any structural reform of the culture itself, all of the proposed interventions follow the strategy of treatment: reengaging families with their adolescent children, setting up developmentally appropriate schools, developing health promotion strategies, strengthening communities, and promoting the constructive potential of the media.

The Carnegie Report relies upon both the "science" of human development to target adolescence as the critical developmental phase in preventing their later socialization problems and "proofs" of programmatic effectiveness to justify its specific interventions. Yet, the literature of human development has offered no convincing proof of the unique, pivotal importance of adolescence. Interventions in early childhood as well as with parents would seem to be a competitive treatment approach that the report does not address.

The report's programmatic proposals are even more problematic than their targeting rationale. There is no proof that those interventions have succeeded, even under optimal demonstration conditions. The Carnegie Report's reliance on psychotherapeutic wisdom, social work, family preservation, counseling, and the rest gains little support from the tatters of evidence that the social sciences have offered. Its source material invokes the authority of science through its organizational manifestations but fails to provide any objective, coherent, or plausible demonstration of effectiveness. The largest portion of its bibliography comprises the reports of other eminent commissions, panels, and citizens groups (including the American Medical Association, City of Chicago, Girl Scouts) and the customary range of outcome studies critiqued in this chapter. It even stoops to ephemeral publications and the media for its authority.

The report also fails to follow its own structural logic. It may be undesirable and programmatically impossible to divorce young adolescence from the development of families and communities. To invest in adolescence without assuring strong families, schools, and other social institutions may be foolhardy and self-defeating.

The Carnegie Report might be excused as a judicious political statement made by a benign philanthropic foundation to coax America into better handling the grievous problems of its adolescents. On the other hand, its very judiciousness, divorced from a rational authority, could be reinterpreted as a comfort for the inertia of current policy. More than a deep criticism of existing provisions for youth, the Carnegie Report provides a sense that customary solutions—the personal social services—offer an appropriate although somewhat underfunded response to their needs. Yet it fails to provide the companion view that those services even when intensified have not achieved their goals. The report's conclusions bolster the United States' assurance of its own fundamental correctness: if its citizens tried a bit harder and if they would be a bit more generous, then many of the nation's social problems could be handled. Thus, by failing to substantiate a credible production function in personal social services, the Carnegie Report becomes a symbol of liberalism's defining insistence that social cohesion can be purchased both cheaply and comfortably.

Such is the life of the personal social services today, torn between political utility and an ennobling role in addressing social problems. The practice of rationality, the child of the Enlightenment enterprise, has been suborned to cobble together the myths of social dialectics. Yet no socially efficient strategy of personal social service has ever been demonstrated to reduce social deviancy or social distress. The course of social problems in America continues blithely unimpeded by any deep response to their consequences.

7 Conclusion: Generosity

Welfare in America is gray both for its ambiguities, paradoxes, and dilemmas, and for its bleak insufficiencies. The effects of the core programs constituting the narrow sense of the American welfare state—AFDC, Food Stamps, and Medicaid—are at best tenuously estimated. Welfare may be implicated in the continuation of social problems but not by creating moral hazards in the manner of Charles Murray. Rather, by its very meanness and its refusal to address the conditions that appear to be associated with poverty, the American welfare state is neglectful and complacent, traits reaffirmed in the 1996 welfare reform, about the continuing deterioration of society.

The conventional wisdom holds that the guarantee and work disincentives of AFDC, Food Stamps, and Medicaid distort labor force participation in "nontrivial" ways. However, the many methodological infractions of the studies, together with their contradictory findings, fail to provide any definitive cachet to this common tenet. In the same way, the effect of welfare on family structure—marriage, divorce, separation, abandonment, out-of-wedlock births, and intergenerational poverty—is poorly defined and misleading. Nor have the minimal work training programs or personal social services demonstrated an ability to increase the work participation of welfare populations or to solve any of the personal problems that seem to interfere with work. Worse, the research fails to adequately defend the centrality of work to social harmony and ignores the effect of existing welfare provisions on any broad concept of social welfare. In turn, the shortcomings of the research obediently reflect the society's refusal to consider the tie between social welfare and the common good, the possibility that public support may be necessary to achieve social cohesion and tranquility.

An alternative understanding seems more plausible. The levels of welfare payments and the intensity of job training and personal social service programs are too low to affect the social or economic behavior of poor people. The cash provisions of AFDC and Food Stamps typically provide a standard of living far below (often only 50 percent) the official poverty threshold, which itself may fall far short of contemporary social standards. Work training programs have provided only the barest kinds of skills which typically fail to command even a minimum wage, let alone a wage sufficient to raise the recipient out of poverty. The personal social services usually provide only a few hours a week of personal attention. In short, direct welfare, training, and personal social services seem to exist as symbols of the society's enforced virtues more than as substantive provisions to ameliorate social problems.

The value of work itself is not understood. Okun's bucket imperfectly defines the relationship between economic efficiency and social adequacy. It is quite plausible that a loss of economic efficiency is an easy price to pay for social progress. The most productive economic system may not create the best society. In the same way, policy decisions affecting the iron triangle of welfare—the relationship among adequacy, work, and fairness (which also implies cost)—have been dictated by social efficiency, the political demand for low cost and compatible social policies. The welfare debate has largely ignored the role of underlying social conditions. In its turn, the intellectual community has timidly internalized the political decision to define social problems as a deficiency of work effort, avoiding the desirability of addressing cultural poverty.

The raw economic determinism of the social sciences has produced a welfare literature that crowds out the social consequences of welfare policy. The social debate has been insulated from the perverse consequences of a social policy that refuses to address deprivation, sacrificing adequate benefits to reduce poverty for work effort. Making more people available for work without providing more jobs at adequate wages may tear at social cohesion and social equality: wages for the least well off decline, the unemployed subsidize each other as they spend down to become eligible for welfare, workers at the bottom end are forced to share jobs, and children in single-parent families are inadequately socialized.

Nevertheless, the body of research has provided overwhelming evidence (see Bane and Ellwood (1994), at least on this point) that the impulse to maximize income cannot explain either social outcomes or personal choices. Unitary measures, such as income, are inadequate to capture the complexity of welfare decisions that reflect motives for social integration along with needs for financial adequacy. The refusal of welfare policy either to provide a livable income, to improve social functioning, or to provide the adjuncts necessary to compensate for family and social failures has probably perpetuated social problems. Yet, the price for deferring solutions has been consistently sidestepped.

The contemporary welfare literature, particularly the influential and sophisticated policy analyses of economics, can be read as a generation's intellectual and moral failure to handle grievous social problems—the ascendancy of technique over meaning and professionalism over social purpose. The battle lines are drawn over the most incremental of mincing steps to address poverty. Recanting a noble vision of society and the common good, contemporary social science cautiously tinkers with existing social preferences, accepting the popular antipathy for redistributional policies as constraints on its own imagination. Only rare statements of comprehensive solutions have been attempted.

SOLOMON'S JUSTICE

Welfare policy in the United States is curiously undisciplined by any unified assumptions about the causes of poverty. Neither structural, subcultural, nor even genetic logic provides coherence for contemporary welfare policy. Rather, welfare policy is Solomon's justice, a compromise among competitive constituencies lacking any rational or consistent theme in addressing social failure. Poverty reduction does not seem to be a central goal, given that payments are stunted. Without incentives, work is hardly a central objective either. Structural change is not pursued; neither serious training opportunities nor jobs are provided; and little has been done to reform the economic and social systems. No substantial effort is made to address subcultural problems through either intensive surrogate care or social services. More disturbing still, welfare programs seem to serve as a rebuke to those who need them, often conveying rigid contempt to recipients.

The political disagreement over the causes of social failure reflects clear ideological differences—the ideological camps commonly defined as structural, subcultural, and genetic or in terms of human motivation, as rational choice, expectancy, and cultural determinism—which remain untested. The poorly designed and poorly conducted research of the social sciences preclude any identification of the initial and sustaining causes of poverty, dependency, human deviance, or social failure. The authority of the research is seriously undermined by threats to its scientific credibility: most notably, the absence of random selection and random assignment and the consequent problem of self-selection, inaccurate and distorted measures, researcher bias, unreplicated studies, and so forth.

Even the definition of cause seems to be arbitrary. There has been no consecutive regression to a point that truly disentangles cultural influences from economic determinants or that identifies factors influencing both economic and personal responses. The effects of interventions are not known beyond Rossi's inclusive suspicion that nothing seems to have worked.

The literature has also failed to come up with a test for deserving-ness—the conditions of free choice under which people can be fairly judged as responsible for their conditions. To the contrary, in one of its few intellectual triumphs, social science has largely succeeded in debunk-ing the notion that worthiness is easily ascribed (Gans 1995). Coontz (1992), as one example, has shredded the conservative's nostalgia for the bastion of the American family and the standing of "people's rotten or ir-redeemable selfishness" as a cause of their dysfunctional behaviors. At the same time, her own theological preference for a myth of cooperation to repair social institutions cannot sustain a similarly rigorous and de-tached analysis. Her "new tradition" built upon the insights of the social sciences seems doomed to the fate of kindred revolutions in human con-sciousness that have attempted to resolve social problems inexpensively. In spite of its Broadway popularity, the Pygmalion myth and, conse-quently, liberal sentimentality have been refuted by centuries of failed good intentions that inspired poorly funded and superficial personal so-cial services.

Liberals have constructed acoustic tiles around any suggestion that the poor are a disproportionately dysfunctional group, internalizing opposi-tional values that it passes on to the next generation. Liberal social wel-fare policy complacently relies upon the unproven assertion that an im-proved economy and more equal income distribution will automatically create a more cohesive society. Yet it seems unlikely that the poor are dif-ferentiated from others simply by their incomes. To the contrary, they may be more troubled, less conforming, less socialized, more opposi-tional, and perhaps even more lawless.[1] A roseate view that denies deep

1. A great amount of research has noted considerable variation between the poor and the nonpoor and among many ethnic groups suggesting that they differ in fundamental ways from the dominant culture. Wilson (1987) and an enormous descendent literature (see Anderson 1990; Brooks-Gunn, Klebanov, and Liaw 1995; Brooks-Gunn et al. 1993; Mincy (in Danziger, Sandefur, and Weinberg 1994; and Osterman 1991) suggest that inner-city residents are so deeply scarred by their environments as to constitute a subculture of dep-rivation. These works "emphasize the importance of family and community influences" (Corcoran et al. 1990). There seem to be neighborhood and family effects in addition to socioeconomic effects (Bumpass and McLanahan 1989; Crane 1991; Hill and O'Neill 1993; and Hogan and Kitagawa 1985). Perhaps as a related phenomenon, there appears to be considerable intergenerational poverty (see discussion above and Dolinsky, Caputo, and O'Kane 1989; Gottschalk, McLanahan, and Sandefur in Danziger, Sandefur, and Weinberg 1994).

Moreover, work participation and fertility patterns and therefore basic social attitudes

social differences and blindly insists upon the effectiveness of minimal provisions deprives social need of its dignity in policy debates.

Researchers who have approached the ambiguities of subcultural influence—notably Moynihan in his famous report on the black family (Rainwater and Yancey 1967) and occasionally Wilson in his suggestion

---

may be different for different ethnic groups (Carliner 1981; Eggebeen and Lichter 1991; Farber 1990). Without attributing cause, Kane (1987) argues that there are important attitudinal differences between the poor and the nonpoor (such as expectancy, motivation, and sense of control).

The underclass may contain only a very small proportion of the population. Yet there may be typical underclass behaviors: low work participation, dropping out of high school by age twenty-two, heavy drug use, criminality, and out-of-wedlock childbearing (Hill and O'Neill 1993; Hopkins 1987). Motivation to seek employment may vary among different groups (Carcagno, Cecil, and Ohls 1982). Political attitudes and participation may vary by ethnic group (Cohen and Dawson 1993; Hill and Leighley 1992) and economic class (*New York Times* 1996). Support groups among the poor may be dysfunctional (Ratcliff and Bogdan 1988).

The homeless differ considerably from the dominant culture and even among themselves (Bassuk 1984; Burt and Cohen 1989; Rossi et al. 1987). Elliott and Krivo (1991) pointedly suggest that many studies fail to "advance a reliable [structural] understanding of the causes of homelessness" for the same methodological reasons discussed throughout this book.

Olson and Scholer (1993) attempt to explain an attitudinal paradox, the "state of being satisfied with objectively unsatisfying conditions" (173). This "satisfaction-paradox" suggests either a conscious decision to opt for poverty or shiftlessness among the poor. Yet the theory of learned helplessness finesses the issue of cause; perhaps it is taught helplessness.

Geronimus and Korenman (1992), Committee on Ways and Means (1994), as well as many others have reported the greater prevalence of out-of-wedlock births among the poor. In contrast, a number of studies report conventional attitudes toward work among the poor (see Cruz 1991; Goodwin 1972; Hagen and Davis 1994). Yet, even Hagen and Davis (1995) report "differences across sites on the [AFDC] women's willingness to work in low-paying jobs without benefits" (663), apparently contradicting a generalized "commitment to the work ethic" (Hagen and Davis 1995:663).

Goodwin (1983) notes an absence of research concern with the social and psychological characteristics of welfare recipients. The PSID has corrected some of these deficiencies. However, as discussed throughout these chapters, it brings additional problems of its own: selection biases, limited descriptors, attrition, reporting inaccuracies, and so forth. Yet taken together, the published differences may suggest different subcultures, complete with different attitudes and behavioral patterns that are transmitted intergenerationally. Whether the differences truly constitute separate subcultures of poverty would seem to rest on the issue of whether these patterns persist even in the absence of structural (environmental) causes for their development, that is, whether they have a life of their own apart from general social and economic influences or whether they are simply expected adaptations to deprivation. This, however, is a very difficult point to verify by experiment. Moreover, regression analyses of nonexperimental data (see Dolinsky, Caputo, and O'Kane 1989) have not been scientifically credible. In the absence of a credible test, the debate continues over whether conditions of society are essentially different for different groups or whether

of a ghetto subculture—have incurred a merciless crusade of vilification from liberals. Yet the determinants of the American class system remain very uncertain. Conservatives continue to deny the defining power of social institutions and liberals refuse to acknowledge the possibility of oppositional subcultures and the role of personal motivation. Both refuse to accept the possibility that only much greater public spending to achieve greater cultural parity is necessary to repair society.

The promise of the liberal vision—rational identification of cause and consequent policy intervention—has not been realized. On the other hand, the hope of the conservative vision to regain a lost Eden, perhaps that of the founding American patriarchs, has also been belied by the impossibility of identifying either initial or sustaining cause. Both visions share the comforting belief in professional "capacities to implement social programs in technically and politically viable ways" (Weir, Orloff, and Skocpol 1988:433); this is undercut by the actual quality of professional knowledge.

Rather than sentimentality or nostalgia, factional political considerations dominate any conceit of professional expertise. The policy community's point of view is essentially determined by social dictates, not by an acultural logic of social science research. The policy community "becomes convinced" through a hard appraisal of its own institutional stakes in social commitments more than through any process of scientific scrutiny.

Yet the social sciences have failed to demonstrate any socially efficient ability to cut corners and their commitment to professional minimalism and to low-cost solutions gets in the way of effective social policy. Program effectiveness may depend more on the intensity of provisions than on any elegance of professional technique or parsimonious application of limited resources. In spite of the hubris of the policy sciences, society is getting what it pays for.

---

different groups choose to interpret similar opportunities differently. Thus, unemployed minority youth from the subcultural perspective are perceived as rejecting social norms and refusing to look for jobs outside their neighborhoods. In contrast, from the structural perspective, they are perceived as being denied knowledge and access to employment.

But whether or not the undesirable differences constitute subcultures, the differences often define social problems. Farley's (1990) documentation of persistent economic differences among ethnic groups does not answer the question of why they exist. The task remains for social policy to identify the conditions under which these differences can be reduced. Either minimizing their importance as linear expressions of structural imperfections or discounting their importance as a question of personal motive would seem to beg the social policy question.

CAUSE AND POLITICS

The failure to identify cause is the result of practical impediments and theoretical limitations on definitive research. No decisive test of cause may be possible. While the randomized experiment may be the method of choice and represents the definitive application of science to policy interventions (Burtless and Orr 1986; Fraker and Maynard 1987), in practice it may be impossible to conduct a truly credible social experiment. Randomization may create perverse and unintended problems of its own while the conditions necessary to validate nonexperimental data may be too rare and difficult to achieve. Consequently, welfare issues will remain political and social policymaking may never be able to answer important questions of fact.

Heckman (in Manski and Garfinkel 1992) convincingly argues that randomization itself may introduce bias. Both the rigors of randomization procedures and their threat to professional control may routinely discourage participation in social experiments and impair the representativeness of research samples. Moreover, patients themselves may seek to discover their status in the experimental group, aborting participation if they find that they are being given placebos. This breech occurred in AIDS experiments where the patients paid for independent blood tests to find out whether they were being treated with an active drug or a placebo (Palca 1989). Even apart from randomization bias, social experiments are expensive and disruptive. The few experiments that have been conducted—NIT, MDRC manpower studies, and the Families First experiment—have failed to produce credible findings.

Recognizing the problems of social experiments, Moffitt (1991) argues that nonexperimental data can provide a credible test of cause under certain conditions: when the data are derived from a natural experiment, when reliable cohort information is available, and when baseline behaviors are known. However, the comparison groups—say, neighborhoods and states—for natural experiments are rarely equivalent. The longitudinal data sets are beset by enormous problems of reliability (especially in collecting sensitive data) and attrition; a large scale, eidetic data set has still not been put together. Finally, baseline behaviors, in part because of the failures of the longitudinal panel surveys, are not known.

SOCIAL SCIENCE AND UNCERTAINTY

The problems of research credibility lead to the conclusion that definitive research may be impossible—a true epistemic fix that argues for the necessarily political nature of social policy truths. The overblown policy recommendations of the social sciences, consistently misconstruing the meaning and authority of their research, underscore this conclusion. Yet while social welfare studies may be indeterminate and perhaps even factional there is little reason to capitulate to subjectivity; an embedded uncertainty does not justify the incoherence of research methods that plague the social sciences.

Mahajan (1992), following the postmodern mood, fails to demonstrate that causal explanation—scientific logic—is inadequate and misleading or that subjective methods—hermeneutics, narratives, and reason-action explanations—provide reliable information for social policymaking. Rather, Mahajan (1992) advances a quest for "practical" research methods that falls far short of providing credible answers to questions of program impact. While these methods may have a literary and expressive value that augment their political meaning, they cannot answer the fundamental question of program efficacy. Simply disparaging the Enlightenment enterprise and its reliance upon scientific truth provides no useful alternative.

It is true that the social sciences have routinely failed to conduct definitive research, investigating "areas in which the major assumptions are hardly ever challenged" (Horowitz 1995–96:57). Yet "the answer to inferior social science is better social science," even while accepting the premise that definitive research may be both pragmatically and theoretically impossible (Horowitz 1995–96:56). The descent into subjectivity—the acceptance of philosophic nihilism as all-embracing—is far more perilous than the choice to discipline policy research with the fiction of an objective reality. Indeed, the major criticisms of welfare research have been occasioned by lapses in social science objectivity—the abandonment of objectivity and susceptibility to personal and political biases. However much Mahajan and others would like to criticize current social science research for obsequiously lining up with regnant orthodoxies, their own "practical" research methods are even more open to the temptations of political conformity. Science provides at least some protection against the caprices of power.

Yet the continuing challenge for the social sciences is not to break the conundrum of rationality but to define a scientifically credible practice of limited rationality that serves the policy needs of a modern democracy. This they have not done, at least in the welfare area. While accepting the political definition of a problem, that is, by developing theories of the middle range, the social sciences have not provided credible tests of even these limited relationships. The deficiency is not primarily a technical one, although there are many remaining methodological challenges.

Rather the problem is largely sociological—the refusal of the community of investigators to withstand partisan distortions in a larger commitment to the public process of social dialectics.

THE POLICY COMMUNITY

Without the possibility of definitive tests, the issue of scientific credibility becomes displaced from the methods to the researcher, conflating objectivity and personal motive. Lamentably, the social science community has followed the tunes of funding sources, permitting intrusions into each step of the research process. Initial conceptualizations of the social problem are usually restricted to a safe series of outcome measures; time frames are short; samples are narrowly drawn; and so forth. However, of greater moment, researchers too often accept hobbling restrictions on the credibility of the investigation and then proceed to report the outcomes of what are essentially pilot studies as if they were fully formed tests. In this way, the social science community becomes complicit in establishing a false authority that translates tentative research into defining social myths. No instance emerges in the literature of an organization refusing to conduct an investigation because of the implicit distortions of inadequate funding, a handcuffing problem definition, or the mistreatment of results. To the contrary, the lure of social prominence that attends novel outcomes is sufficient to overcome intellectual probity.

The frequent failures of research suggest a serious communal problem in the social sciences. MDRC, the National Academy of Sciences, and the "shadow government" of private consulting firms, think tanks, and policy institutes (such as the Brookings Institution, the Heritage Foundation, the Hudson Institute, and the Institute for Research on Poverty) along with academic social science generally accept the limitations of research funding. These funding sources—government, foundations, private donors, and corporations—naturally transmit the preferences of the dominant culture.

The preferences of the American culture for socially efficient remedies perfuse its many institutions as blood saturates the body's organs. Wiseman's (1993) "social science bickers" count for very little against the insistence that interventions be inexpensive and compatible with social mores. The experience with welfare programs provides a reminder that policy remains political, in the grip of social rather than rational forces and nurtured on the parental lap of intellectuals. The intellectual's role is to create the symbolic justifications of the social will not to challenge it. Neither Blank's (in Daniger, Sandefur, and Weinberg 1994) arrogance nor Barr's (1993) hope that the policy community is fulfilling a

tutelary role on behalf of the common good or that its opinions are decisive over public policy can be sustained. Unrepresentative, unelected, and
beholden to orthodox funding streams, the policy community is shel-
tered in the cocoon of academia from the harshness of life in the United
States.

In the end, the issue of whether to accept the liberal or conservative
position, or a more generous alternative, remains largely intuitive, subjective, and political. The current level of empirical proof in the social
sciences does not constitute an informed middle ground between rationality and politics. The literature looks more like the cloak of rationality
than the real thing, an unacceptably porous instance of a limited rationality in service to social forces, not the Enlightenment enterprise.

IMPLICATIONS FOR POLICY

The rational deficits of the welfare policy process may be a defining case
of social policymaking in the United States. There is no clear way to adjudicate between the different reform proposals or to select an appropriate strategy to handle poverty and dependency in the United States. As a
consequence, the different reform proposals are political symbols of self-
interest fashioned to fit the mood of the nation rather than rational statements either of goals that serve the common good or of cost-effective
methods to achieve any political end. The policy sciences have not acknowledged their failed authority, however, but rather have pumped ambiguous and uncertain propositions into the public debate as if they were
the revealed truths of modern humanism.

The policy community has not responded credibly to any of the central questions preparatory to decisions on welfare. None of the relationships of welfare in a narrow sense is empirically well substantiated; none
of the empirical assumptions undergirding the reform proposals is adequately tested; none of the broader relationships between welfare and socialization, social cohesion, and the general good is understood.

To the contrary, the skeptical position remains persistently credible.
Little if anything seems to have been effective. The conservative's nostalgia and the liberal's sentimentality—two inspirations of social efficiency—have both failed as welfare strategies. All of their relatively superficial interventions continue the history of thin attempts to deal with
poverty and its associated problems. No welfare response has provided
more than a maintenance level below absolute economic poverty. Cultural poverty has been ignored along with underlying social conditions.

The definition of poverty limits policy responses. Characteristic of contemporary social thought, the National Academy of Sciences (Citro and

Michael 1995) skip over cultural deprivation, making the very suspect assumption that a modestly increased threshold of economic poverty will work to assure cultural sufficiency.

In spite of the ambiguous research, the United States may have more or less addressed absolute economic poverty. The current system in a curious way may already have achieved Bane and Ellwood's (1994) reforms, although certainly not in the straightforward way that they propose. Edin may be correct that the reported incomes of welfare recipients greatly underestimate their actual family incomes. Recipients seem to be treating their AFDC and Food Stamp benefits as if they were Garfinkel's (1992) assured child support payment and then supplementing this income with work and contributions from their families, former spouses, and partners. Yet in spite of the likelihood that economic poverty has declined, social problems continue to increase. While economic deprivation may be an important ingredient in personal deviance and social failure, other cultural factors may play a far more vital role.

There is a need to consider cultural failure more broadly as the critical factor in social problems. Inadequate participation in the institutions of society may lie at the root of most pressing issues. Rather than simply a bare level of economic subsistence, healthy families, communities, schools, work places, and the other essential institutions of American life may be the crucial determinant of social goals. Yet the resources necessary to undertake a strategy of cultural sufficiency are politically out of the question.

The monomaniacal search for ways to reduce welfare rolls and welfare expenditures has defeated any longer-term consideration of the social good, social equality, and social harmony. The blanketing white noise of a work test inhibits a more reasoned social debate over the conditions necessary to address social problems. Out of a pious self-certainty that work redeems, the policy arena is deprived of serious policy proposals. The nation simply does not wish to entertain the possibility that a solution to its pressing social problems requires far greater expenditures.

Deprived of the resources to address cultural poverty, welfare programs, particularly the personal social services and job training programs, are playing out the ceremonies of processing social claims and denying greater equality. This role is performed through the substance of the services as well as the selection of recipients. The adjudication of deservingness occurs in eligibility criteria and their discretionary application—some are declared eligible for relief and some are not (Handler 1995). More subtle, the actual process of service itself provides a test of social worth. Services are offered to elicit particular behaviors; failure to conform implies personal failure. By providing an opportunity to correct deviant behavior, society seems to absolve itself of responsibility for the individual's failure.

The social service process as a screening device is clearest with psychotherapy but it also occurs with the other attempts to reform personal behavior. Services typically exhort change but fail to provide sufficient resources (notably for a new environment) for that change to take place. In this way, most social services adhere to the assumption that change is spiritual (motivational) and not material. This is a safe position since no amount of empirical evidence of ineffectiveness (the number of people who do not change) can refute the basic dogma that change is related less to the quality of the service and more to deep moral characteristics of the recipient. Social science research is thus transformed into a morality survey, a census of the condition of the human soul.

Yet, it is unreasonable to expect a re-socialization without providing sustained opportunities to learn new behaviors that are repatterned in a protective subculture. At a minimum, the research has not challenged the notion that populations treated in similar manners will produce similar behaviors. Indeed, greater cultural parity has probably never been an experimental condition of research. In essence, similar access to basic institutional experiences has been denied to Americans; those coming from inadequate families, communities, and schools are far more likely to engage in socially undesirable acts than those raised in nurturing families, safe and supportive communities, good schools, and so forth.

The long-term remedy would seem to lie in providing all Americans with assurances of more equal participation in basic social institutions and at levels adequate to protect the nation's civic society. Yet, the nation is perversely moving in the opposite direction even while its wealth is increasing. Underlying social conditions—the differences in institutional participation—are deteriorating, especially for those on the bottom rungs of society: more broken families, less adequate schools, fewer jobs, more jails, and so forth. Without redistributive policies that assure better socialization—that is, without attacking the problems of cultural insufficiency—the nation will likely suffer greater turmoil, producing ever greater numbers of the disaffected, even while its material wealth increases.

The pervasive adherence to social efficiency denies investment in basic social institutions. The exquisite insensibility to the possibility of oppositional and dysfunctional subcultures produces a distorting reliance on structural factors that are blind to social reality. There is evil; many social problems are not automatically dispelled by higher incomes. At the same time, subcultural explanations are doomed by their fanciful notions of human choice. The relationship between seemingly uncontrollable economic and social forces on the one hand and personal adaptation on the other may be impossible to tease apart. As a result, the interventive assumption needs to be made that both types of factors require attention.

The caste-like social attitudes that administer the stigma of deservingness are the greatest barriers to a broad social attack on cultural inequality, reinforcing society's commitment to social efficiency. A generous policy to address need probably awaits a social disaster, one that inspires that realization that American civic culture is the nation's most cherished achievement and that it requires the deep sustenance of public welfare—programs in support of family, community, jobs, and so forth. This seems to be the only strategy left that has not been discredited by the natural histories of live social policy. Yet nothing will occur unless the nation dispels its grand illusion that a Darwinian fate operates for the greater glory and social majesty of the United States of America. Destiny is negotiable.

REFERENCES
INDEX

References

Aaron, H. 1978. *Politics and the Professors*. Washington, DC: Brookings Institution.

Abraham, K. G., and J. C. Haltiwanger. 1995. "Real Wages and the Business Cycle." *Journal of Economic Literature* 33:1215–64.

Alexander, P. C., R. A. Neimeyer, V. M. Follette, M. K. Moore, and S. Harter. 1989. "A Comparison of Group Treatments of Women Sexually Abused as Children." *Journal of Consulting and Clinical Psychology* 57(4): 479–83.

Almond, G. A. 1988. "The Return to the State." *American Political Science Review* 82(3):853–74.

Amatetti, S. K. 1989. *Prevention Plus 2*. Rockville, MD: Office of Substance Abuse Prevention.

American Psychiatric Association. 1989. *Treatments of Psychiatric Disorders: A Task Force Report of the American Psychiatric Association*. Washington, DC: American Psychiatric Association.

Anderson, E. 1990. *Streetwise*. Chicago: University of Chicago Press.

Anderson, M. 1978. *Welfare*. Stanford, CA: Hoover Institution Press.

Andrews, D. A., I. Zinger, R. D. Hoge, J. Bonta, P. Gendreau, and F. T. Cullen. 1990. "Does Correctional Treatment Work? A Clinically Relevant and Psychologically Informed Meta-analysis." *Criminology* 28(3):369–404.

Andrews, G., and R. Harvey. 1981. "Does Psychotherapy Benefit Neurotic Patients." *Archives of General Psychiatry* 38 (November):1203–8.

Auletta, Ken. 1982. *The Underclass*. New York: Vintage Books.

Auspos, P. 1988. *Maine: Final Report on the Training Opportunities in the Private Sector Program*. New York: Manpower Demonstration Research Corporation.

Bane, M. J., and D. T. Ellwood. 1983. "The Dynamics of Dependence: The Routes to Self Sufficiency." Report prepared for the U.S. Department of Health, Education, and Welfare by Urban Systems Research and Engineering, Inc. Cambridge, MA: Harvard University.

Bane, M. J., and D. T. Ellwood. 1994. *Welfare Realities: From Rhetoric to Reform*. Cambridge, MA: Harvard University Press.

Barr, N. 1993. *The Economics of the Welfare State.* Stanford, CA: Stanford University Press.

Barr, N., and R. E. Hall. 1981. "The Probability of Dependence on Public Assistance." *Economica* 48:109–23.

Barth, R. P., M. Courtney, J. D. Berrick, and V. Albert. 1994. *From Child Abuse to Permanency Planning.* New York: Aldine de Gruyter.

Bassi, L. J., M. C. Simms, L. C. Burbridge, and C. L. Betsey. 1984. *Measuring the Effect of CETA on Youth and the Economically Disadvantaged.* Washington, DC: Urban Institute.

Bassuk, E. L. 1984. "The Homeless Problem." *Scientific American* 251:40–5.

Baum, E. 1991. "When the Witch Doctors Agree: The Family Support Act and Social Science Research." *Journal of Policy Analysis and Management* 10 (4):603–15.

Becker, G. 1974. "A Theory of Marriage: Part 11." *Journal of Political Economy.* 82:S11–S26.

Becker, G. 1981. *A Treatise on the Family.* Cambridge, MA: Harvard University Press.

Behrman, J. R., and P. Taubman. 1990. "The Intergenerational Correlation between Children's Adult Earnings and Their Parents' Income: Results from the Michigan Panel Survey of Income Dynamics." *Review of Income and Wealth* 36(2):115–27.

Bennett, N. G., D. E. Bloom, and P. H. Craig. 1989. "The Divergence of Black and White Marriage Patterns." *American Journal of Sociology* 3:692–722.

Bennett, N. G., D. E. Bloom, and C. K. Miller. 1995. "The Influence of Nonmarital Childbearing on the Formation of First Marriages." *Demography* 32(1):47–62.

Bennett, W. J. 1994. *The Index of Leading Cultural Indicators.* New York: Simon and Schuster.

Bergin, A. E., and A. E. Garfield (eds.). 1971 [1978, 1986, 1994]. *Handbook of Psychotherapy and Behavior Change.* New York: John Wiley.

Bernstam, M. S., and L. Swan. 1986. *The Production of Children as Claims on the State: A Comprehensive Labor Market Approach to Illegitimacy in the United States 1960–1980.* Working Paper in Economics No. E-86-1. Hoover Institution, Stanford University.

Beschner, G. M., and A. S. Friedman (eds.) 1979. *Youth Drug Abuse: Problems, Issues and Treatment.* Lexington, MA: Lexington Books.

Blank, R. 1989a. "Analyzing the Length of Welfare Spells." *Journal of Public Economics* 39:245–73.

Blank, R. 1989b. "The Effect of Medical Need and Medicaid on AFDC Participation." *Journal of Human Resources* 24(1):54–87.

Blank, R. M., and P. Ruggles. 1993. *When Do Women Use AFDC and Food Stamps? The Dynamics of Eligibility vs. Participation.* Working Paper 4429. Washington, DC: National Bureau of Economic Research.

Blankenthorn, D. 1995. *Fatherless America.* New York: Basic Books.

Blankenthorn, D., S. Bayme, and J. B. Elshtain. 1990. *Rebuilding the Nest.* Milwaukee, WI: Family Service America.

Bloom, M., and J. Fischer. 1982. *Evaluating Practice: Guidelines for the Accountable Professional.* Englewood Cliffs, NJ: Prentice Hall.

Bloom, H., L. Orr, G. Cave, S. Bell, F. Doolittle, and W. Lin. 1994. *The National JTPA Study: Overview: Impacts, Benefits and Costs of Title 11-A.* Bethesda, MD: Abt Associates.

Bouchard, T. J., Jr. 1994. "Genes, Environment, and Personality." *Science* 264: 1700–1701.

Bouchard, T. J., Jr., D. T. Lykken, M. McGue, N. L. Segal, and A. Tellegen. 1990. *Science* 250:223.

Bourgois, Philippe. 1995. *In Search of Respect: Selling Crack in El Barrio.* New York: Cambridge University Press.

Brasilevsky, A., and D. Hum. 1984. *Experimental Social Programs.* New York: Academic Press.

Braybrooke, D., and C. E. Lindblom. 1963. *A Strategy of Decision.* New York: Free Press of Glencoe.

Brom, D., R. J. Kleber, and P. B. Defares. 1989. "Brief Psychotherapy for Posttraumatic Stress Disorders." *Journal of Consulting and Clinical Psychology* 57(5):607–12.

Brooks-Gunn, J., G. J. Duncan, P. K. Klebanov, and N. Sealand. 1993. "Do Neighborhoods Influence Child and Adolescent Development?" *American Journal of Sociology* 99(2):353–95.

Brooks-Gunn, J., P. K. Klebanov, and F. Liaw. 1995. "The Learning, Physical, and Emotional Environment of the Home in the Context of Poverty: The Infant Health and Development Program." *Children and Youth Services Review* 17(1/2):251–76.

Bumpass, L., and S. McLanahan. 1989. "Unmarried Motherhood: Recent Trends, Composition, and Black-White Differences." *Demography.* 26(2): 279–86.

Burden, D. S., and L. V. Klerman. 1984. "Teenage Parenthood: Factors That Lessen Economic Dependence." *Social Work* 29(1):11–16.

Burt, M. R., and B. E. Cohen. 1989. "Differences among Homeless Single Women, Women with Children, and Single Men." *Social Problems* 36(5): 508–24.

Burtless, G. 1989. "The Effect of Reform on Employment, Earnings, and Income." In Cottingham and Ellwood (1989).

Burtless, G. 1990. *A Future of Lousy Jobs.* Washington, DC: Brookings Institution.

Burtless, G., and L. L. Orr. 1986. "Are Classical Experiments Needed for Manpower Policy?" *Journal of Human Resources* 21(4):606–39.

Butler, G., M. Fennell, P. Robson, and M. Gelder. 1991. "Comparison of Behavior Therapy and Cognitive Behavior Therapy in the Treatment of Generalized Anxiety Disorder." *Journal of Consulting and Clinical Psychology* 59(1): 167–75. (Audio.)

Caplow, T. 1994. *Perverse Incentives: The Neglect of Social Technology in the Public Sector*. Westport, CT: Praeger.

Carcagno, G. J., R. Cecil, and J. C. Ohls. 1982. "Using Private Employment Agencies to Place Public Assistance Clients in Jobs." *Journal of Human Resources* 17(1):132–43.

Carliner, G. 1981. "Female Labor Force Participation Rates for Nine Ethnic Groups." *Journal of Human Resources* 16(2):287–93.

Carnegie Council on Adolescent Development. 1995. *Great Transitions: Preparing Adolescents for a New Century*. New York: Carnegie Corporation of New York.

Chan, S. 1990. *Income and Status Differences between White and Minority Americans*. New York: Edwin Mellen Press.

Citro, C. F., and G. Kalton. 1993. *The Future of the Survey of Income and Program Participation*. Washington, DC: National Academy of Sciences Press.

Citro, C. F., and R. T. Michael. 1995. *Measuring Poverty: A New Approach*. Washington, DC: National Academy Press.

Cohen, C. J., and M. C. Dawson. 1993. "Neighborhood Poverty and African American Politics." *American Political Science Review* 87(2):286–302.

Cole, O. J., and V. Washington. 1986. "A Critical Analysis of the Assessment of the Effects of Head Start on Minority Children." *Journal of Negro Education* 55(1):91–106.

Committee on Ways and Means. 1994. *Overview of Entitlement Programs* (1994 Green Book). Washington, DC: U.S. House of Representatives.

Consortium for Longitudinal Studies. 1978. *Lasting Effects after Preschool*. Washington, DC: U.S. Department of Health, Education, and Welfare.

Consortium on Developmental Continuity. 1977. *Lasting Effects after Preschool*. Washington, DC: U.S. Department of Health, Education, and Welfare.

Consumer Reports. 1995. "Mental Health: Does Therapy Help?" November: 734–39.

Cook, F. L., and E. J. Barrett. 1992. *Support for the American Welfare State*. New York: Columbia University Press.

Coontz, S. 1992. *The Way We Never Were: American Families and the Nostalgia Trap*. New York: Basic Books.

Corcoran, M., R. Gordon, D. Laren, and G. Solon. 1990. "Effects of Family and Community Background on Economic Status." *AEA Papers and Proceedings*. 80(2):362–66.

Costin, L., H. J. Karger, and D. Stoesz. 1996. *The Politics of Child Abuse in America*. New York: Oxford University Press.

Cottingham, P. H., and D. T. Ellwood (eds.). 1989. *Welfare Policy for the 1990's*. Cambridge, MA: Harvard University Press.

Coughlin, E. K. 1995. "Understanding East Harlem's Culture of Crack." *The Chronicle of Higher Education*, December 8, p. 17.

Cox, M., and R. Cox. 1984. "Foster Care and Public Policy." *Journal of Family Issues* 5:2 (June):182–99.

Cruz, J. E. 1991. *Implementing the Family Support Act: The Perspective of Puerto Rican Clients.* Washington, DC: National Puerto Rican Coalition.

Danziger, S., and P. Gottschalk. 1986. "Do Rising Tides Lift All Boats? The Impact of Secular and Cyclical Changes on Poverty." *AEA Papers and Proceedings* 76(2):405–10.

Danziger, S., R. H. Haveman, and R. Plotnick. 1981. "How Income Transfer Programs Affect Work, Savings, and the Income Distribution: A Critical Review." *Journal of Economic Literature* 19(3):975–1028.

Danziger, S., G. Sandefur, and D. Weinberg (eds.). 1994. *Confronting Poverty: Prescriptions for Change.* Cambridge, MA: Harvard University Press.

Danziger, S., G. Jakubson, S. Schwartz, and E. Smolensky. 1982. "Work and Welfare as Determinants of Female Poverty and Household Headship." *Quarterly Journal of Economics* 92(3):519–34.

Dawes, R. M. 1994. *House of Cards: Psychology and Psychotherapy Built on Myth.* New York: Free Press.

deLeon, P. 1988. *Advice and Consent.* New York: Russell Sage Foundation.

Divers-Stammes, A. C. 1995. *Lives in the Balance.* Albany, NY: State University Press of New York.

Dolan, M. P., J. L. Black, W. E. Penk, R. Rabinowitz, and H. A. Deford. 1985. "Contracting for Treatment Termination to Reduce Illicit Drug Use among Methadone Maintenance Treatment Failures." *Journal of Consulting and Clinical Psychology* 53(4):549–51.

Dolinsky, A. L., R. K. Caputo, and P. O'Kane. 1989. "Competing Effects of Culture and Situation on Welfare Receipt." *Social Service Review* 63(3):359–71.

Dryden, W., and C. Feltham. 1992. *Psychotherapy and Its Discontents.* Buckingham, England: Open University Press.

Duncan, G. J. 1976. "Unmarried Heads of Households and Marriage." in G. J. Duncan and J. N. Morgan (eds.), *Five Thousand American Families,* Volume 4 (Ann Arbor, MI: Survey Research Center, Institute for Social Research, University of Michigan).

Duncan, G. J., and S. D. Hoffman. 1990a. "Wefare Benefits, Economic Opportunities, and Out-of-Wedlock Births among Black Teenage Girls." *Demography* 27(4):519–35.

Duncan, G. J., M. S. Hill, and S. D. Hoffman. 1988. "Welfare Dependence within and across Generations." *Science* 239:467–71.

Edin, K. 1991. "Surviving the Welfare System: How AFDC Recipients Make Ends Meet in Chicago." *Social Problems* 38(4):462–74.

Eggebeen, D. J., and D. T. Lichter. 1991. "Race, Family Structure, and Changing Poverty among American Children." *American Sociological Review* 56:801–17.

Elkin, I., I. T. Shea, J. T. Watkins, S. D. Imber, S. M. Sotsky, J. F. Collins, D. R. Glass, P. A. Pilkonis, W. R. Leber, J. P. Docherty, S. J. Fiester, and M. B. Parloff. 1989. "National Institute of Mental Health Treatment of Depression Collaborative Research Program." *Archives of General Psychiatry* 46 (November):971–83.

Elliot, M., and L. J. Krivo. 1991. "Structural Determinants of Homelessness in the United States." *Social Problems* 38(1):113–31.

Ellwood, D. T. 1988. *Poor Support: Poverty in the American Family.* New York: Basic Books.

Ellwood, D. T., and M. J. Bane. 1984. *The Impact of AFDC on Family Structure and Living Arrangements.* Cambridge, MA: John F. Kennedy School of Government.

Ellwood, D. T., and M. J. Bane. 1985. *The Impact of AFDC on Family Structure and Living Arrangements.* In R. G. Ehrenberg (ed.), *Research in Labor Economics, Vol. 7* (Greenwich, CT: JAI Press).

Epstein, W. M. 1984. "Technology and Social Work, Part 1: The Effectiveness of Psychotherapy." *Journal of Applied Social Sciences* 8(2):155–75.

Epstein, W. M. 1993a. *The Dilemma of American Social Welfare.* New Brunswick, NJ: Transaction Publishers.

Epstein, W. M. 1993b. "Randomized Controlled Trials in the Human Services." *Social Work Research and Abstracts* 29(3):3–10.

Epstein, W. M. 1995. *The Illusion of Psychotherapy.* New Brunswick, NJ: Transaction Publishers.

Epstein, W. M. 1996. "Passing into Proverbs" *Society* 33(5):19–22.

Evans, P. B., D. Rueschemeyer, and T. Skocpol. (eds.). 1985. *Bringing the State Back in.* New York: Cambridge University Press.

Eysenck, H. F. 1952. "The Effects of Psychotherapy: An Evaluation." *Journal of Consulting Psychology* 16:319.

Eysenck, H. F. 1961. "The Effects of Psychotherapy" in H. F. Eysenck (ed.), *Handbook of Abnormal Psychology* (New York: Basic Books).

Eysenck, H. F. 1965. "The Effects of Psychotherapy." *International Journal of Psychiatry* 1:97.

Farber, N. 1990. "The Significance of Race and Class in Marital Decisions among Unmarried Adolescent Mothers." *Social Problems* 37(1):51–63.

Farley, R. 1990. "Blacks, Hispanics, and White Ethnic Groups: Are Blacks Uniquely Disadvantaged?" *AEA Papers and Proceedings* 80(2):237–41.

Farley, R. (ed.). 1995a. *State of the Union. Volume 1: Economic Trends.* New York: Russell Sage Foundation.

Farley, R. (ed.). 1995b. *State of the Union. Volume 2: Social Trends.* New York: Russell Sage Foundation.

Feldman, L. H. 1991. *Assessing the Effectiveness of Family Preservation Services in New Jersey within an Ecological Context.* Trenton, NJ: New Jersey Division of Youth and Family Servies, Bureau of Research, Evaluation, and Quality Assurance.

Fischer, J. 1973. "Is Casework Effective: A Review." *Social Work* 18(1):5–20.

Fischer, J. 1981. "The Social Work Revolution." *Social Work* 26(3):199–209.

Fitzgerald, J. 1991. "Welfare Durations and the Marriage Market." *Journal of Human Resources* 26:545–61.

Fitzgerald, J., P. Gottschalk, and R. Moffitt. 1996. "An Analysis of Sample Attrition in Panel Data: The Michigan Panel Study of Income Dynamics." December. Unpublished paper.

Fraker, T., and R. Maynard. 1987. "The Adequacy of Comparison Group Designs for Evaluations of Employment-Related Programs." *Journal of Human Resources* 22(2):194–227.

Fraker, T., and R. Moffitt. 1988. "The Effect of Food Stamps on Labor Supply." *Journal of Public Economics* 35:25–56.

Fraser, S. (ed.). 1995. *The Bell Curve Wars.* New York: Basic Books.

Freedman, S., and D. Friedlander. 1995. *The JOBS Evaluation: Early Findings on Program Impacts in Three Sites.* New York: Manpower Demonstration Research Corporation.

Friedlander, D. 1988. *Subgroup Impacts and Performance Indicators for Selected Welfare Employment.* New York: Manpower Demonstration Research Corporation.

Friedlander, D., and G. Burtless. 1995. *Five Years After.* New York: Manpower Demonstration Research Corporation.

Friedlander, D., G. Hoerz, J. Quint, and J. Riccio. 1985a. *Arkansas: Final Report on the Work Program in Two Counties.* New York: Manpower Demonstration Research Corporation.

Friedlander, D., G. Hoerz, D. Long, and J. Quint. 1985b. *Maryland: Final Report on the Employment Initiatives Evaluation* (December). New York: Manpower Demonstration Research Corporation.

Friedlander, D., M. Erickson, G. Hamilton, and V. Knox. 1986. *West Virginia: Final Report on the Community Work Experience Demonstrations.* New York: Manpower Demonstration Research Corporation.

Friedman, A. S., and G. M. Beschner. 1985. *Treatment Services for Adolescent Drug Abusers.* Rockville, MD: National Institute on Drug Abuse.

Funiciello, T. 1993. *Tyranny of Kindness.* New York: Atlantic Monthly Press.

Gans, H. J. 1995. *The War against the Poor.* New York: Basic Books.

Garfinkel, I. 1992. *Assuring Child Support.* New York: Russell Sage Foundation.

Garfinkel, I., and S. McLanahan. 1986. *Single Mothers and Their Children.* Washington, DC: The Urban Institute.

Garrett, C. J. 1985. "Effects of Residential Treatment on Adjudicated Delinquents: A Meta-analysis." *Journal of Research in Crime and Delinquency* 22:287–308.

Garrity, J. A. 1978. *Unemployment in History.* New York: Harper and Row.

Gay, R. S., and M. E. Borus. 1980. "Validating Performance Indicators for Employment and Training Programs." *Journal of Human Resources* 15(1):29–48.

Geronimus, A. T., and S. Korenman. 1992. "Socioeconomic Consequences of Teen Childbearing Reconsidered." *The Quarterly Journal of Economics* 107(4):1187–1214.

Gerstein, D. R., and H. J. Harwood (eds.). 1990. *Treating Drug Problems, Vol. 1: A Study of the Evolution, Effectiveness and Financing of Public and Private Drug Treatment Systems.* Washington, DC: National Academy Press.

Giannarelli, L., and S. Clark. 1992. "Changes in AFDC Eligibility and in AFDC

Participation Rates, 1981–1990." Conference paper presented at the Association for Public Policy Analysis and Management, Washington, DC, January.

Giblin, P., D. H. Sprenkle, and R. Sheehan. 1985. "Enrichment Outcome Research: A Meta-Analysis of Premarital, Marital and Family Interventions." *Journal of Marital and Family Therapy* 11(3):257–71.

Gilder, G. 1971. *Naked Nomads*. New York: Quadrangle Books.

Gilder, G. 1981. *Wealth and Poverty*. New York: Basic Books.

Gilder, G. 1986. *Men and Marriage*. Gretna, NY: Pelican Publishing.

Glazer, N. 1988. *The Limits of Social Policy*. Cambridge, MA: Harvard University Press.

Goldman, B. 1981. *Impacts of the Immediate Job Search Assistance Experiment: Louisville WIN Research Laboratory Project*. New York: Manpower Demonstration Research Corporation.

Goldman, B., D. Friedlander, J. Gueron, and D. Long. 1985. *Findings from the San Diego Job Search and Work Experience Demonstration*. New York: Manpower Demonstration Research Corporation.

Goodwin, L. 1972. *Do the Poor Want to Work?* Washington, DC: Brookings Institution.

Goodwin, L. 1983. *Causes and Cures of Welfare*. Lexington, MA: Lexington Books.

Gottfredson, G. D. 1987. "Peer Group Interventions to Reduce the Risk of Delinquent Behavior: A Selective Review and New Evaluation." *Criminology* 25: 671–714.

Gottschalk, P. 1990. "AFDC Participation across Generations." *AEA Papers and Proceedings* 80(2):367–71.

Gottschalk, P. 1992. "The Intergenerational Transmission of Welfare Participation: Facts and Possible Causes." *Journal of Policy Analysis and Management* 11(2):254–72.

Greenberg, D., and H. Halsey. 1983. "Systematic Misreporting and Effects of Income-Maintenance Experiments on Work Effort—Evidence from the Seattle-Denver Experiment." *Journal of Labor Economics* 1(4):380–407.

Greenberg, D., R. Moffitt, and J. Friedmann. 1981. "Underreporting and Experimental Effects on Work Effort: Evidence from the Gary Income Maintenance Experiment." *Review of Economics and Statistics* 53(4):581–90.

Groeneveld, L. P., M. T. Hannan, and N. B. Tuma. 1983. "Marital Stability" (Volume 1 Part 5) in *Final Report of the Seattle-Denver Income Maintenance Experiment*. Menlo Park, CA: SRI International.

Grossman, J. B., R. Maynard, and J. Roberts. 1985. *Reanalysis of the Effects of Selected Employment and Training Programs for Welfare Recipients*. Princeton, NJ: Mathematica Policy Research, Inc.

Grunbaum, A. 1984. *The Foundations of Psychoanalysis*. Berkeley, CA: University of California Press.

Gueron, J. 1986a. *Work Initiatives for Welfare Recipients: Lessons from a Multistate Experiment*. New York: Manpower Demonstration Research Corporation.

Gueron, J. 1986b. "Work for People on Welfare." *Public Welfare* 44(1):7–12.

Gueron, J. 1987. "Reforming Welfare with Work." *Public Welfare* 45(4):13–25. (Reprinted from a monograph published by the Ford Foundation, Occasional Paper 2, Ford Foundation Project of Social Welfare and the American Future, 1987.)

Gueron J. 1990. "Work and Welfare: Lessons on Employment Programs." *Journal of Economic Perspectives* 4(1):79–98.

Gueron, J. M. 1995. "Testimony of Judith M. Gueron before the Senate Committee on Finance." New York: Manpower Demonstration Research Corporation.

Gueron, J. M., and E. Pauley. 1991. *From Welfare to Work*. New York: Russell Sage Foundation.

Hagen, J. L., and L. V. Davis. 1994. "Women on Welfare Talk about Reform." *Public Welfare* 52(2):30–40.

Hagen, J. L., and L. V. Davis. 1995. "The Participants' Perspective on the Jobs Opportunities and Basic Skills Training Program." *Social Service Review* 69:656–78.

Hall, A., and A. H. Crisp. 1987. "Brief Psychotherapy in the Treatment of Anorexia Nervosa: Outcome at One Year." *British Journal of Psychiatry* 151:185–91.

Handler, J. F. 1995. *The Poverty of Welfare Reform*. New Haven, CT: Yale University Press.

Harrington, M. 1962. *The Other America*. New York: Macmillan.

Harris, K. M. 1993. "Work and Welfare among Single Mothers in Poverty." *American Journal of Sociology* 99(2):317–52.

Harvey, P. 1989. *Securing the Right to Employment: Social Welfare Policy and the Unemployed in the United States*. Princeton, NJ: Princeton Universit Press.

Haskins, R. 1991. "Congress Writes a Law: Research and Welfare Reform." *Journal of Policy Analysis and Management* 10(4):616–32.

Hauser, R. M., and D. L. Featherman. 1977. *The Process of Stratification*. New York: Academic Press.

Hausman, J. 1981. "Labor Supply." In *How Taxes Affect Economic Behavior* H. J. Aaron and J. A. Wise (eds.), (Washington, DC: Brookings Institution).

Hausman, J. A., and D. A. Wise. 1985. *Social Experimentation*. Chicago: University of Chicago Press.

Haveman, R. H. 1986c. "Social Experimentation and Social Experimentation." "Review of *Social Experimentation*." *Journal of Human Resources* 21(4):586–605.

Haveman, R. H. 1987a. *Poverty Policy and Poverty Research: The Great Society and the Social Sciences*. Madison, WI: University of Wisconsin Press.

Haveman, R. H. 1987b. "Policy Analysis and Evaluation Research after Twenty Years." *Policy Studies Journal* 16(2):191–218.

Haveman, R. H. 1987c. "The War on Poverty and the Poor and Non-poor." *Political Science Quarterly* 102(1):65–78.

Haveman, R. H. 1988. *Starting Even: An Equal Opportunity Program to Combat the Nation's New Poverty*. New York: Twentieth Century Fund.

Haveman, R. H. 1992. "Review of *Assets and the Poor: A New American Welfare Policy.*" *Journal of Economic Literature* 30(3):1520–21.

Haveman, R. H. 1994. "Transfers, Taxes, and Welfare Reform." *National Tax Journal* 47(2):417–34.

Haveman, R. H., and B. Wolfe. 1984. "Disability Transfers and Early Retirement: A Causal Relationship." *Journal of Public Economics* 24(1):47–66.

Haveman, R. H., and B. Wolfe. 1994. *Succeeding Generations: On the Effects of Investments in Children.* New York: Russell Sage Foundation.

Hawkins, J. D. 1988. "Delinquency and Drug Abuse: Implications for Social Services." *Social Service Review* 60(2):258–85.

Hayes, C. (ed.). 1987. *Risking the Future.* Washington, DC: National Academy Press.

Heckman, J. 1979. "Sample Selection Bias as a Specification Error." *Econometrica* 47 (January):153–61.

Heineman, M. B. 1981. "The Obsolete Scientific Imperative in Social Work." *Social Service Review* 55(3):371–97.

Heineman Pieper, M. 1989. "The Heuristic Paradigm: A Unifying and Comprehensive Approach to Social Work Research." *Smith College Studies in Social Work* 60(1):8–34.

Heineman Pieper, M., and W. J. Pieper. 1990. *Intrapsychic Humanism: An Introduction to a Comprehensive Psychology and Philosophy of the Mind.* Chicago: Falcon Press.

Herman, E. 1995. *The Romance of American Psychology.* Berkeley, CA: University of California Press.

Hernandez, D. J. 1993. *America's Children: Resources from Family, Government, and the Economy.* New York: Russell Sage Foundation.

Herrnstein, R. J., and C. Murray. 1994. *The Bell Curve.* New York: Free Press.

Hill, K. Q., and J. E. Leighley. 1992. "The Policy Consequences of Class Bias in State Electorates." *American Journal of Political Science* 36(2):351–65.

Hill, M. A., and J. O'Neill. 1993. *Underclass Behaviors in the United States: Measurement and Analysis of Determinants.* Unpublished paper. Baruch College, City University of New York.

Himmelfarb, G. 1983. *The Idea of Poverty.* New York: Knopf.

Hixson, W. B. 1992. *The Search for the American Right Wing.* Princeton, NJ: Princeton University Press.

Hofferth, S. L. 1991. "Programs for High Risk Adolescents: What Works?" *Evaluation and Program Planning* 14(1–2):3–16.

Hoffman, S. D., and G. J. Duncan. 1988. "A Comparison of Choice-Based Multinomial and Nested Logit Models: The Family Structure and Welfare Use Decisions of Divorced or Separated Women." *Journal of Human Resources* 23(4):550–62.

Hoffman, S., and J. Holmes. 1976. "Husbands, Wives and Divorce." In *Five Thousand American Families,* Vol. 4, edited by G. J. Duncan and J. N. Morgan. Ann Arbor, MI: Institute for Social Research.

Hogan, D. P., and E. M. Kitagawa. 1985. "The Impact of Social Status, Family

Structure, and Neighborhood on the Fertility of Black Adolescents." *American Journal of Sociology* 90(4):825–55.

Hollister, R. G., Jr., P. Kemper, and R. A. Maynard (eds.). 1984. *The National Supported Work Demonstration.* Madison, WI: University of Wisconsin Press.

Honig, M. 1976. "A Reply." *Journal of Human Resources* 11:250–60.

Hopkins, K. R. 1987. *Welfare Dependency.* Alexandria, VA: Hudson Institute.

Horowitz, I. L. 1990. *Daydreams and Nightmares: Reflections on a Harlem Childhood.* Jackson, MS: University of Mississippi Press.

Horowitz, I. L. 1995–96. "Are the Social Sciences Scientific?" *Academic Questions* Winter:21–7.

Hosek, J. R. 1980. "Determinants of Family Participation in the AFDC-Unemployed Fathers Program." *Review of Economics and Statistics* 52(3):466–70.

Hudson Institute. 1995. *Hudson Institute Report* (summer). Indianapolis, IN: Hudson Institute.

Hutchens, R. M. 1979. "Welfare, Remarriage, and Marital Search." *American Economic Review* 69(3):369–79.

Hutchens, R. M. 1981. "Entry and Exit Transitions in a Government Transfer Program: The Case of Aid to Families with Dependent Children." *Journal of Human Resources* 16:217–37.

Hutchens, R. M., G. Jakubson, and S. Schwartz. 1989. "AFDC and the Formation of Subfamilies." *Journal of Human Resources* 24(4):599–628.

Imber, S. D., P. A. Pilkonis, S. M. Sotsky, I. Elkin, J. T. Watkins, J. F. Collins, M. T. Shea, W. R. Leber, and D. R. Glass. 1990. "Mode-Specific Effects among Three Treatments for Depression." *Journal of Consulting and Clinical Psychology* 58(3):352–9.

Izzo, R. L., and R. R. Ross. 1990. "Meta-analysis of Rehabilitation Programs for Juvenile Delinquents—A Brief Report." *Criminal Justice and Behavior* 17(1):134–42.

Jacoby, R., and N. Glauberman (eds.). 1995. *The Bell Curve Debate.* New York: Times Books.

Jencks, C. 1992. *Rethinking Social Policy: Race, Poverty and the Underclass,* Cambridge, MA: Harvard University Press.

Jencks, C., and P. E. Peterson. 1991. *The Urban Underclass.* Washington, DC: Brookings Institution.

Kane, T. J. 1987. "Giving Back Control: Long-Term Poverty and Motivation." *Social Service Review* 61(3):405–19.

Katz, M. 1986. *In the Shadow of the Poorhouse.* New York: Basic Books.

Katz, M. 1989. *The Undeserving Poor: From the War on Poverty to the War on Welfare.* New York: Pantheon.

Kaus, M. 1992. *The End of Equality.* New York: Basic Books.

Kavaler, F., and M. Swire. 1983. *Foster Child Health Care.* Lexington, MA: Lexington Books.

Kazdin, A. E., D. Bass, T. Siegel, and C. Thomas. 1989. "Cognitive-Behavioral

Therapy and Relationship Therapy in the Treatment of Children Referred for Antisocial Behavior." *Journal of Consulting and Clinical Psychology* 57(4): 522–35.

Ketron, Inc. 1980. *The Long-Term Impact of Win 11: Longitudinal Evaluation of the Employment Experiences of Participants in the Work Incentive Program*. Wayne, PA: Ketron.

Killingsworth, M. R. 1983. *Labor Supply*. New York: Cambridge University Press.

Kline, P. 1988. *Psychology Exposed or the Emperor's New Clothes*. London: Routledge.

Kozol, J. 1995. *Amazing Grace*. New York: Crown Publishers.

Lab, S. P., and J. T. Whitehead. 1988. "An Analysis of Juvenile Correctional Treatment." *Journal of Research in Crime and Delinquency* 24 (January): 60–83.

Lab, S. P., and J. T. Whitehead. 1989. "From 'Nothing Works' to 'The Appropriate Works': The Latest Stop on the Search for the Secular Grail." *Criminology* 28(3):405–18.

Lafer, G. 1994. "The Politics of Job Training: Urban Poverty and the False Promise of JTPA." *Politics and Society* 22(3):349–88.

Landman, J. T., and R. M. Dawes. 1982. "Psychotherapy Outcome: Smith and Glass' Conclusions Stand Up under Scrutiny." *American Psychologist* 37(5):504–16.

Lasch, C. 1965. *The New Radicalism in America (1889–1963): The Intellectual as a Social Type*. New York: Knopf.

Lasch, C. 1978. *The Culture of Narcissism*. New York: Norton.

Leiby, J. 1978. *A History of Social Welfare and Social Work in the United States*. New York: Columbia University Press.

Lemieux, T., B. Fortin, and P. Frechette. 1994. "The Effect of Taxes on Labor Supply in the Underground Economy." *American Economic Review* 84(1): 231–54.

Lerman, P. 1975. *Community Treatment and Social Control: A Critical Analysis of Juvenile Correctional Policy*. Chicago: University of Chicago Press.

Lerman, R. I. 1990. Review of *The Prisoners of Welfare: Liberating America's Poor from Unemployment and Low Wages*, by D. R. Riemer. *Journal of Economic Literature* 28(4):1243–4.

Levy, F. 1987. *Dollars and Dreams: The Changing American Income Distribution*. New York: Russell Sage Foundation.

Lewinsohn, P. M., G. N. Clarke, H. Hops, and J. Andrews. 1990. "Cognitive-Behavioral Treatment for Depressed Adolescents." *Behavior Therapy* 21: 385–401.

Lewis, O. 1967. *Children of Sanchez*. Boston: Little, Brown.

Liebow, E. 1962. *Tally's Corner*. Boston, MA: Little, Brown.

Lind, M. 1995. "Drums along the Potomac." *New York Times Book Review*, July 23, p. 3.

Lindsey, D. 1994. *The Welfare of Children*. New York: Oxford University Press.

Lipton, D., R. Martinson, and J. Wilks. 1975. *The Effectiveness of Correctional Treatment.* New York: Praeger.

Littrell, J. 1991. *Understanding and Treating Alcoholism, Volume 1: An Empirically Based Clinician's Handbook for the Treatment of Alcoholism.* Hillsdale, NJ: Lawrence Erlbaum Associates.

Luborsky, L., B. Singer, and L. Luborsky. 1975. "Comparative Studies of Psychotherapies: Is It True that 'Everybody Has Won and All Must Have Prizes'?" *Archives of General Psychiatry* 32 (August):995–1008.

Lubove, R. 1965. *The Professional Altruist.* Cambridge, MA: Harvard University Press.

Magura, S., C. Casriel, and D. S. Goldsmith. 1987. "Contracting with Clients in Methadone Treatment." *Social Casework* 68 (October):485–93.

Mahajan, G. 1992. *Explanation and Understanding in the Human Sciences.* Delhi: Oxford University Press.

Malgady, R. G., L. H. Rogler, and G. Costantino. 1990. "Culturally Sensitive Psychotherapy for Puerto Rican Children and Adolescents: A Program of Treatment Outcome Research." *Journal of Consulting and Clinical Psychology* 58(6):704–12.

Manski, C. F., and I. Garfinkel (eds.). 1992. *Evaluating Welfare and Training Programs.* Cambridge, MA: Harvard University Press.

Manski, C. F., and S. R. Lerman. 1977. "The Estimation of Choice Probabilities from Choice Based Samples." *Econometrica* 45 (8):1977–88.

Marchione, K. E., L. Michelson, M. Greenwald, and C. Dancu. 1987. "Cognitive Behavioral Treatment of Agoraphobia." *Behavioral Research and Therapy* 255:319–28. (Audio.)

Marcuse, H. 1964. *One Dimensional Man.* Boston: Beacon Press.

Martinson, R. 1974. "What Works—Questions and Answers about Prison Reform." *Public Interest* (Spring):22–54.

Massey, D. S., and N. A. Denton. 1993. *American Apartheid.* Cambridge, MA: Harvard University Press.

Masters, S. 1981. "The Effects of Supported Work on the Earnings and Transfer Payments of Its AFDC Target Group." *Journal of Human Resources* 16(4):600–36.

Mattera, P. 1985. *Off the Books: The Rise of the Underground Economy.* New York: St. Martin's Press.

Maynard, R. 1995. "Teenage Childbearing and Welfare Reform: Lessons from a Decade of Demonstration and Evaluation Research." *Children and Youth Services Review* 17(1/2):309–32.

McAuliffe, W. E. "A Randomized Controlled Trial of Recovery Training and Self-help for Opioid Addicts in New England and Hong Kong." *Journal of Psychoactive Drugs* 22 (2):197–208.

McDonald, W. R., and Associates. 1990. *Evaluation of AB 1562 In-Home Care Demonstration Projects: Final Report.* Sacramento, CA: W. R. McDonald and Associates.

McFate, K., R. Lawson, and W. J. Wilson (eds.). 1995. *Poverty, Inequality and the Future of Social Policy.* New York: Russell Sage Foundation.

McKey, R. H., L. Condelli, H. Ganson, B. J. Barrett, C. McConkey, and M. C. Plantz. 1985. *The Impact of Head Start on Children, Families, and Communities.* Washington, DC: U.S. Department of Health and Human Services.

McLanahan, S. S. 1988. "Family Structure and Dependency: Early Transitions to Female Household Headship." *Demography* 25(1):1–16.

McLean, P. D., and A. R. Hakstian. 1990. "Relative Endurance of Unipolar Depression Treatment Effects: Longitudinal Follow-up." *Journal of Consulting and Clinical Psychology* 58(4):482–8.

McLean, P., and S. Taylor. 1992. "Severity of Unipolar Depression and Choice of Treatment." *Behavioral Research and Therapy* 30(5):443–51.

McLelland, A. T., A. I. Alterman, D. S. Metzger, G. R. Grissom, G. E. Woody, L. Luborsky, and C. P. O'Brien. 1994. "Similarity of Outcome Predictors across Opiate, Cocaine, and Alcohol Treatments: Role of Treatment Services." *Journal of Consulting and Clinical Psychology* 62(6):1141–58.

Mead, L. M. 1986. *Beyond Entitlement.* New York: Free Press.

Mead, L. M. 1988a. "The Potential for Work Enforcement: A Study of WIN." *Journal of Policy Analysis and Management* 7(2):264–88.

Mead, L. 1988b. "Jobs for the Welfare Poor." *Policy Review* Winter:60–69.

Mead, L. M. 1992. *The New Politics of Poverty.* New York: Basic Books.

Mead, L. M. 1994. "Poverty: How Little We Know." *Social Service Review* 68:322–50.

Merton, R. 1957. *Social Theory and Social Structure.* Glencoe, IL: Free Press.

Meezan, W., and J. McCroskey. 1993. *Family Centered Home Based Interventions for Abusive and Neglectful Families in Los Angeles.* Los Angeles: University of Southern California School of Social Work.

Metcalf, C. E. 1973. "Making Inferences from Controlled Income Maintenance Experiments." *American Economic Review* 63 (June):478–83.

Metcalf, C. E. 1974. "Predicting the Effects of Permanent Programs from a Limited Duration Experiment." *Journal of Human Resources* 9(4):530–55.

Michel, R. 1980. "Participation Rates in the Aid to Families with Dependent Children Program, Part 1." Working Paper 1387-02. Washington: Urban Institute.

Miller, W. R. 1980. "Focused versus Broad-Spectrum Behavior Therapy for Problem Drinkers." *Journal of Consulting and Clinical Psychology* 48(5):590–601.

Miller, W. R., and N. K. Heather (eds.). 1986. *Treating Addictive Behaviors: Processes of Change.* New York: Plenum.

Minarik, J. J., and R. S. Goldfarb. 1994. "AFDC Income, Recipient Rates, and Family Dissolution: A Comment." *Journal of Human Resources* 11:243–50.

Mitchell, J. E., R. L. Pyle, E. D. Eckert, D. Hatsukami, C. Pomeroy, and R. Zimmerman. 1990. "A Comparison Study of Antidepressants and Structured Intensive Group Psychotherapy in the Treatment of Bulimia Nervosa." *Archives of General Psychiatry* 47 (February):149–57.

Moffitt, R. 1980. "Disequilibrium in Labor Supply: The Effect of the Negative Income Tax Experiments on Hours of Work." Unpublished paper. New Brunswick, NJ: Rutgers University.

Moffitt, R. 1983. "An Economic Model of Welfare Stigma." *American Economic Review* 73(5):1023–35.

Moffitt, R. 1985. "Evaluating the Effects of Changes in AFDC: Methodological Issues and Challenges." *Journal of Policy Analysis and Management* 4(4): 537–53.

Moffitt, R. 1986a. "Work Incentives in the AFDC System: An Analysis of the 1981 Reforms." *AEA Papers and Proceedings* 76(2):219–23.

Moffitt, R. 1986b. "Work Incentives in Transfer Programs (Revisited)." In R. G. Ehrenberg (ed.), *Research in Labor Economics, Volume 8* (Greenwich, Connecticut: JAI Press).

Moffitt, R. 1990. "The Effects of the US Welfare System on Marital Status." *Journal of Public Economics* 41:101–24.

Moffitt, R. 1991. "Program Evaluation with Nonexperimental Data." *Evaluation Review* 15(3):291–314.

Moffitt, R. 1992. "Incentive Effects of the US Welfare System: A Review." *Journal of Economic Literature* 30:1–61.

Moore, K. A. 1980. *Policy Determinants of Teenage Childbearing.* Washington, DC: Urban Institute.

Moore, K. A., and S. B. Caldwell. 1977. "The Effect of Government Policies on Out-of-Wedlock Sex and Pregnancy." *Family Planning Perspectives* 9(4): 164–72.

Moynihan, D. P. 1996. "Congress Builds a Coffin." *New York Review of Books,* January 11, pp. 14–16.

Murray, C. 1984. *Losing Ground.* New York: Basic Books.

Murray, C. 1992. "Restore Personal Responsibility." *Youth Policy* 14(7,8): 126–39.

Murray, C. 1993. "Welfare and the Family: The US Experience." *Journal of Labor Economics* 11(1):S224–62.

Murray, C. 1996. "Keeping Priorities Straight on Welfare Reform." *Society* 33(5):10–12.

Nathan, R. P. 1988. *Social Science in Government: Uses and Misuses.* New York: Basic Books.

National Commission on Children. 1991. *Beyond Rhetoric: A New American Agenda for Children and Families.* Washington, DC: National Commission on Children.

New York Times. 1996. "Stand Up and Be Counted." August 11, p. A26.

Nezu, A. M., and M. G. Perri. 1989. "Social Problem-Solving Therapy for Unipolar Depression: An Initial Dismantling Investigation." *Journal of Consulting and Clinical Psychology* 57(3):408–13.

Nirenberg, T. D., and S. A. Maisto (eds.). 1987. *Developments in the Assessment and Treatment of Addictive Behaviors.* Norwood, NJ: Alex Publishing.

Nozick, R. 1993. *The Nature of Rationality.* Princeton, NJ: Princeton University Press.

Office of Policy Planning and Research. 1965. *The Negro Family: The Case for National Action.* (The Moynihan Report.) Washington, DC: U.S. Department of Labor.

Okun, A. 1975. *Equality and Efficiency: The Big Tradeoff.* Washington, DC: Brookings Institution.

Olasky, M. N. 1992. *The Tragedy of American Compassion.* Washington, DC: Regnery Gateway.

Oliker, S. J. 1994. "Does Workfare Work? Evaluation Research and Workfare Policy." *Social Problems* 41(2):195–213.

Olson, G. I., and B. I. Scholer. 1993. "The Satisfied Poor." *Social Indicators Research* 28(2):173–93.

O'Neill, J. 1990. *Work and Welfare in Massachusetts: An Evaluation of the ET Program.* Boston: Pioneer Institute for Public Policy Research.

O'Neill, J. 1994. "Report Concerning New Jersey's Family Development Program." Unpublished paper. Baruch College, City University of New York.

Orloff, A. S., and Skocpol, T. 1984. "Why Not Equal Protection? Explaining the Politics of Public Social Spending in Britain, 1900–1911, and the United States, 1880's–1920." *American Sociological Review* 49(6):726–50.

Osberg, L. 1991. *Economic Inequality and Poverty: International Perspectives.* Armonk, NY: M. E. Sharpe.

Osterman, P. 1991. "Welfare Participation in a Full Employment Economy: The Impact of Neighborhood." *Social Problems* 38(4):475–91.

Palca, J. 1989. "AIDS Drug Trials Enter New Age." *Science* 246:19–21.

Palmer, J. L., and J. A. Pechman, eds. 1978. *Welfare in Rural Areas: The North Carolina-Iowa Income Maintenance Experiment.* Washington, DC: Brookings Institution.

Palmer, T. 1974. "The Youth Authority's Community Treatment Program." *Federal Probation* 38(1):3–14.

Papadimitriou, D. B., and E. N. Wolff (eds.). 1993. *Poverty and Prosperity in the USA in the Late Twentieth Century.* New York: St. Martin's Press.

Parrott, S. 1995. *What Do We Spend on "Welfare"?* Washington, DC: Center on Budget and Policy Priorities.

Patterson, J. T. 1981. *America's Struggle against Poverty 1900–1980.* Cambridge, MA: Harvard University Press.

Pavetti, L., and A. Duke. 1995. *Increasing Participation in Work and Work-Related Activities: Lessons from Five State Welfare Reform Demonstration Projects.* Washington, DC: Urban Institute.

Pecora, P. J., M. Fraser, and D. A. Haapala. 1992. "Intensive Home-Based Family Preservation Services: An Update from the FIT Project." *Child Welfare* 71(2):177–88.

Pelton, L. H. 1989. *For Reasons of Poverty.* New York: Praeger.

Percy, W. A. 1973 (or 1974). *Lanterns on the Levee: Recollections of a Planter's Son.* Baton Rouge, LA: Louisiana State University Press.

Piel, G. 1993. "Can History Stop Repeating Itself?" Review of *Preparing for the 21st Century* by Paul Kennedy. *Scientific American* 269 (1–July):114–17.

Piven, F. F., and R. A. Cloward. 1993. *Regulating the Poor*. New York: Vintage Books.

Platt, J. J., S. D. Husband, and S. Taube. 1990–91. "Major Psychotherapeutic Modalities for Heroin Addiction: A Brief Overview." *International Journal of the Addiction* 25 (12A):1453–77.

Plotnick, R. 1983. "Turnover in the AFDC Population: An Event History Analysis." *Journal of Human Resources* 18:65–81.

Plotnick, R. D. 1990. "Welfare and Out-of-Wedlock Childbearing: Evidence from the 1980's." *Journal of Marriage and the Family* 52:735–46.

Polit, D. F. 1989. "Effects of a Comprehensive Program for Teenage Parents: Five Years after Project Redirection." *Family Planning Perspectives* 21(4):164–9.

Polsky, A. J. 1991. *The Rise of the Therapeutic State*. Princeton, NJ: Princeton University Press.

Popenoe, D. 1988. *Disturbing the Nest*. New York: Aldine de Gruyter.

Prioleau, L., M. Murdock, and N. Brody. 1983. "An Analysis of Psychotherapy versus Placebo Studies." *Behavioral and Brain Sciences* 6:275–310.

Proctor, E. K. 1990. "Evaluating Clinical Practice: Issues of Purpose and Design." *Social Work Research and Abstracts* 26(1):32–40.

Public Agenda. 1996. *The Values We Live by: What Americans Want from Welfare Reform*. New York: Public Agenda Foundation.

Quadagno, J. 1984. "Welfare Capitalism and the Social Security Act of 1935." *American Sociological Review* 49(5):632–47.

Quint, J., J. Musick, and J. Ladner. 1994. *Lives of Promise, Lives of Pain*. New York: Manpower Demonstration Research Corporation.

Rachman, S. 1971. *The Effects of Psychological Treatment*. Oxford: Perragon Press.

Rainwater, L. 1974. *What Money Buys: Inequality and the Social Meanings of Income*. New York: Basic Books.

Rainwater, L., and W. L. Yancey. 1967. *The Moynihan Report and the Politics of Controversy*. Cambridge, MA: MIT Press.

Rainwater, L., and T. M. Smeeding. 1995. *Doing Poorly: The Real Income of American Children in a Comparative Perspective*. Syracuse, NY: The Maxwell School of Citizenship and Public Affairs, Syracuse University.

Rainwater, L., M. Rein, and J. Schwartz. 1986. *Income Packaging in the Welfare State*. Oxford: Clarendon Press.

Rank, M. R. 1989. "Fertility among Women on Welfare: Incidence and Determinants." *American Sociological Review* 54 (April):296–304.

Rank, M. R. 1994. *Living on the Edge: The Realities of Welfare in America*. New York: Columbia University Press.

Reid, W. J., and P. Hanrahan. 1982. "Recent Evaluations of Social Work: Grounds for Optimism." *Social Work* 27(4):328–40.

Reimer, D. R. 1992. *Prisoners of Welfare*. New York: Praeger.

Rein, M., and L. Rainwater (eds.). 1986. *Public/Private Interplay in Social Protection: A Comparative Study*. Armonk, NY: M. E. Sharpe.

Riccio, J., D. Friedlander, and S. Freedman. 1994. *GAIN: Benefits, Costs, and Three-year Impacts of a Welfare-to-Work Program.* New York: Manpower Demonstration Research Corporation.

Rorty, R. 1991. *Objectivity, Relativism, and Truth.* New York: Cambridge University Press.

Rosenthal, R., and D. B. Rubin. 1978. "Interpersonal Expectancy Effects: The First 345 Studies." *Behavioral and Brain Sciences* 3:377–415.

Ross, H. L., and I. V. Sawhill. 1975. *Time of Transition: The Growth of Female Headed Families.* Washington, DC: Urban Institute.

Rossi, P. H. 1991. *Evaluating Family Preservation Programs: A Report to the Edna Mcconnell Clark Foundation.* Unpublished report. Social and Demographic Research Institute, University of Massachusetts.

Rossi, P. H., J. D. Wright, G. A. Fisher, and G. Willis. 1987. The Urban Homeless: Estimating Composition and Size." *Science* 235:1336–41.

Rowe, J., H. Cain, M. Hundleby, and A. Keane. 1984. *Long Term Foster Care.* New York: St. Martin's Press.

Rubin, A. 1985. "Practice Effectiveness: More Grounds for Optimism." *Social Work* 30(6):469–76.

Ruggles, P., and R. C. Michel. 1987. *Participation Rates in the Aid to Families with Dependent Children Program: Trends for 1967 through 1984.* Washington, DC: Urban Institute.

Rutter, M., and H. Giller. 1984. *Juvenile Delinquency.* New York: Guilford Press.

Sawhill, I., G. E. Peabody, C. A. Jones, and S. B. Caldwell. 1975. *Income Transfers and Family Structure.* Washington, DC: Urban Institute.

Schuerman, J. R., R. L. Rzepnicki, and J. H. Littell. 1994. *Putting Families First.* New York: Aldine de Gruyter.

Schwartz, I. M., P. AuClaire, and L. J. Harris. 1991. "Intensive Home-Based Service as an Alternative to Out-of-Home Placement of Adolescents: The Hennepin County Experience." In K. Wells and D. E. Beigel (eds.), *Family Preservation Services: Reseach and Evaluation* (Newbury Park, CA: Sage)

Scott, K. G., T. Field, and E. G. Robertson (eds.). 1981. *Teenage Parents and Their Offspring.* New York: Grune and Stratton.

Sechrest, L., S. O. White, and E. D. Brown (eds.). 1979. *The Rehabilitation of Criminal Offenders.* Washington, DC: National Academy Press.

Segal, S. 1972. "Research on the Outcome of Social Work Therapeutic Interventions: A Review of the Literature." *Journal of Health and Social Behavior* 13 (March):3–17.

Seligman, M. E. P. 1995. "The Effectiveness of Psychotherapy: The *Consumer Reports* Study." *American Psychologist* 50:965–74.

Sells, S. B., and D. D. Simpson. 1979. "Evaluation of Treatment Outcome for Youths in the Drug Abuse Reporting Program (DARP): A Follow-up Study." In Beschner and Friedman (1979).

Shapiro, D. A. 1985. "Recent Applications of Meta-analyses in Clinical Research." *Clinical Psychology Review* 5:13–34.

Sheehan, S. 1993. *Life for Me Ain't Been No Crystal Stair.* New York: Pantheon.

Sheldon, B. 1986. "Social Work Effectiveness Experiments: Review and Implications." *British Journal of Social Work* 16(2):223–42.

Shockley, W. 1965. "Is Quality of US Population Declining." *U.S. News and World Report,* November 22, pp. 68–71.

Shockley, W. 1966. "Population Control or Eugenics." In J. D. Roslansky (ed.), *Genetics and the Future of Man* (New York: Appleton-Century-Crofts).

Shockley, W. 1970. "A 'Try Simplest Cases' Approach to the Heredity-Poverty-Crime Problem." In V. L. Allen (ed.), *Psychological Factors in Poverty* (Chicago: Markham).

Sidney, S. 1990. "Discrepant Data Regarding Trends in Marijuana Use and Supply." *Journal of Psychoactive Drugs* 22(3):319–24.

Siegel, L. J., and J. J. Senna. 1991. *Juvenile Delinquency.* St. Paul, MN: West Publishing.

Skocpol, T. 1992. *Protecting Soldiers and Mothers: The Political Origins of Social Policy in the United States.* Cambridge, MA: Belknap Press.

Skocpol, T., and E. Amenta. 1985. "Did Capitalists Shape Social Security?" *American Sociological Review* 50(4):572–5.

Slemrod, J. 1994. *Tax Progressivity and Income Inequality.* New York: Cambridge University Press.

Smeeding, T. M., M. O'Higgins, and L. Rainwater (eds.). 1990. *Poverty, Inequality and Income Distribution in Comparative Perspective.* Washington, DC: Urban Institute.

Smith, M. L., G. V. Glass, and T. I. Miller. 1980. *The Benefits of Psychotherapy.* Baltimore, MD: Johns Hopkins University Press.

Smith, S. R., and M. Lipsky. 1993. *Nonprofits for Hire.* Cambridge, MA: Harvard University Press.

Solon, G. 1992. "Intergenerational Income Mobility in the United States." *American Economic Review* 82(3):393–408.

Solon, G., M. Corcoran, R. Gordon, and D. Laren. 1988. "Sibling and Intergenerational Correlations in Welfare Program Participation." *Journal of Human Resources* 23(3):388–96.

Sotsky, S. M., D. R. Glass, T. Shea, P. A. Pilkonis, J. F. Collins, I. Elkin, J. T. Watkins, S. D. Imber, W. R. Leber, J. Moyer, and M. E. Oliveri. 1991. "Patient Predictors of Response to Psychotherapy and Pharmacotherapy: Findings in the NIMH Treatment of Depression Collaborative Research Program." *American Journal of Psychiatry* 148(8):997–1008.

Stein, L. I., and M. A. Test. 1980. "Alternatives to Mental Hospital Treatment." *Archives of General Psychiatry* 37 (April):392–412.

Stevens, A. H. 1994. "The Dynamics of Poverty Spells: Updating Bane and Ellwood." *AEA Papers and Proceedings* 84(2):34–7.

Stuart, R. B. 1970. *Trick or Treatment.* Champaign, IL: Research Press.

Szanton, P. L. 1991. "The Remarkable 'Quango': Knowledge, Politics, and Welfare Reform." *Journal of Policy Analysis and Management* 10:590–602.

Szapocznik, J., E. Murray, M. Scopetta, O. Hervis, A. Rio, R. Cohen, A. Rivas-

Vazquez, V. Posada, and W. Kurtines. 1989. "Structural Family versus Psychodynamic Child Therapy for Problematic Hispanic Boys." *Journal of Consulting and Clinical Psychology* 57(5):571–8.

Thomlison, R. J. 1984. "Something Works: Evidence from Practice Effectiveness Studies." *Social Work* 29(1):51–6.

Thompson, L. W., D. Gallagher, and J. S. Breckenridge. 1987. "Comparative Effectiveness of Psychotherapies for Depressed Elders." *Journal of Consulting and Clinical Psychology* 55(3):385–90.

Thrope, R. 1980. "The Experiences of Children and Parents Living apart: Implications and Guidelines for Practice." in J. Triseliotis (ed.), *New Developments in Foster Care and Adoption* (London: Routledge and Kegan Paul).

Tonry, Michael. 1995. *Malign Neglect*. New York: Oxford University Press.

Townsend, P. 1992. *The International Analysis of Poverty*. Hemel Hempstead, England: Harvester-Wheatsheaf.

U.S. Bureau of the Census. 1995. *Income, Poverty, and Valuation of Noncash Benefits: 1993*. Washington, DC: U.S. Department of Commerce.

U.S. Department of Health and Human Services. 1995. *Characteristics and Financial Circumstances of AFDC Recipients, FY 1993*. Washington: USGPO.

U.S. National Center for Health Statistics. 1995. *Vital Statistics of the United States*. Washington, DC: U. S. Department of Health and Human Services.

Videka-Sherman, L. 1988. "Meta-analysis of Research on Social Work Practice in Mental Health." *Social Work* 33(4):325–38.

Wakefield, J. C. 1993a. "Psychoanalytic Fallacies: Reflections on Martha Heineman Peiper and William Joseph Peiper's Intrapsychic Humanism." *Social Service Review* 67:127–55.

Wakefield, J. C. 1993b. "Philosophy of Science and the Evaluation of Clinical Theory: A Reply to the Piepers." *Social Service Review* 67:656–66.

Weir, M., A. S. Orloff, and T. Skocpol. 1988. *The Politics of Social Policy in the United States*. Princeton, NJ: Princeton University Press.

Westinghouse Learning Corporation. 1969. *The Impact of Head Start: An Evaluation of the Effects of Head Start on Children's Cognitive and Affective Development*. ERIC #ED 036321. Washington, DC: Clearinghouse for Federal Scientific and Technical Information.

Whitehead, J. T., and S. P. Lab. 1989. "A Meta-analysis of Juvenile Correctional Treatment." *Journal of Research in Crime and Delinquency* 26:276–95.

Wilson, W. J. 1987. *The Truly Disadvantaged*. Chicago: University of Chicago Press.

Wilson, W. J., and K. M. Neckerman. 1986. "Poverty and Family Structure: The Widening Gap between Evidence and Public Policy Issues." In *Fighting Poverty: What Works and What Doesn't*, edited by S. H. Danziger and D. H. Weinberg. Cambridge, MA: Harvard University Press.

Winkler, A. E. 1989. "The Incentive Effects of Medicaid on Women's Labor." *Journal of Human Resources* 29:308–37.

Wiseman, M. 1993. "The New State Welfare Initiatives." Discussion paper. Madison, WI: Institute for Research on Poverty.

Wiseman, M. 1995. "State Strategies for Welfare Reform: The Wisconsin Story." Discussion paper. Madison, WI: Institute for Research on Poverty.

Wolf, C., Jr. 1988. *Markets or Governments*. Cambridge, MA: MIT Press.

Wolff, E. N. 1995. *Top Heavy*. New York: Twentieth Century Fund.

Wolfhagen, C., and B. Goldman. 1983. *Job Search Strategies: Lessons from the Louisville WIN Laboratory*. New York: Manpower Demonstration Research Corporation.

Wood, K. M. 1978. "Casework Effectiveness: A New Look at the Research Evidence." *Social Work* 23 (November):437–58.

Woody, G. E., A. T. McLellan, and L. Luborsky. 1987. "Twelve-Month Follow-Up of Psychotherapy for Opiate Dependence." *American Journal of Psychiatry* 144 (5–May):590–6.

Wootton, B. 1959. *Social Science and Pathology*. London: George Allen and Unwin.

Wu, L., and B. C. Martinson. 1993. "Family Structure and the Risk of a Premarital Birth." *American Sociological Review* 58 (April):210–32.

Zigler, E., and S. Muenchow. 1992. *Head Start: The Inside Story of America's Most Successful Educational Experiment*. New York: Basic Books.

Zigler, E., and J. Valentine. 1979. *Project Head Start*. New York: Free Press.

Index

Rutter, M., 210
Rzepnicki, R. L., 200, 201, 202*n16*

Sandefur, G., 136
San Diego (California), 163, 168
Sawhill, I., 126, 130
Scared Straight, 212
Scholer, B. I., 225*n1*
Schuerman, J. R., 200, 201
Schwartz, I. M., 129–30
Scientific credibility: reform proposals, 4;
  social science, 4, 5–6, 8, 25–26, 32–34,
  49, 50, 59, 68–69, 72–73, 86, 217,
  223–26, 227–30; causality, 5, 11–12,
  13, 31, 89, 96–100, 227; limited rationality, 5, 33–35; rationality, 8, 11, 15,
  18, 26, 32, 55, 180, 185, 219; postmodernism, 32, 196, 228; researcher bias,
  32–33, 167, 189, 223; randomized controlled trials (RCT) in poverty research,
  27–29, 31, 32, 91; family structure, 29,
  88, 112, 113, 115–16, 119, 120–21,
  122–25, 126–28, 128, 129, 130, 131,
  137–40, 221; fugitive literature, 45*n5,*
  103, 104*n8;* social services, 55, 187–90,
  221; welfare/work research, 77–79, 83–
  84, 86–88, 96–104 *passim,* 221; selectivity bias, 78, 85, 87, 102, 128, 134,
  177; dynamic studies, 79, 80, 87, 96,
  102; experimental data, 79, 87; static
  studies, 79, 80–82, 84–85, 87; sampling
  bias, 84; time studies, 85; welfare spells,
  86–88*n3;* simulation research, 89, 90;
  unreported income, 95; surveys, 96*n5;*
  ex post facto analysis, 107; intergenerational dependency, 134–36, 221; training program research, 145–46, 148,
  150, 158, 159–61, 164–75 *passim;* Supported Work, 155–58, 177–81, 221;
  psychotherapy research, 193, 194; social
  work, 196, 198–200; family preservation research, 203–5; drug and alcohol
  treatment research, 206–9; juvenile
  delinquency research, 211; illegitimacy
  research, 212–15; Head Start, 215–17
Seattle/Denver Income Maintenance Experiment (SIME), 78, 79, 86–87*n3,*
  91–92, 94, 126–28, 131
Segal, S., 197, 198, 205

Seligman, M. E. P., 194*n11*
Sells, S. B., 206
Shockley, W., 46
Silverlake experiment, 211
Simpson, D. D., 206
Skidmore, F., 154
Skocpol, T., 30–31, 34–35
Smith, S. R., 187–90, 187*n4,* 205
Social cohesion, 94, 104, 109, 177–79,
  220, 221
Social conditions: cause, 10, 26–27;
  scarcity of resources, 12, 22; poverty
  rates, 15–16, 24; living standard decline,
  16–17; inequality, 16–17, 22; housing,
  18–19; youth, 19–20, 21; education,
  20, 22; addiction, 20–21; crime, 20–21;
  family structure, 21, 116–19, 125, 140;
  civic participation, 21–22; defining as
  a social problem, 37, 197; social dissatisfaction, 99; social cohesion, 101–
  2; mentioned, 132, 230–33; subculture,
  134–35; failure of basic institutions,
  144
Social efficiency: conservative proposals, 9,
  39–41, 108–9, 113, 230; liberal proposals, 9, 39–41, 59, 72, 113, 230; training
  programs, 142, 145, 151, 172–75, 179;
  social services, 184, 186, 193, 194, 220;
  social work, 195, 196, 197, 205, 215;
  juvenile delinquency programs, 211; policy decisions dictated by, 222; program
  effectiveness, 226; mentioned, 229; adherence to, 232–33
Social institutions, 144, 182, 226
Social insurance programs. *See* Social
  Security
Socialization, 7, 20, 75, 94, 104, 109, 128,
  179, 232
Social policy, 3, 29–31, 74, 80, 97, 98, 103,
  158, 180, 233
Social problems, 4, 5, 10, 11, 13, 19, 22,
  25–26, 40, 65, 76, 104, 109, 221, 222.
  See also Social conditions
Social Security, 24, 35*n11,* 106, 154, 158,
  177
Social services. *See* Program effectiveness;
  Scientific credibility; Social efficiency;
  Social welfare, social services
Social welfare: defined, 3, 12–13; Food